MW00974533

Marking the Church

Marking the Church

Essays in Ecclesiology

EDITED BY

Greg Peters

AND

Matt Jenson

PICKWICK *Publications* · Eugene, Oregon

MARKING THE CHURCH
Essays in Ecclesiology

Copyright © 2016 Wipf and Stock Publishers. All rights reserved. Except for brief quotations in critical publications or reviews, no part of this book may be reproduced in any manner without prior written permission from the publisher. Write: Permissions, Wipf and Stock Publishers, 199 W. 8th Ave., Suite 3, Eugene, OR 97401.

Pickwick Publications
An Imprint of Wipf and Stock Publishers
199 W. 8th Ave., Suite 3
Eugene, OR 97401

www.wipfandstock.com

PAPERBACK ISBN: 978-1-4982-7969-7
HARDCOVER ISBN: 978-1-4982-7971-0
EBOOK ISBN: 978-1-4982-7970-3

Cataloguing-in-Publication data:

Names: Peters, Greg. | Jenson, Matt.

Title: Marking the church : essays in ecclesiology / edited by Greg Peters and Matt Jenson.

Description: Eugene, OR: Pickwick Publications, 2016 | Includes bibliographical references and index.

Identifiers: ISBN 978-1-4982-7969-7 (paperback) | ISBN 978-1-4982-7971-0 (hardcover) | ISBN 978-1-4982-7970-3 (ebook)

Subjects: LSCH: Church. | Evangelicalism.

Classification: BR1640 M22 2016 (print) | BR1640 (ebook)

Manufactured in the U.S.A.   12/06/16

Kent Eilers' "Embodying Faithfulness: New Monastic Retrieval and the Christian Imagination" is taken from *Theology as Retrieval* by W. David Buschart and Kent Eilers. Copyright (c) 2015 by W. David Buschart and Kent D. Eilers. Used by permission of InterVarsity Press, P.O. Box 1400, Downers Grove, IL 60515, USA.www.ivpress.com

An earlier version of Kent Eilers' "Embodying Faithfulness: New Monastic Retrieval and the Christian Imagination" was published as Kent Eilers, "New Monastic Social Imaginary: Theological Retrieval for Ecclesial Renewal," in *American Theological Inquiry* 6/2 (2013): 45–57. Used by permission.

To the evangelicals who taught us to love the church

Contents

One

Holy

Lists of Illustrations

Contributors

John Hammett is John L. Dagg Senior Professor of Systematic Theology and Associate Dean for Theological Studies at Southeastern Baptist Theological Seminary. He is the author of *Biblical Foundations for Baptist Churches: A Contemporary Ecclesiology* (2005).

Robert Herrington is Executive Pastor of Mercy Hill Church in Greensboro, NC. He is completing a Ph.D. in Theology at Southeastern Baptist Theological Seminary.

Taylor Worley is the Associate Vice President for Spiritual Life and University Ministries and Visiting Associate Professor of Faith and Culture at Trinity International University. He is editor (with Robert MacSwain) of *Theology, Aesthetics, and Culture: Responses to the Work of David Brown* (2012).

Jim Larsen is Minister at North Garland Baptist Fellowship in Texas and an adjunct professor at Criswell College. He completed his Ph.D. in Theological Studies from Dallas Theological Seminary.

Matt Jenson is Associate Professor of Theology in the Torrey Honors Institute of Biola University. He is the author of *The Gravity of Sin* (2007) and (with David Wilhite) *The Church: A Guide for the Perplexed* (2010).

Kent Eilers is Associate Professor of Theology at Huntington University. He is the author (with W. David Buschart) of *Theology as Retrieval: Receiving the Past, Renewing the Church* (2015) and editor (with Kyle Strobel) of *Sanctified by Grace: A Theology of the Christian Life* (2014).

John Halsey Wood Jr. is an independent scholar who works in retail and wholesale food business. He completed his Ph.D. in Theological Studies from St. Louis University.

W. Bradford Littlejohn is an independent scholar and President of The Davenant Trust. He is the author of *Richard Hooker: A Companion to His Life and Work* (2015) and *The Mercersburg Theology and the Quest for Reformed Catholicity* (2009).

James M. Arcadi is a Postdoctoral Research Fellow in the Analytic Theology Project at Fuller Theological Seminary. He completed his Ph.D. in Theology and Religious Studies from the University of Bristol.

Joseph L. Mangina is Professor of Systematic Theology at Wycliffe College, Toronto. He is the author of *Karl Barth: Theologian of Christian Witness* (2004) and *Revelation* (2010). He is the editor of *Pro Ecclesia: A Journal of Catholic and Evangelical Theology.*

Eugene R. Schlesinger is an independent scholar who specializes in ecclesiology and sacramental theology. He is the author of *Missa Est! A Missional Liturgical Ecclesiology* (2017).

Joel Scandrett is Assistant Professor of Historical Theology and Director of the Robert E. Webber Center at Trinity School for Ministry. He is the former Project Research Director and Translations Coordinator for the *Ancient Christian Commentary on Scripture.*

Acknowledgments

You cannot count or recall all the gifts, big and small, that go into making a book. The time taken to write and edit is time given, by God, yes, but also by so many people. We thank each of them for their gifts of time, and with that support, encouragement, and accountability. Thanks in particular to the Evangelical Theological Society for sponsoring an Ecclesiology Consultation for the last seven years, and to those who have given, listened to, and discussed papers at our annual meeting. The editors are grateful, too, for the Torrey Honors Institute and Biola University, a home in which we have found such remarkable intellectual fellowship. Financial assistance for the publication of this book was provided by the Ressourcement Institute.

Abbreviations

ANF   *The Ante-Nicene Fathers*, edited by Alexander Roberts and James Donaldson. 1885–1887. 10 vols. Reprint, Peabody, MA: Hendrickson, 1994.

CD   Karl Barth, *Church Dogmatics*, edited by G. W. Bromiley and T. F. Torrance. Edinburgh: T&T Clark, 1957–1975.

NPNF[1]   *The Nicene and Post-Nicene Fathers*, Series 1, edited by Philip Schaff. 1886–1889. 14 vols. Reprint, Peabody, MA: Hendrickson, 1994.

NPNF[2]   *The Nicene and Post-Nicene Fathers*, Series 2, edited by Philip Schaff and Henry Wace. 1890–1900. 14 vols. Reprint, Peabody, MA: Hendrickson, 1994.

Introduction

Reading about the church can be like reading the phonebook. Yes, the information matters; it needs to be gathered in one place for easy reference, and there may come a day when we need to take the book off the shelf to answer a question. But whereas discussions of Christology and theological anthropology—even discussions of eschatology—go to the heart of the matter, the center of the Christian thing, and have manifold and far-reaching implications, ecclesiological discussions seem at best incidental, at worst distractions from what *really* matters.

Spoken like a true Evangelical Protestant, you might say. Roman Catholic and Eastern Orthodox Christians know that the church *is* the heart of the matter, that you cannot speak of Christ or the human person without speaking of the church in which both find their home. While that is certainly true, the Evangelical reluctance at times to attend to the church need not imply negligence; it might rather reflect diligence in attending to the One who stands over-against the church and the ones to whom the church seeks to proclaim this One. It might reflect obedience to Jesus' call to "be my witnesses in Jerusalem and in all Judea and Samaria, and to the end of the earth" (Acts 1:8).

Still, the integrity of the church's witness requires even the most apostolically-minded of churches to reflect from time to time on what it is to be the church. And in the midst of their missional zeal Evangelicals have at times been guilty of a lack of self-awareness. Often, this only means that we have not had many intelligent things to say about the being of the church. If that is intellectually embarrassing, it is not dangerous. This kind of self-forgetfulness can be more insidious, though; a church that forgets herself can fail to know her place, can exalt herself above her Lord above those whom her Lord calls her to serve. Failing to consider itself, then, can lead the church into idolatry and defection.

Ecclesial self-awareness is required for faithful witness. Proper self-awareness is neither self-forgetfulness nor self-absorption. For the church to know itself, it must consider itself; but it must not be fascinated by itself. Consider, then, talking, reading, and writing about the church to be a way to cultivate proper ecclesial self-awareness for the sake of the worship and witness of the church. The church has other things to talk about, most important things even; but among the things she talks about, she must talk about herself.

The essays in this volume were originally delivered at the annual meeting of the Evangelical Theological Society in the Ecclesiology Consultation from 2011–2014. The consultation itself was founded with the purpose of having more intentional discussions about ecclesiology at the largest annual gathering of Evangelical theologians. It was decided in 2010 that the next four years would be dedicated to the Nicene marks of the church: unity, holiness, catholicity, and apostolicity. The steering committee for the consultation then invited scholars to speak on these topics, giving the speakers as much latitude as possible in the content of their talks, hence the diversity represented in this volume. The essays do not present one particular methodology or approach to the marks of the church. The various approaches to the marks are, we believe, the strength of this volume for just as the church is diverse in its form and expression so too are these essays.

One

What Makes a Multi-Site Church One Church?

–John Hammett

Introduction

One of the most rapidly growing movements in North American Christianity is that of multi-site churches. A recent dissertation on the movement says, "The Multi-Site Church Revolution era began with a trickle of new multi-site churches; it now burgeons with a torrent of them."[1] Growth has been especially steep since 2000. The results of a 2007 survey of 1000 multi-site churches indicate that "for every one multi-site church begun before 2000, ten more emerged between 2000 and 2007."[2] Those who have been tracking the movement estimate the total number of multi-site churches as 2000 in 2007, growing to 2500 by 2008, and 3000 by 2009, leading them to call multi-site churches "the new normal."[3]

What is distinctive or new about multi-site churches? As the phrase implies, it is "being one church in many locations."[4] But this phrase raises questions, because from the New Testament onward, individual churches were often described in terms of a single location, from "the church in Cenchrea" (Rom 16:1) to "the church that meets at their house" (the house of Priscilla and Aquila, Rom 16:5). Paul and Barnabas won disciples in Lystra,

1. Frye, *The Multi-Site Phenomenon*, 104.

2. Ibid., 104–5.

3. Surratt, Ligon, and Bird, *A Multi-Site Road Trip: Exploring the New Normal*, 217–18.

4. "Being one church in many locations" is the subtitle of the book by Surratt, Ligon, and Bird, *The Multi-Site Church Revolution*.

Iconium, and Antioch, and regarded the groups of believers in each place as individual churches, for whom they appointed elders "in each church" (Acts 14:23). Robert Banks believes that for Paul, "*ekklēsia* cannot refer to a group of people unless they all do in fact actually gather together."[5] How then can groups of believers in divergent locations be one church? This article will present the answer given to that question by those in the multi-site movement and evaluate it. It will, first of all, give a brief historical survey of what it has meant to affirm belief in one church. Second, it will give what multi-site churches mean when they affirm that they are "one church in many locations." Third, it will explore the single most common objection raised against the multi-site understanding of the oneness of the church. Finally, it will evaluate the multi-site church understanding of the oneness of the church.

Historical Survey:
"We Believe in One Church"

The affirmation of belief in one church, found in the Nicene-Constantinopolitan Creed, has deep roots in New Testament teaching. Jesus' use of the singular "church" in Matthew 16:18 ("I will build my church") is an implicit argument that the church is one, and is strengthened by Jesus' prayer in John 17:21 that all those who believe in him would be one. Paul's teaching on the church as a body highlights both the multiplicity of members and the oneness of the body (Rom 12:5; 1 Cor 12:12), and the oneness of the body is one of the aspects of unity that Paul proclaims as fact, and commands us to maintain and preserve (Eph 4:3–5).

At the same time, the New Testament also speaks of churches in the plural on twenty-seven occasions. Obviously, belief in the oneness of the church did not preclude the recognition that, in some sense, the oneness of the church had some boundaries. When groups of Christians crossed those boundaries, it was proper to speak of them as "churches." So, in what sense is the church in the New Testament one? Christian history gives a variety of answers.

In the early church, it was obvious that there were a multitude of scattered churches, but they sensed as well that each local church was somehow related to a larger, universal Church, the one body of Christ. While some early fathers appealed to their common proclamation of one faith as the

---

5. Banks, *Paul's Idea of Community*, 40.

4

basis of their unity,[6] increasingly the unity of the church was grounded in communion with the bishops. Those who walked in communion with the bishops were part of the one Church; those who rebelled against the authority of the bishops were outside the Church.[7] The unity of the church was seen as that of a visible, empirical institution. Little theological consideration was given to the oneness of a local congregation; rather, oneness was a mark of the Church (capital C).

The Reformers' break with the Catholic Church signaled a new understanding of the oneness of the Church. Unity was no longer based on communion with a visible institution and its bishops, but on possession and embrace of the gospel. Paul Avis says,

> For Luther, the Church was created by the living presence of Christ through his word the gospel. Where the gospel is found Christ is present, and where he is present the Church must truly exist. This conviction lay at the root of the whole Reformation struggle and was shared by all the Reformers—Lutheran and Reformed, Anglican, and Anabaptist. They were prepared to sacrifice the visible unity of the Western church if only by so doing they could save the gospel.[8]

In place of a visible unity, the Reformers and their Evangelical descendants have largely seen the oneness of the church as a spiritual and invisible reality. The preaching of the word and the right administration of the sacraments have been seen as the visible marks of a true church, but how the scattered true churches possess unity is not visible or institutional. It lies in their common embrace of the gospel.[9]

In the centuries following the Reformation, Protestants split irrepressibly into dozens, then hundreds, even thousands of denominations. Such Protestants could still affirm the oneness of the church, because they assumed the distinction between the visible and invisible church, and attributed oneness to the latter.[10] Still, strongly connectional denominations

6. Such as Irenaeus, *Against Heresies*, 1.10.2.

7. This is a major theme of Cyprian's important work, *The Unity of the Catholic Church*, written in response to the schism of Novatian.

8. Avis, *Church in the Theology of the Reformers*, 3.

9. For a contemporary expression of this idea of the oneness of the church, see Phillips, Ryken, and Dever, *The Church: One, Holy, Catholic and Apostolic*.

10. Tinder, "Denominationalism," in *Evangelical Dictionary of Theology*, 335. He notes, "The theological distinction between the church visible and invisible, made by Wycliffe and Hus and elaborated by the Protestant Reformers, underlies the practice

introduced some ambiguity into the idea of oneness, because while never claiming to be the one universal church, they nevertheless claimed to be one church. For example, the Presbyterian Church (U.S.A.) affirms and seeks "to deepen communion with all other churches within the one, holy, catholic, and apostolic Church" and yet also affirms that "the particular congregations of the Presbyterian Church (U.S.A.) wherever they are, taken collectively, constitute one church, called the church."[11] How are the associated congregations of a denomination one church? Overall governance by the General Assembly is one obvious aspect, but some denominations might also claim "common vision, mission, and ministry."[12]

Less connectional denominations, while not calling their associated congregations one church, did see the act of associating as giving some manifestation of unity on a larger than local church level. Perhaps the most striking statement of the close relationship associated churches bear to one another comes from the seven English Particular Baptist churches who formed the first Particular Baptist Association. In their 1644 Confession, they affirmed the autonomy and full ecclesial nature of each local congregation, yet also saw a value in associations of congregations. They wrote:

> And although the particular Congregations be distinct and severall Bodies, every one a compact and knit Citie in it selfe; yet are they all to walk by one and the same Rule, and by all meanes convenient to have the counsel and help one of another in all needful affaires of the Church, *as members of one body* in the common faith under Christ their onely head.[13]

Since it is the local congregations who are the "members of one body," the unity of that one body is one that extends beyond the local church level. Yet it cannot be the full unity of the universal church, which extends far beyond the scope of the seven churches which signed the 1644 Confession. Rather, the statement seems to imply that the unity of associated churches

---

and defense of denominationalism that emerged among seventeenth century English Puritans."

11. *The Constitution of the Presbyterian Church (U.S.A)*, 3, 13.

12. This phrase is from the web site of the United Methodist Church, describing their structure and organization. It states, "The United Methodist Church is able to maintain a common vision, mission, and ministry through the worldwide connectional system." See http://www.umc.org/site/c.1wL4KnN1LtH/b.1720697/k.734E/Structure_Organization_Organizaation.htm, accessed September 14, 2011.

13. W. Lumpkin, ed., *Baptist Confessions of Faith*, 168–69.

is nonetheless valuable and desirable because it manifests, even if in a limited way, something of the oneness of the larger body of Christ.

While many decry denominations as detrimental to the unity of the church,[14] Richard Phillips sees them as positively enabling unity on two levels. He cites Bruce Shelley's view that "Denominations were created . . . to make unity in the church possible," and explains, "Denominations allow us to have organizational unity where we have full agreement, and allow us to have spiritual unity with other denominations, since we are not forced to argue our way to perfect agreement but can accept our differences of opinion on secondary matters."[15] But while Phillips may be correct that denominations have enabled like-minded congregations to enjoy organizational unity, others would say that organizational unity is not the type of unity the New Testament calls for, nor is it the type of unity given to the church by the Spirit, and thus it is not the unity we are to recognize and maintain (Eph 4:3–4).[16]

What makes a local church one church has not been a major topic in theological discussions. From early on, those discussions focused on the oneness of the Church universal. Perhaps the fact that the church was born in an imperial context, where the local was subordinated to the imperial, had some impact. At any rate, while the unity of local congregations has not received much attention from theologians, it was an important issue in the New Testament. One important element of unity was a common faith. Paul reacted strongly to the threat to the oneness of the faith represented by the heterodox preaching in the churches in Galatia.[17] One of the elements of unity highlighted in Ephesians 4 is "one faith" (Eph 4:5) and many of Paul's letters to churches included theological instruction and correction so that they could be one in faith, both internally and in relationship to other churches.

But most often, the oneness of a local congregation in the New Testament seems to be relational, rooted in the relationships among the

---

14. The Book of Order of the Presbyterian Church (U.S.A.) states, "Divisions into different denominations obscures but does not destroy unity in Christ." See *Constitution of the Presbyterian Church*, 3.

15. Phillips, Ryken, and Dever, *Church*, 27.

16. Banks, *Paul's Idea of Community*, 48.

17. Theological unity is given both primacy and greatest prominence in the list of five areas of church unity advocated by Driscoll and Breshears in *Vintage Church*, 137–40. In addition to theological unity, they highlight relational, philosophical, missional, and organizational unity.

members. So, in Acts 2:44, we read that "all who believed were together and had all things in common." Acts 4:32 continues, "the full number of those who believed were of one heart and soul." The image of the one body with many members in Romans 12 and 1 Corinthians 12 emphasizes equality in value and honor despite diversity in gifts, and is given as an incentive to mutual care. In fact, one of the major themes of 1 Corinthians is Paul's appeal to all the members there to "agree, and that there be no divisions among you, but that you be united in the same mind and the same judgment" (1 Cor 1:10). Similarly, the Philippian church is exhorted to make Paul's joy complete "by being of the same mind, having the same love, being in full accord and of one mind" (Phil 2:2). Unity seems very much a matter of the quality of relationships members have with each other, and little to do with organizational matters.

The living out of such relationships would seem to require some level of interaction among the members, as in Acts 2:44, where all the believers "were together." This assumption of interaction among members for local church oneness raises the question this chapter addresses. While there are some multi-site churches whose sites are limited geographically to one city, and a smaller number who think it is important for all the sites to meet jointly on occasion, the dominant model does not consider geographical proximity of sites as an issue. When Surratt, Ligon, and Bird list seven criteria multi-site churches should consider in choosing a new site, geographical proximity does not make the list; rather, they endorse a number of multi-sites who are "going global."[18] So for the growing number of multi-site churches whose members are widely scattered and never interact, what makes such a church one church?

How Can a Church Be One in Many Locations? The Multi-Site Answer

Advocates of multi-site churches have given a clear answer to the question posed above. They say, "A multi-site church shares a common vision, budget, leadership, and board."[19] To clarify, they add, "If your new campus has a vision, budget, leader, or board that's not part of the sending campus, then you've started a new church or a mission campus, not a multi-site church."[20]

18. Surratt, Ligon, and Bird, *Multi-Site Road Trip*, 61–63; 129–45.

19. Surratt, Ligon, and Bird, *Multi-Site Church Revolution*, 18.

20. Ibid., 51.

Perhaps the most striking part of this definition of the unity of a multi-site church is the almost complete absence of relational or theological elements, and the strongly organizational emphasis. Such a definition could fit restaurant and hotel franchises, a drug store chain, or banks with multiple branches. In fact, Surratt, Ligon, and Bird explicitly link the development of multi-site churches to franchising concepts and add, "multi-site extensions of trusted-name churches are something that connect well with our times."[21] Brian Frye notes the similarities and raises the question of whether or not it is "acceptable for a new church model to emerge from a secular business model," but concludes that "it could be that the multi-site church concept is simply a sacred crossover of a twentieth-century marketplace phenomenon."[22] One of the main criticisms of multi-site churches by Thomas White and John Yeats is the similarity of multi-site churches to the business model and the consumerism it encourages. They charge that multi-site churches, in accepting the franchise model, also buy into franchise model standards: "In order to keep up the calculability and meet the demands of predictability, the congregations are forced to become more efficient and sacrifice people on the altar of success."[23]

Gregg Allison argues for a much more positive view of multi-site unity. He notes that biblical teaching says that love, unity, cooperation, and interdependence should characterize local churches individually. Multi-site churches allow for the visible expression of those virtues in a larger than local church level, as congregations show their unity visibly by working together for the good of their city. Allison states, "This theological emphasis on unity is often cited as a key reason for preferring multiplying campuses rather than multiplying church plants: when a new church is spun off, the mother church and the daughter church quickly move away from each other and stop cooperating."[24]

However, Allison's statement is open to question. First, the "theological emphasis on unity" he cites has not been mentioned in any of the literature on multi-site churches this author has seen other than Allison. Rather, the organizational idea of unity seems much more prevalent. Second, as noted above, the desire for visible expression of larger than local church unity is not something new. But in the past, this desire sparked the development

21. Ibid., 10.
22. Frye, "Multi-Site Church Phenomenon," 76.
23. White and Yeats, *Franchising McChurch*, 82–83.
24. Allison, "Theological Defense of Multi-Site," 12.

of associations, conventions, or denominations, not multi-site churches. Third, Allison's observation that mother and daughter churches move away from each other and stop cooperating is not in any way necessarily linked to the phenomenon or model of church planting itself. Separate churches certainly can and often do cooperate. If such churches cease to cooperate, the culprit would seem to be attitudes of independence and pride or rivalry and dissension. Such attitudes, sadly, are equally possible in multi-site churches. Thus, in the end, the key elements of unity in a multi-site church remain primarily organizational (a common vision, budget, board, and leadership). Theological expressions of unity, such as cooperation in ministry, may be present, but are not distinctive to multi-site churches, nor are they intrinsically linked to the multi-site model, and would seem problematic for multi-site churches whose sites are geographically scattered.

Still, the recognition that multi-site churches, like associations, can give some type of a tangible expression of unity on a larger than local church level leads to an important but, as far as this author has read, unacknowledged point. Multi-site churches, as most such churches are developing, are *not* local churches and in fact cannot be. The very definition of one church in many *locations* excludes "local" as a proper adjective for them. The fact that some multi-site churches are extending their campuses across multiple states, and some are even going international, require us to see them as something other than local churches, but they are not the universal Church. So if they are neither a local church nor the universal Church, what are they? Part of the difficulty with multi-site churches is they fit neither of the traditional categories for church.

Perhaps multi-site churches that are expansive geographically are more akin to denominations than local churches. The fact that multi-site churches see their oneness in terms of sharing a common vision, budget, board, and leaders makes for interesting comparison to the unity of associations, conventions, and denominations. The parallel is not exact, for multi-site churches have one budget, board, and leaders, while individual congregations in most denominations have their own individual budgets, boards, and leaders, but there are some similarities. Denominations do often seek to foster a common vision, and as a denomination, they operate under one denominational budget, with one set of denominational leaders, similar to multi-sites.[25] While a common theological heritage is often part

---

25. For example, the United Methodist Church website states, "The United Methodist Church is able to maintain a common vision, mission, and ministry throughout the

of the common vision of denominations, their unity, like that of multi-site churches, seems to be largely organizational. The reason why it is difficult to find biblical or theological grounds for the unity of multi-site churches is the same reason why it is difficult to find biblical or theological grounds for the unity of denominations: "the Bible in no way envisages the organization of the church into denominations."[26] Likewise, multi-site churches, at least once they go beyond the city level, are not envisaged in the New Testament.

Then is the oneness of multi-site churches simply a semantic problem that would evaporate if multi-site churches gave up the claim to be local churches and accepted the designation of being networks or associations or even denominations of churches? It would clarify things on one level, but would raise other questions, issues of polity, the role of a "campus pastor," and the importance of a congregation providing its own teaching ministry, issues that lie beyond the purview of this chapter.

It is this author's belief that part of the difficulty in evaluating most multi-site churches, especially those that are widely scattered geographically, is that they fit neither of the common categories of biblical teaching about the church. They are neither clearly local nor universal. If we ask, then, "are multi-site churches biblical?" the answer is no, at least not as most multi-site churches are developing, in terms of having a clear biblical precedent. However, if a multi-site church limits itself geographically to an area the size of a city, the possibility of biblical precedent becomes much stronger, as will be discussed below. But the presence or lack of biblical precedent does not necessarily validate or invalidate multi-site churches *per se*. For example, it is very difficult to find a biblical precedent for denominations, yet most would grant at least some limited value and validity to them. The question should then rather be, is there anything inherent in the multi-site church model that is contrary to biblical teaching on the church, or destructive of the New Testament idea of the church? Specifically, for this chapter, is there something about multi-site churches that violates biblical teaching on the oneness of the church?[27] In fact, there are many who think the multi-site model is fatally at odds with the New Testament model of the church, precisely on that issue. In the next section, we will consider the

worldwide connectional system." For the location of the website, see n. 12 above.

26. Tinder, "Denominationalism," 335. He sees this as the explanation why historically, "there has never been much theological reflection on denominationalism."

27. Thus, I am taking something of a normative, as opposed to a regulative approach to assessing multi-site churches. It would seem that this is the tacit approach most Protestants have taken with respect to denominations.

single most commonly offered objection to the multi-site model, which is related to the oneness of the multi-site church.

Are Multi-Site Churches Contrary to New Testament Teaching on the Oneness of the Church?

The most common objection to multi-site churches comes from the claim that the basic meaning of the word for church in the New Testament, *ekklēsia*, is assembly. But multi-site churches, by their very nature as "one church in many locations," do not assemble.[28] Therefore, it is argued, they are contrary to the basic New Testament idea of the church. This argument is employed by Thomas White, Grant Gaines, Jonathan Leeman, and Bobby Jamieson in their articles in the May/June 2009 issue of *9Marks eJournal*, and in books by Mark Dever, and Thomas White and John Yeats.[29] As quoted earlier, Robert Banks believes that for Paul, "*ekklēsia* cannot refer to a group of people unless they all do in fact actually gather together."[30] Roger Gehring similarly affirms that in Pauline teaching the church "comes into existence in the act of gathering."[31]

There is, however, an interesting pattern of usage of *ekklēsia* in the New Testament that qualifies the application of this objection. This is the fact that Paul always uses the singular for the church in a city (thus, the church in Cenchrea, Corinth, and Thessalonica) and always uses the plural for groups of Christians scattered across an area larger than a city (thus, the churches of Asia, Galatia, etc.). The usage by Luke in Acts follows the same pattern, with the single exception of Acts 9:31, where the singular "church" is used in a regional sense, to refer to the Christians in Judea, Galilee, and Samaria.

Multi-site advocates have claimed the use of the singular for all the Christians in a city as support for their model: "Aubrey Malphurs observes that Corinth and other first-century churches were multi-site, as a number of multi-site house churches were considered to be part of one citywide

---

28. The exceptions to this are the multi-site models offered by Allison, "Theological Defense," 17–18.

29. See articles by White, Gaines, Leeman, and Jamieson in *9Marks eJournal*, 42–66; Dever and Alexander, *The Deliberate Church*, 87; and White and Yeats, *Franchising Mc-Church*, 102–03.

30. Banks, *Paul's Idea of Community*, 40.

31. Gehring, *House Church and Mission*, 164.

church."[32] The size of the church in Jerusalem has caused many to posit that the one local church of Jerusalem must have included a plurality of house churches, if for no other reason than the sheer difficulty of finding a place large enough for three thousand or more to meet. Roger Gehring, whose book *House Church and Mission: The Importance of Household Structures in Early Christianity* is the most detailed study of this issue that I have found, concludes that "a plurality of house churches existed alongside the local church as a whole in Jerusalem."[33] In addition to the sheer practical difficulties in gathering a church of the size of what the church in Jerusalem certainly came to be, he notes how frequently houses pop up in the description of the church in Jerusalem. On the day of Pentecost, we are told that the sound of a violent wind "filled the entire house" where the believers were gathered (Acts 2:2). The habitual practice of the early church was to attend "the temple together" and break bread "in their homes" (Acts 2:46). Paul ravaged the church in Jerusalem by "entering house after house" to drag believers off to prison (Acts 8:3). Gehring says, "We can assume that Saul did not randomly choose some houses but, rather, precisely the houses in which he suspected Christian assemblies, in hopes of catching them in flagrante delicto."[34] Finally, in Acts 12, upon his miraculous release from prison, Peter knew to go "to the house of Mary, the mother of John whose other name was Mark, where many were gathered together and were praying" (Acts 12:12). It seems likely that this house was the location of one of the house churches of the church in Jerusalem. Gehring believes "It is almost certain that a plurality of house churches existed in Rome," and "we can be certain that a plurality of house churches existed alongside the whole local church in Corinth," with indications of a similar plurality in Antioch, Thessalonica, Ephesus, Philippi, and Laodicea.[35]

On the basis of such claims, Brian Frye thinks the objection to multi-site churches on the grounds that they do not assemble falls. He says,

> no definitive evidence exists that would forbid or disqualify dividing a single church into multiple worship gatherings . . . If both house church gathering and local church gathering took place concurrently within the early church without harm, it stands to

---

32. Surratt, Ligon, and Bird, *Multi-Site Church Revolution*, 27, citing Malphurs, *Being Leaders: The Nature of Authentic Christian Leadership*, 22–26.

33. Gehring, *House Church and Mission*, 89.

34. Ibid., 88.

35. Ibid, 296.

reason that the multi-site practice of segmenting a congregation into smaller groups for corporate worship is an acceptable and viable expression of church worship.[36]

But he and other multi-site advocates who make this claim overlook an important limitation in their theory. While I think it is likely that Gehring is right, his findings only validate *citywide* multi-site churches, and the fact that Paul uses the plural "churches" for gatherings of Christians beyond the city level implies that oneness only applies to a church in one location (i.e. city) and the universal church. Multi-site churches that go beyond a city are neither, and going beyond a city is characteristic of most multi-site churches. In fact, among multi-site advocates, Gregg Allison is the only one I know of who limits the spread of a multi-site church to a city, and who advocates the various sites gathering as one church on a regular basis.

Here we must ask the question why Paul consistently used the plural (churches) for groups that were scattered over areas larger than a city. While there is no explicit answer in Paul's letters, a good argument can be made that to be one local church, there must be some level of relational unity. Thus, there is something in the nature of a local church that involves relational interaction or gathering, and when the geographic expansion of a group of Christians exceeds the ability of the persons involved to gather, it is more appropriate to see them as separated into different churches rather than as distributed in the sites of a single church. While Gehring does see a plurality of house churches composing the one church in various cities, he also states, "Paul, however, also places a high value on a regular assembly of the whole local church there [Corinth]."[37] Robert Banks is even stronger. While he acknowledges the probability that the whole church in Corinth and Jerusalem met together in smaller groups from time to time, he also insists on the importance of an actual gathering of the whole as well. He says, "The word [*ekklēsia*] does not describe all the Christians who live in a particular locality if they do not in fact gather or when they are in fact not gathering. Nor does it refer to the sum total of Christians in a region or scattered throughout the world at any particular point of time."[38] Such gathering is not envisioned for most multi-site churches. Thus, the objection to the possibility that one church can meet in many locations seems to have some weight, at least for those multi-site churches who see no impor-

36. Frye, "The Multi-Site Phenomenon," 228–29.

37. Gehring, *House Church and Mission*, 296.

38. Banks, *Paul's Idea of Community*, 41.

tance in gathering their members, or those whose expansion makes such gathering impossible. Such multi-site churches are missing the relational element involved in making a group of believers one church, and would be more accurate to describe themselves as one network of churches in many locations, as one prominent former multi-site church has recently done.[39]

Conclusion

This paper has argued that two factors question the appropriateness of calling multi-site churches "one church in many locations." First is the New Testament teaching on the unity of a local church, which includes a strongly relational element, referring to the quality of relationships among the members, relationships that assume some level of interaction. A second and related idea is the importance of gathering to the nature of a church.[40] Even Brian Frye, whose dissertation supports multi-site churches, recommends that "*multi-site churches should attempt to gather the entire church body periodically as the context allows.*"[41] These findings do question the appropriateness of calling a widely scattered multi-site church one local church. Some are coming close to resembling associations or mini-denominations.[42] However, we did find support for the idea that some New Testament churches were composed of multiple house churches in one city, and

39. In the summer of 2011, as they were planning to expand into more widely scattered locations, Mars Hill Church decided to do away with "campus" terminology and call each of its sites a church. They see this as more biblical, more natural, and more accurate, because every Mars Hill church "fulfills the biblical criteria for a church." But these former campuses will not lose all relationship with each other and the home church. "Though by definition we may be many different churches, the Mars Hill Network of churches remains a single, united church. We share a common infrastructure, a common mission, common teaching, and a common belief that we can reach more people by working together than existing separately." This seems a positive development, though questions remain concerning the relationship of the individual churches to the Mars Hill Network. See "No More Mars Hill 'Campuses,'" http://blog.marshill.com/2011/08/08/no-more-mars-hill-%2%80%9ccampuses%e2%80%9d/, accessed August 9, 2011.

40. Gehring, *House Church and Mission*, 296; Banks, *Paul's Idea of Community*, 41.

41. Frye, "Multi-Site Phenomenon," 229. Italics in original. In the absence of a clear biblical command that churches must gather, Frye is unwilling to give more than a recommendation, but it is a recommendation that many multi-site models will not be able to put into practice.

42. Surratt, Ligon, and Bird, *Multi-Site Road Trip*, 222, list as one of their predictions for what is next for multi-site churches, "A few multi-site churches will become mini-denominations."

were regarded as one local church. Thus, multi-site churches whose sites are close enough to allow for relational unity and at least occasional gathering do seem to have some New Testament support.

Finally, the wide diversity of multi-site models and the varied circumstances that have led churches to go in that direction call for adding some limitations to this critique of multi-site churches. For example, in the case of churches who have gone to multiple sites because of extraordinary response to a gifted preacher, going to multiple sites seems to this author preferable to the options of turning people away, or building ever bigger and more expensive auditoriums. In other cases, a multi-site model adopted as a temporary expedient while leadership is being developed to allow additional sites to become healthy local churches seems an acceptable church planting strategy. But a church that extends its sites across states and even internationally needs to recognize the difficulty involved in calling itself a single local church. If it recognizes this difficulty and begins to see itself as a denomination or network of churches, this would be a positive step, but if it still retains one budget, leadership, and board for its associated churches, it faces other questions of polity, the proper role of pastors, and the importance of local churches providing their own teaching. But we will leave those questions for another day and another article.

Online Churches and
Christian Community

Does Christian Fellowship
Require Embodied Presence?

—Robert Herrington

This chapter will attempt to accomplish three things. First, this chapter will outline how society has gotten to a place where virtual community and online church is an important topic of discussion. Second, this chapter will examine one of the fundamental assumptions that online churches make: that media itself is neutral. Lastly, this chapter will attempt to analyze the medium of the Internet in order to determine whether Christian community can authentically be expressed through this medium.

How Have We Gotten Here?

Since the start of the 21st century there has been a shift in the primary medium used for communication. This shift, which began with the invention of the telegraph, is from print based to electronic image based media. The dominance of print media lasted for nearly two hundred years, from the time of Gutenberg's printing press to Morse's telegraph.[1] Since the invention of the telegraph, electronic media has evolved to include television and, more recently, the Internet. Like the printing press, the Internet will likely have a major influence on society and the church.

Just as Gutenberg's printing press, the Internet has both religious and non-religious uses. Nearly two-thirds of all U.S. Internet users have used

---

1. Postman, *Amusing Ourselves to Death*, 41.

the Internet for religious purposes.[2] In fact, the same amount of people use the Internet for religious purposes as they do for online banking.[3] As of right now most statistics show that the use of the Internet for religious purposes acts as a supplement, not a substitute, to offline religious practices. [4] Furthermore, those who most actively use the Internet for religious purposes are also the most active offline religious participants.[5]

While for many people online religious activity acts as a supplement to offline religion, there are a growing number of people that use the Internet as a replacement for offline religion. For the most part this divide is generational. For example, while electronic technology complements face to face communication for many in the Baby Boomer generation, it acts more as a replacement for face to face communication for younger generations like Generation X, The Net Generation, and Generation Next.[6] The difference is that many Baby Boomers were well into adulthood before the Internet became widespread, while younger generations were born into this technology.[7] As a result, those who are ages eleven through thirty one spend upwards of thirty hours a week online.[8]

Additionally, the Internet is rapidly replacing television as the dominant communication medium in society, especially among the Net Generation.[9] Furthermore, traditional phone usage is also being replaced by Internet technology, which includes text messaging, Facebook messaging, Skype, GTalk, and AIM.[10] The result from this shift is that those in the Net Generation have adapted to communicating largely through electronic media.

Not only are people communicating online, but millions are attempting to have community through this medium. The social networking site Facebook has played a major role in this shift. By 2011 there were more

2. Hoover et al., "Faith Online," 2.

3. Larsen, "Wired churches, Wired temples," 6.

4. Hoover et al., "Faith Online," 3.

5. Larsen, "CyberFaith," 3.

6. Tapscott, *Grown Up Digital*, 16. Those in Generation X were born between January 1965 and December 1976; the Net Generation were born between January 1977 and December 1997; Generation Next were born between January 1998 and the present. *Grown Up Digital* is the continuation of Tapscott's book *Growing up Digital*.

7. Ibid., 17.

8. Ibid., 42.

9. Ibid.

10. Ibid.

than 800 million users on Facebook.[11] In terms of time spent on the social media site, "Facebookers around the world were using the site up to three billion minutes a day."[12] Of course the use of social media in general, Facebook included, has only grown since then. This shift in communication media has led to a shift in how community is defined and experienced. Facebook has allowed people to think of the Internet in terms of community not just communication. Douglas Groothuis notes, "Community was once reserved for persons closely associated geographically and culturally. Cyberspace technologies, however, have pushed the concept of community beyond these physical limits."[13] These new technologies have changed the very nature of what it means to be in community with others.[14]

Online Churches

Churches have responded to the increased use of the Internet by increasing their presence online. In fact, there are some churches that now exist exclusively online through, for example, Second Life, an online virtual community.[15] And when discussing online churches, it is important to make distinctions. With the prevalence of the Internet almost every church has some presence online. Pastors have email addresses and most churches have websites. Furthermore, many churches even post their entire service online. While such churches are online this does not necessarily mean they are online churches; this is an important distinction. J.K Hadden and D.E. Cowan distinguish between the two; they note that religion online "Provides the interested web traveler with information about religion: doctrine, polity, organization, and belief; service and opportunities for service; religious books and articles; as well as other paraphernalia related to one's

---

11. http://www.facebook.com/press/info.php?factsheet, accessed November 13, 2011.

12. Rice, *Church of Facebook*, 74.

13. Groothuis, *Soul in Cyber-Space*, 125.

14. Veith and Stamper, *Christians in a .com World*, 49

15. Andreé Robinson-Neal notes, "Second Life, the product of California-based Linden Lab, came online publicly in 2003 and boasts of an active variety of communities including clubs, casinos, stores and malls, education facilities, and churches. These virtual communities are created and maintained by real-world people who appear (virtually) in Second Life as men, women, mechanized creations, and furry humanoids, collectively known as avatars" ("Impact of Virtual Worship," 228).

religious tradition."[16] In contrast, they note that online churches are those that "invite the visitor to participate in the religious dimension of life via the Web; liturgy, prayer, ritual, mediation, and homiletics come together and function with the e-space itself acting as a church."[17]

Additionally, it is important to distinguish whether or not an online church uses virtual technology.[18] Online churches that do not use virtual technology post their old video feed from previous live services or simulcast a live service from a physical location on the Internet. Most of these churches have an online campus pastor along with some low tech means through which the congregants are able to communicate with one another, like the use of instant messenger. Furthermore, many of these churches are connected to a physical church.[19]

In contrast, churches that use virtual technology interact through online avatars. Some proponents of online churches argue that this type of communication provides more authentic community than the text based interactions of other online churches.[20] Typically, these churches are not connected to a physical church; they exist completely in cyberspace. Instead of watching simulcast sermons that are broadcast from a physical location these services are done completely online, including a pastor preaching and interacting through an online avatar. Most of these churches can be found on Second Life.[21]

Is Media Neutral?

The possibility of reaching millions of persons with the gospel is the primary argument put forth in defense of online and virtual churches.[22] The Internet is seen as the next great mission field, with many online churches

---

16. Hadden, and Cowan, "Promised Land or Electronic Chaos?," 9.

17. Ibid.

18. For a detailed explanation of this distinction see Estes, *SimChurch.*

19. There are many churches that are moving to this model. For example, Saddleback Church now has an online campus. See http:// http://saddleback.com/visit/locations/onlinecampus.

20. Estes, *SimChurch,* 72.

21. A search of the word "church" on Second Life's website returned 526 results. See http://search.secondlife.com/web/search/?q=church&s=secondlife_com&m=N&lang=en-US, accessed November 13, 2011.

22. Surratt et al., *Multi-Site Church Road Trip,* 94.

describing the online community as a neighborhood of lost people in need of a church.[23] Additionally, many online churches believe the Internet has the ability to restore the breakdown of community. Samuel Ebersole and Robert Woods note this sentiment:

> The growth of computer networking, the Internet, and the World Wide Web (WWW) has been accompanied by an increased interest in the idea that these communication networks can facilitate community. Online communities are said to be springing up in every corner of the 'Net,' promising to restore the intimacy that was believed to have been lost through technological advance first introduced by writing and later by print.[24]

Most online churches believe authentic community can be mediated through the Internet without undermining its authenticity. This view assumes that embodied presence is not required for authentic community. Along with this assumption comes a more fundamental assumption, an assumption about media itself. It is the assumption that media is neutral.

A neutral view of media believes that changes in methods do not bring about changes to the nature of what is being communicated, or affect those doing the communicating.[25] There is an assumption that what could be done face to face can just as well be done online. A neutral view of media sees media essentially like a pipeline or conduit.[26] As an example, Geoff Surratt, in *The Multi-Site Church Revolution*, defends simulcast preaching by putting forth a neutral view of media, stating, "I was connecting to the content; the container didn't really matter."[27] In an article written by Simon Jenkins, a creator of one of the first publicized Second Life churches, Jenkins also assumes a neutral view of media. Jenkins states that "Just as the Methodist church leader John Wesley took his preaching out of churches and into the fields and streets in the 18th century, we wanted to take church to where people are in the 21st century—on the Net."[28] Both of the previous statements assume that the church can be transported or mediated through a different medium without any fundamental changes taking place. By

---

23. Ibid., 91.

24. Ebersole and Woods, "Virtual Community," 185.

25. Hipps, *Hidden Power of Electronic Culture*, 29.

26. Ibid., 38.

27. Surratt et al., *Multi-Site Revolution*, 164.

28. Jenkins, "Rituals and Pixels," 101.

overlooking the effects of media, online churches underestimate the influence the medium of the Internet has on authentic community.

Media Ecology

In contrast to such a view, media ecology disputes the idea that media are neutral. Media ecology was developed in the middle of the 20th century to analyze the impact of media on culture, apart from the specific content of the media.[29] Media ecology argues that media do three things. First, media influence the message being communicated. Second, new media bring ecological changes to society. Lastly, media affects not only society, but the individuals using a particular medium. Marshall McLuhan, the father of media ecology, argued that the relationship between content and form was so intertwined that he coined the phrase "the medium is the message."[30] What McLuhan means is that the medium itself communicates something along with the content that is communicated.

Similar to McLuhan's idea that the "medium is the message," Neil Postman argues that each medium has a bias of content.[31] Each medium has a

29. Some of the major works on media ecology are: McLuhan, *Understanding Media*; Harold Innis, *The Bias of Communication* (Toronto: University of Toronto Press, 1951); Walter Ong, *The Presence of the Word: Some Prolegomena for Cultural and Religious History* (New Haven: Yale University Press, 1967); Postman, *Amusing Ourselves to Death*; Lewis Mumford, *Technics and Civilization* (New York: Harcourt, Brace & World, 1934); Jacques Ellul, *The Technological Society* (New York: Knopf, 1964); Elizabeth L. Eisenstein, *The Printing Press as an Agent of Change: Communications and Cultural Transformations in Early Modern Europe, Vols. I and II* (Cambridge: Cambridge University Press, 1979); Joshua Meyrowitz, *No Sense of Place: The Impact of Electronic Media on Social Behavior* (New York: Oxford University Press, 1985).

30. For the use of this phrase see McLuhan, *Understanding Media*. Marshall McLuhan was a professor at the University of Toronto and was known for his work on how media influenced society. He held a Ph.D. from Cambridge in English Literature, and received ten honorary doctorates in his lifetime. Between 1965 and 1975 no other figure in popular culture held more sway regarding media than McLuhan. In one week in the year of 1967 he was the feature story in *Newsweek* and *Life*. Some of McLuhan's major works are McLuhan and Fiore, *The Medium is the Message*; Marshall McLuhan and Eric McLuhan, *Laws of Media: The New Science* (Toronto: University of Toronto Press, 1988); and Marshall McLuhan, *The Gutenberg Galaxy: The Making of Typographic Man* (Toronto: University of Toronto Press, 1962).

31. Postman, *Amusing Ourselves to Death*, 84. Neil Postman was a cultural critic and communication theorist who wrote extensively in the field of media ecology. He founded the first ever program for media ecology at New York University. Some of Postman's major works are Postman, *The Disappearance of Childhood*; Neil Postman, *Building a*

built in bias towards how it best communicates. For example, print based media is biased towards communicating logical, deductive content, which the television is not as well equipped to communicate, with its time restrictions of thirty minutes to an hour and its focus on the image. Another way to say this is that "every technology has embedded deep within it some kind of ideology . . . ideas that lie behind every technology that will make their way known over time."[32] Essentially, media have built in values.[33] For example, the medium of Twitter is an online social networking service that allows its users to post 140 character tweets.[34] Twitter has a bias toward short, efficient messages, because of the 140 character restriction and the overall nature of the medium. This bias restricts the type of content a person can communicate through Twitter. According to McLuhan, societies are shaped just as much by the nature of the media used to communicate as they are by the content of the communication.[35] For this reason, media ecology argues that each medium introduced to society brings ecological change to that society. It is not the old society plus the new medium.[36]

Shane Hipps provides a good explanation as to why the term ecology is used:

> As we begin to perceive the power of media regardless of the message, we soon discover that the metaphor of media forms as conduits or containers is not adequate. Instead, it is more helpful to borrow a principle from the environmental science of ecology. The principle of ecology refers to the ways in which environments change and adapt. For example, imagine two adjacent rooms separated by a wall. In one room the temperature is 20 degrees; in the adjacent room the temperature is 90 degrees. If the dividing wall is removed, the two temperatures are blended to form a completely new climate. In the same way, communication media often serve

---

Bridge to the 18th Century (New York: Vintage Books, 1999); Neil Postman, *Conscientious Objections: Stirring Up Trouble About Language, Technology, and Education* (New York: Vintage Books, 1988); and Neil Postman, *Technopoly: The Surrender of Culture to Technology* (New York: Vintage Books, 1993).

32. Challies, *Next* Story, 37.

33. Dyer, *From the Garden to the City*, 96.

34. See http://twitter.com/.

35. McLuhan and Fiore, *Medium is the Message*, 8.

36. Dyer, *From the Garden to the City*, 16.

to remove the walls of time and distance. As a result, formerly separate worlds collide, creating entirely new cultural ecologies.[37]

In addition to ecological effects, media also have biological effects. [38] Media change people and societies. For example, the introduction of the printing press during the Reformation changed the way people think. Postman describes it like this: "The Bible became an instrument to think about, but also an instrument to think with."[39] The very manner in which people began to think and learn was shaped by the form of print based media introduced by the printing press. John Dyer provides a helpful explanation as to why media have biological effects on its users:

> Our brains work just like our muscles; when we perform a mental task repeatedly, our neural pathways rewire themselves to become better at that task. For example, people who spend long hours reading books with complex ideas tend to become good at that activity. Likewise, people who spend their days consuming small pieces of information such as text messages or status updates tend to have minds particularly suited to performing that task.[40]

Along with proponents of media ecology, it should be noted that the biblical writers themselves make a distinction between media, which means they do not hold to a neutral view of media. The apostle John recognizes that what can be done through one medium cannot necessarily be done through another medium. There are two instances when John seems to prefer the nature of embodied presence over the medium of typography. In 2 John 12, he says, "I have much to write to you, I would rather not use paper and ink. Instead I hope to come to you and talk face to face, so that our joy may be complete." John recognizes that writing to someone is different than talking with them face to face.

That there will be times when face to face communication is necessary should not be surprising, seeing that God has created humans as embodied persons. The recognition of this reality should lead online churches to ask an important question: "what, if anything, is lost when human beings relate

---

37. Hipps, *Hidden Power of Electronic Culture*, 40.

38. Tim Challies uses the term "biological" to describe how media change people. See Challies, *Next Story*, 44–46.

39. Postman, *Disappearance of Childhood*, 34.

40. Dyer, *From the Garden to the City*, 37.

to each other by way of teletechnology"?[41] Does the medium of the Internet allow it to authentically mediate Christian community online?

Does Community Require Presence?

When it comes to having Christian community online, most online churches do not attempt to provide theological justification for online *koinonia*. They simply assume that *koinonia* can be mediated online without becoming something fundamentally different than biblical *koinonia*. The only book length theological defense of online Christian community is *SimChurch: Being the Church in the Virtual World* by Douglas Estes.[42] Estes defines a virtual church as "a virtually localized assembly of the people of God dwelling in meaningful community with the task of building the kingdom."[43] Estes argues that there is no reason to deny the authenticity of virtual community: "the everyday *koinonia*, or intimate community, referred to in Acts 2 is possible and even commonplace in virtual churches."[44] In fact, Estes argues that there are times when virtual community can be more authentic than embodied community, especially among the Millennial generation (those born between 1982–2001).[45]

In the New Testament *koinonia* can refer to "fellowship, association, community, communion, joint participation, and intercourse."[46] Yet, "The root idea of *koinonia* is 'taking part in something with someone.'"[47] The foundation for *koinonia* is the "the common life shared by all believers on the ground that they all, by their calling as Christians, participate in Jesus Christ."[48] Therefore, it must be noted that community is created by God not humans. As Ralph Martin notes, "It is not a collection of folk associated because they share a common interest in religion, but the society or fellowship—or even body —of those whom God has called into *koinonia* with Himself through His Son and in Him with one another."[49] The believer's

41. Dreyfus, *On the Internet*, 52.

42. Estes, *SimChurch*.

43. Ibid., 37.

44. Ibid., 43.

45. Ibid., 27.

46. Thayer, *Thayer's Greek-Lexicon of the New Testament*, 352.

47. Martin, *Family and the Fellowship*, 36.

48. Ibid., 37.

49. Ibid., 8.

koinonia with God, Christ, and the Holy Spirit, enables and provides a foundation for *koinonia* with one another (1 John 1:3; 1 Cor 1:9; 2 Cor 13:14).[50]

Through faith in the gospel people are brought into community with God and one another. All Christians are adopted into the same family and are all baptized into one body (Gal 3:26; 1 Cor 12:12–13). This is the community that God creates. However, in light of this community, Christians are commanded to express and be in community with one another. This is the imperative of community.

This chapter does not want to question the community that God has created through the gospel in online or virtual churches. If members of online churches have placed their faith in the gospel they surely have community with God and one another. What is in question is whether or not online churches can rightly express community? Can the Internet provide a legitimate means through which to express and maintain the community that God has created through the gospel?

Sharing

Immediately apparent in Acts, as an implication and expression of *koinonia*, is the sharing of goods. This sharing of goods is "an outward expression of their sharing in divine things: this community of material possessions stemmed from the *koinonia* of Christ."[51] Furthermore, the New Testament uses *koinonia* to express the sharing of material needs more than any other usage.[52] John Hammett notes, "Serving one another in terms of the practical, material needs of life is an expression of fellowship."[53]

Concerning the sharing of material needs through the medium of the Internet, there are obvious limitations. Using Neil Postman's terminology of the bias of media, it is fair to say that the Internet has a bias towards the non-material. While online relationships provide some avenues for sharing, these do not compare to the amount that face to face interactions provide. Virtual reality simply does not provide tangible ways to share with one another. Furthermore, even when people take advantage of the limited means of sharing provided through online interaction, this sharing loses its

---

50. Ibid.

51. Davies, *Members One of Another*, 28.

52. Hammett, *Biblical Foundations for Baptist Churches*, 234.

53. Ibid.

visible expression, which keeps it from fully picturing the unity the church has in Christ.

Gathering

A second visible expression of Christian *koinonia* in the New Testament is the church gathering. This is why Paul says in Hebrews 10:25, let us not neglect "to meet together, as is the habit of some, but encouraging one another." Philip Ryken rightly notes that "The first Christians understood that within the communion of the saints, covenant assembly is required."[54] One reason covenant assembly is important is because it is a visible expression of the unity that Christians have through the work of Christ (Eph 2:1–12).

Online churches are certainly gathering, but it is not reflective of the gathering commanded in the New Testament. Can an avatar sitting across from another avatar in a virtual world picture the unity that Christians have in Christ in the same way that Jews sitting across from Gentiles, or African Americans sitting across from Caucasians, picture the unity that Christians have in Christ? For this reason, Gene Veith is right to note that "It may be 'meeting' to log into a Christian chat room, but it is not 'meeting together.' The biblical model for the Church is clearly one of actual—not virtual—relationships between its members, being in each other's presence and in the presence of Christ."[55]

Not only is the medium of the Internet not able to visibly express the unity that Christians have in Christ, but it seems likely that it actually has a bias against physical presence. And if this is the case, then it very well could lead to ecological changes in society. With the onset of online community will people feel inclined to be in the physical presence of others? Why physically gather when you can gather on online? In terms of this bias against embodied presence, Hipps states that "Digital social networking inoculates people against the desire to be physically present with others in real social networks-networks like a church or a meal at someone's home. Being together becomes nice but nonessential."[56] As evidence of this shift, Challies notes, "A study from the University of Stanford found that for

54. Ryken, *Communion of the Saints*, 78.

55. Veith and Stamper, *Christians in a .com World*, 159.

56. Hipps, *Flickering Pixels*, 115.

every hour we spend on our computers, traditional face-to-face interaction falls by nearly thirty minutes."[57]

Baptism and Communion

Two of the most important visible expressions of the *koinonia* that Christians have are the sacraments of baptism and communion.[58] In fact, baptism and communion are a celebration of the fact that Christians have fellowship with God and each other in the gospel. Baptism is the physical expression of one's union with Christ and entrance into the body of Christ.[59] Ryken states that, "Since believers are united to Christ through baptism, we are also united to one another through baptism."[60] Baptism is a visualization of a spiritual reality.[61] Thus, online baptism loses the visual significance of one's death, burial, and resurrection with Christ (Rom 6:3–4). Furthermore, online baptism also loses the public significance of someone entering into the fellowship through the work of Christ. Yes, online church members are baptized into the universal body of Christ. Yet, there is no tangible, local body of believers to represent the body of Christ. Instead, there is a disembodied virtual body with members who cannot see one another.

In terms of communion this is the renewal of what began with baptism. Communion is a physical expression of one's union with Christ and fellow believers, through the gospel. In 1 Corinthians 10:16–17 Paul states, "The cup of blessing that we bless, is it not a participation in the blood of Christ? The bread that we break, is it not a participation in the body of Christ? Because there is one bread, we who are many are one body, for we all partake of the one bread." Based on this, Banks states, "The most visible and profound way in which the community gives physical expression to its fellowship is in the common meal in which the members share."[62] Banks further notes, "Thus the meal they shared together not only reminded the members of their relationship with Christ and one another but actually

---

57. Challies, *Next Story*, 76.

58. Ryken, *Communion of the Saints*, 83.

59. Banks, *Paul's Idea of Community*, 80–82.

60. Ryken, *Communion of the Saints*, 30.

61. Ibid.

62. Banks, *Paul's Idea of Community*, 83.

deepened it, much as participation in a common meal by a family or group not only symbolizes but really cements the bond between them."[63]

Communion, like baptism, loses the richness of its physical expression when it is practiced alone and online. The physical expression of this celebration points to the wonder of what God has done through Christ. Online churches cannot take of the "one loaf" because the church members are physically separated from one another.

The Body of Christ and the Church as a Family

New Testament metaphors for the church are also important for understanding the nature of Christian community. The New Testament describes the church as the body of Christ and as a spiritual family. These metaphors not only describe the community God has created through the gospel, but they also command community. One aspect of being the body of Christ is the use of spiritual gifts for the betterment of the body. Kirkpatrick notes, "The *koinonia* brought together a variety of individual gifts, as Paul notes on more than one occasion. But these gifts are to be exercised for the community itself, for its common good (Acts 4:32 and 1 Cor 12:7). To convey the unity of the community Paul invokes the image of the body with its many organs and functions."[64] Davies notes,

> The spiritual gifts are therefore to be understood in terms of the *koinonia*, i.e. in terms of the fellowship of believers who share in the Spirit—the Spirit's presence being revealed by the gifts of which he is the source: the gifts, in their turn, being bestowed in order that the *koinonia* might develop to its maturity, its members being thereby more closely knit the one to the other and progressively refashioned in Christlikeness.[65]

The very medium of the Internet restricts the gifts that can be used in the church. Can the whole spectrum of the gifts in the body of Christ be utilized without physical presence? Unfortunately, it is only natural that online churches will lack maturity because only a few people will be able to actively use their gifts for the building up of the body.

---

63. Ibid., 86.

64. Kirkpatrick, *Ethics of Community*, 16–17.

65. Davies, *Members One of Another*, 19.

Another important metaphor for the church in the New Testament is the church as family. Joseph Hellerman, in *When the Church Was a Family: Recapturing Jesus' Vision for Authentic Christian Community*, argues that authentic Christian community requires Christians to place their church family before their natural family. Furthermore, the apostle Paul was particularly fond of using this family imagery to describe believer's relationships, with at least 274 references in his writings alone.[66] Regarding Paul's terminology, Banks states, "All Paul's 'family' terminology has its basis in the relationship that exists between Christ, and as a corollary the Christian, and God. Christians are to see themselves as members of a divine family."[67] Since the New Testament describes Christian community in such intimate terms it seems unlikely that the Internet can mediate such relationships. While there are times when the Internet proves useful in keeping people connected, the Internet cannot ultimately sustain familial relationships.

It could even be argued that the medium of the Internet is biased against these types of deep authentic relationships. Hipps notes, "Authentic community involves high degrees of intimacy, permanence, and proximity. While relative intimacy can be gained in virtual settings, the experiences of permanence and proximity have all but vanished."[68] Similarly, Robert D. Putnam notes, "The poverty of social cues in computer-mediated communication inhibits interpersonal collaboration and trust, especially when the interaction is anonymous and not nested in a wider social context. Experiments that compare face-to-face and computer-mediated communication confirm that the richer the medium of communication, the more sociable, personal, trusting, and friendly the encounter."[69] Proponents of online churches are trying to make the Internet do something it simply is not capable of doing.

One Another Commitments

Ultimately, the true expression of the *koinonia* that God has created through the gospel requires very serious commitments between members of the church, represented by at least thirty-one other commands in the New

---

66. Hellerman, *When the Church Was a Family*, 77.

67. Banks, *Paul's Idea of Community*, 54.

68. Hipps, *Flickering Pixels*, 114.

69. Putnam, *Bowling Alone*, 176.

Testament.[70] Many of these commitments require physical presence in one another's lives. The Internet has a bias of efficiency that could actually work against these one another commitments. Deep committed relationships are not efficient and take hours of investment. The medium of the Internet does not allow for this type of commitment level. After an extensive amount of research on people who have been involved in both online and offline community, Heidi Campbell introduces the concept "Chocolate Chip Cookie Factor." Campbell created this phrase to make the point that physical presence cannot simply be replaced online. An act, such as making a friend chocolate chip cookies when they are sad, has no equal on the Internet.[71]

Moreover, the Internet might have some rather serious effects on the way people interact with one another. As Challies notes, "By the times today's digital native reaches his twenties, he will have spent some 20,000 hours accessing the Internet and 10,000 hours playing video games."[72] In terms of these effects a number of studies have demonstrated that "many young people are actually losing their ability to relate to one another in an offline context . . . Many of our new media technologies are designed for speed and urgency, not for thoughtful reflection and undistracted conversation."[73]

Conclusion

Ultimately, relating through the medium of the Internet and relating face to face are fundamentally different. Hubert L. Dreyfus, in *On the Internet*, notes that "two human beings conversing face to face depend on a subtle combination of eye movements, head motion, gesture, and posture . . . studies suggest that a holistic sense of embodied interaction may well be crucial to everyday human encounters."[74] Unfortunately, many online churches fail to see the difference between mediated communication and face to face communication, which has led online churches to believe that the church can do without embodied community.

Lastly, it is important to note that there is nothing inherently wrong with using media and technology to further the Great Commission. Yet, as

---

70. Hammett, *Biblical Basics for Baptist Churches*, 36.

71. Campbell, *Exploring Religious Community Online*, 178.

72. Challies, *Next Story*, 44.

73. Ibid., 77.

74. Dreyfus, *On the Internet*, 58.

this chapter has tried to demonstrate, before Christians use media towards this end they must "take seriously the role of technology and media in our culture and in the church."[75]

75. Hipps, *Flickering Pixels*, 14.

Who is Bonhoeffer for Us Today?

The Ecclesiological Center of
Dietrich Bonhoeffer's Theology

—Taylor Worley

Introduction

The title of this essay comes from a letter Dietrich Bonhoeffer wrote to his best friend on April 30, 1944. This letter would begin a legendary series of theological reflections by the young pastor and imminent martyr, but before there was any talk of enigmatic phrases like a "non-religious interpretation of Christianity" or a "world come of age," this letter took up one question: "Who is Christ for us today?" It is a simple enough question in its own right, but as careful readers of Bonhoeffer know, it forms the center of a theological project almost twenty-five years in the making.[1] You will find it on the pages of his doctoral dissertation and on the last fragments that emerge from his prison cell. In his letter to Eberhard Bethge, Bonhoeffer writes:

> What keeps gnawing at me is the question, what is Christianity, or who is Christ actually for us today? The age when we could tell people that with words—whether with theological or with pious words—is past, as is the age of inwardness and of conscience, and that means the age of religion altogether. We are approaching a

---

1. In 1920, at the age of 14 Bonhoeffer expressed to his family a desire to become a theologian.

completely religionless age; people as they are now simply cannot be religious anymore.[2]

Though these words have incited huge debates over the last half-century, their theological value has gone almost completely unnoticed by Evangelicals. Like other large portions of Bonhoeffer's theological corpus, these theological letters are routinely avoided by Evangelical commentators, biographers, and students. The most recent example of this trend is Eric Metaxas' 2010 biography *Bonhoeffer: Pastor, Martyr, Prophet, Spy*. It has been extraordinarily successful in provoking the ire of Bonhoeffer scholarship's senior guard. Among that cast of scholars, perhaps Martin Marty is the most generous of all when he describes the work as written "from an emphatically Evangelical point of view, avoiding or downplaying the radical questioning and proposals by Bonhoeffer in his late letters."[3] Rather than debating the merits of this recent biography, it should suffice to say that this recent biography is merely part of a consistent trajectory among Evangelicals to avoid or dismiss the critical contributions of Bonhoeffer to modern theology.

While Evangelicals continue to draw inspiration from his courageous life and his devotional literature, we have seen very little substantive engagement with Bonhoeffer's theology, let alone his rich ecclesiology. Bonhoeffer's insights into the nature of Christian discipleship and community are only valuable to Evangelical thought and practice inasmuch as they are seen as part of a much larger theological project—namely the mutuality between Bonhoeffer's ecclesiocentrism and his foundational Christocentrism. As one commentator has said, "for Bonhoeffer, it [the project] was Christ from beginning to end."[4] There is no better arena in which to view his Christology than the ecclesiological implications that it bears out. For this reason we must ask ourselves: Who is Bonhoeffer for us today?[5]

---

2. Bonhoeffer, *Dietrich Bonhoeffer Works in English Vol. 8: Letters and Papers from Prison*, 326. Hereafter all references to the Dietrich Bonhoeffer Works in English volumes will be indicated by the abbreviation *DBWE* with the volume number.

3. Marty, *Bonhoeffer's* Letters and Papers from Prison, 163.

4. De Lange, *Waiting for the Word*, 2.

5. It seems not to matter that at this point in the history of Bonhoeffer scholarship there exists more carefully presented and historically preserved stores of his theological and personal writings than ever before (i.e., the sixteen-volume Dietrich Bonhoeffer Works in English series published by Augsburg Fortress), nor does it matter that these volumes have been the catalyst for what is surely a grand renaissance in Bonhoeffer studies. To borrow an expression from Bonhoeffer himself, the time when people could read

Nowhere has this trend been more carefully documented and studied than Stephen Haynes' book *The Bonhoeffer Phenomenon: Portraits of a Protestant Saint.* In his book, Haynes actually demonstrates the validity of Harvey Cox's much-repeated maxim that Bonhoeffer functions as the Rorschach test of modern theology. In this manner, Haynes documents the various streams of reception and the very different pictures of the man they produce. In contrast to the radical Bonhoeffer as seer or the liberal Bonhoeffer as prophet, the conservative Bonhoeffer stands as an apostle to the secularizing influence of modernity's degenerations. Haynes notes Evangelicals like Chuck Colson and James Dobson manage to overlook aspects of the story to appropriate for their purposes Bonhoeffer's moral courage in resisting the Nazi reign of terror and his concern for the unprotected Jews of Europe as a kind of proto-Zionism.[6] Despite the peculiarities of the conservative Bonhoeffer, Evangelicals are not unique in their selective appropriations of the man. In comparison to Paul Tillich and Rudolf Bultmann, Haynes notes, Bonhoeffer's significance has endured a popular reception far beyond what a theologian might expect. Unlike most of his theological contemporaries, Bonhoeffer attracts a great deal of popular attention to his life and thought due to the remarkable circumstances that brought his life to a tragically premature end. Indeed, Haynes claims that, "what continues to make Bonhoeffer so widely known, admired, read, and studied is his unique *combination* of innovative theology and committed living."[7] For this reason, Haynes ultimately concludes that such a potent combination means that "the conservative Bonhoeffer is probably impervious to scholarly critique, even that of concerned Evangelicals."[8] Along with Eberhard Jüngel, we can lament the sad fact that "Probably due to his life story and its terrible end, a halo of theological unassailability has surrounded the works of Bonhoeffer, much to their own detriment. One should destroy that halo,

---

The Cost of Discipleship or *Life Together* without an appropriately critical lens, whether theological or philosophical, is over, and so is the time of reductionist hagiographies of Bonhoeffer in general.

6. Bonhoeffer's life and thought do not always mesh well the ethos of Evangelicalism (e.g., his educational background and affinities with Protestant Liberalism, his peace activism and ecumenical spirit, and the controversial nature of his late theology).

7. Haynes, *The Bonhoeffer Phenomenon*, 9. "Martyr or theologian?" he asks. "The drama of his life and its unity of action and belief remain at the heart of the Bonhoeffer phenomenon" (7).

8. Ibid., 93.

for Bonhoeffer's sake."[9] At the risk of attempting to destroy that halo, we do well to consider what possibilities for a theological engagement actually remain with Bonhoeffer's thought, especially as regards the nexus of his thinking about Christ and the church.

Bonhoeffer's Binding Together of Ecclesiology and Christology

While the vital connections between Bonhoeffer's theology of the church and his foundational Christology will be evident to those who have read widely in his works, let us take the opportunity to bear out the relationship more clearly. Here are offered both an anecdotal and a thematic witness to their interdependence. First, let us take the most troublesome sample of Bonhoeffer's reflections on Christ and explore it for connections to his thinking about the church. At the same time that Bonhoeffer is probing the implications of his theme "Who is Christ for us today?" he is also asking questions about the future of the church. Contrary to the once-popular reading of *Letters and Papers from Prison* as sourcebook for secular theology, Bonhoeffer cannot pursue the question of who Christ is without simultaneously questioning the implications of his answer for the life and practice of the church. Bonhoeffer is not done with the church, and on one occasion he writes: "The questions needing answers would surely be: What do a church, community, a sermon, a liturgy, a Christian life mean in a religionless world?"[10] Indeed, the question of the church remains, and much of his concentration toward the end of his theological letters focuses on how the church might continue to practice her "arcane discipline," a notion that remains only partially elucidated for us but hints at the enduring value of liturgy as the community's social imaginary.[11] In the magisterial biography of his friend and colleague, Bethge reflects at length on what he calls Bonhoeffer's "unfinished ecclesiology."[12] He notes that Bonhoeffer greatly

9. Quoted in De Lange, *Waiting for the Word*, 13.

10. *DBWE* 8:364.

11. Bethge, *Dietrich Bonhoeffer*, 880. Bethge elaborates on the connection with the "arcane discipline" of the church in this way: "the mystery of a 'participation in the suffering of God on this earth." In other words, the non-religious interpretation of Christianity frees the church from the problems of religion by affirming to the ecclesiological ramifications of the life and worship of the church.

12. Ibid. Bethge writes: "While Bonhoeffer developed his ideas on the nonreligious interpretation of Christianity in a world come of age, he never considered abandoning

hoped that his theological reflections would aid others in thinking about the church when he writes, "I hope that in doing so [conversing theologically with Bethge] I can be of some service for the future of the church."[13] To be sure "religionless Christianity," as Bethge quips, is no "churchless Christianity."[14] So, in as much as Bonhoeffer probes the reality of Christ for us, he also seems to be asking, "What is the church for us today?"

Secondly, Bonhoeffer's entire body of work began by questioning the theological bond between Christ and the church. With that concern, his dissertation *Sanctorum Communio* provides a theological definition of the church in the simple phrase: "Christ existing as community." We will return to this theme later, but here, note the profound connection between these two realities. Not only are these concerns fundamentally bound together for Bonhoeffer, but his successive writings demonstrate a profound mutuality and interdependence between them.[15] Let us treat each briefly. Bonhoeffer's Christology provides, in the phrase he borrowed from music history, a *cantus firmus* or underlying foundation, for the structure of his

---

his connection with the traditional words and customs of the church" (881). Later, he continues: "At the end Bonhoeffer arrived at a stage that was highly critical of the church. His ecclesiology seemed entirely absorbed within the *theologia crucis*. Once his thinking had begun ecclesiologically; then this ecclesiology yielded to Christology, but during the period of *Discipleship* and the church struggle it once more aroused quite distinct connotations. Now he entered a phase where it was once again being called into question by Christology, but it would be wrong to conclude from this situation that Bonhoeffer was not interested in ecclesiology. For him everything depended on the *theologia crucis*, but the only form in which he knew this was in its urging us toward the concrete fellowship of those who share Christ's sufferings in the world" (887–88).

13. *DBWE* 8:504. "All this [his theological sketches in letters] is put very roughly and only outlined. But I am eager to attempt for once to express certain things simply and clearly that we otherwise like to avoid dealing with. Whether I shall succeed is another matter, especially without the benefit of our conversations. I hope that in doing so I can be of some service for the future of the church."

14. Bethge, "'Bonhoeffer's Christology and His 'Religionless Christianity,'" 64.

15. De Lange, *Waiting for the Word*, 74: "His theology is pervaded with Christocentrism, even if it is not continually explicit Christology. That Christocentrism is in turn fed by a faith experience, which can best be called a form of Christ mysticism, provided that one does not take it to be a sort of escapism." And Plant, *Bonhoeffer*, 146: "Finally, the Christology Bonhoeffer formed in his 1933 lectures constitutes the central light that illuminates many of the political, theological, and ethical subjects he attends to. Christ is at the centre of the *Sanctorum Communio*; Christology is *the* academic discipline because with Christology alone is the one central question of human life asked 'Who is Jesus Christ for us today?'" "Christ is the *cantus firmus* in the polyphony of Bonhoeffer's theology."

ecclesiology.[16] As Andreas Pangritz and others have noted, Bonhoeffer's Christology is the golden thread that runs throughout his entire body of thought.[17] Pangritz even points to the novel way in which Christology directed Bonhoeffer's project when he states:

> Throughout his life Bonhoeffer participated in the movement towards Christological concentration inaugurated by Karl Barth and dialectical theology after the First World War. However, in Bonhoeffer's thought this concentration does not lead to isolation from other theological and non-theological themes. Rather the centrality of Christ serves as the decisive motive for opening the horizons of the church towards the world in its concrete reality.[18]

Many of the most respected commentators on Bonhoeffer's project—from Eberhard Bethge and John de Gruchy to more recent voices like Stephen Plant—confirm the way in which Christology provides a foundation for all other aspects of Bonhoeffer's theology, especially his theology of the church.[19] By the same token, Bonhoeffer's ecclesiology creates a space for the concrete application of his Christological themes. Indeed, ecclesiology

16. *DBWE* 8:394–95: "God requires that we should love him eternally with our whole hearts, yet not so as to compromise or diminish our earthly affection, but as a kind of *cantus firmus* to which the other melodies of life provide the counterpoint . . . where the ground bass is firm and clear, there is nothing to stop the counterpoint from being developed to the utmost of its limits . . . only a polyphony of this kind can give life a wholeness, and assure us that nothing can go wrong so long as the *cantus firmus* is kept going . . . put your faith in the *cantus firmus*."

17. Andreas Pangritz, "Who is Jesus Christ, for us, today?," 134 and 151. Pangritz begins: "It has become customary to regard Christology as the centre of Bonhoeffer's thought. And indeed, the question 'Who is Jesus Christ?' forms the *cantus firmus* of Bonhoeffer's theological development from the beginning to the end." And he concludes: "Bonhoeffer's quest for social concreteness of Christology endures in this simile of *cantus firmus* and counterpoint in musical polyphony. Yet the earlier, sometimes almost compulsive identifications of Christ and community, Christ and peace, Christ and David, are relaxed and finally liquefied by a new conception, in which 'divine and human nature,' love of 'God and his eternity,' and 'earthly, erotic love' can communicate with consummate ease in a Christological interplay."

18. Ibid., 134–35.

19. De Gruchy, "Introduction," in *DBWE* 8:27. De Gruchy explains: "Bonhoeffer never ceased to believe in the church even when he was most disillusioned by its failures. Christian faith was never for him simply a matter of individual piety. Christology always implied an ecclesiology, which meant that Christian faith was invariably the faith of a community of disciples. This conviction was deeply embedded in *Sanctorum Communio* and was fundamental to his books *Discipleship* and *Life Together,* as it was to his involvement in the Church Struggle."

represented for Bonhoeffer the best arena in which to engage the reality of Christ and seek the theological turn he described in a letter to his friend dated April 22, 1944 as a move "from the phraseological to the real."[20] Such a notion can only be understood in the context of Bonhoeffer's growing disgust with the tragic impotence of religion in his day. For Bonhoeffer, the church is a dwelling place for faith, a space to be protected from the insincerities of religion. So, with the balance of this essay, we must examine Bonhoeffer's ecclesiocentrism as the primary vehicle for recovering a theological appreciation of his legacy. Here is a brief sketch of his ecclesiocentrism under the headings of life under the Word of Christ, life in the community of Christ, and life in the world with Christ.

Bonhoeffer's Ecclesiocentrism: Life in Christ

Commenting on Martin Luther's influence in Bonhoeffer's theology, Peter Berger highlights the Reformation foundations of his ecclesiology. In Bonhoeffer, he notes: "The Church . . . is not just a means to an end (say, an institutional means to a religious end—as liberal theologians would have had it). It is an end in itself, bearing within the real presence of Jesus Christ. 'To be in Christ' and 'to be in the church' is one and the same thing."[21] Indeed, Bonhoeffer's distinct reflections on the church serve to underscore this solidarity with Christ by stressing the reality of spiritual encounter; that is an encounter *under* the word, an encounter *in* the community, and an encounter *among* the world. In this way, Bonhoeffer sees the church as the sole means of encounter with Christ.

Life under the Word of Christ

"With Christ and the forgiveness of sins to fall back on, the church is free to give up everything else."[22] Statements like this signal Bonhoeffer's unqualified confidence in the Word of Christ and the priority he gives to it as the

---

20. *DBWE* 8:358.

21. Berger, "Sociology and Ecclesiology," in Marty, *The Place of Bonhoeffer*, 66–67.

22. Bonhoeffer, "Worldliness and Christianity of the Church," in Kelly and Nelson, *Testament to Freedom*, 87.

signature encounter of God that the church offers to the world.[23] For our purposes, there is no better source for understanding Bonhoeffer's sense of divine encounter through the Word than his Christology lectures of 1933 published as *Christ the Center*. There he asserts: "The question, 'How can the Man Jesus or the God Christ be present here and now?' is quite inadmissible. The fact of his presence is not in question. The question is really about the kind of structure of his person which enables Christ to be present within the Church."[24] Such confidence directs him to consider the relationship between the Word of Christ and Christian Scripture. He reflects: "Christ is not only present *in* the Word of the Church, but also *as* Word of the Church, that means the spoken word of preaching . . . Christ's presence is his existence as proclamation . . . His presence is not that power of the congregation or its objective spirit, out of which the preaching is made, but his existence as preaching."[25] For Bonhoeffer, the givenness of Christ is the new reality of heaven and earth—the center of humanity, history, and nature.[26] Everything in his theology begins and ends here, and Bonhoeffer builds his entire understanding of the church on this very proposition. Christ is present to the church *in* Word and Sacrament and *as* Word and Sacrament. To be present to the church is to be present in the church. Thus, affirming Christ as the center and the church as the place of divine encounter is for Bonhoeffer the proper application of Luther's *theologia crucis*.

Life in the Community of Christ

The second encounter with Christ that defines the church emerges through experiences of genuine Christian brotherhood and fellowship, what Bonhoeffer identifies exclusively as spiritual community in and through Jesus

---

23. And such encounters testify to the givenness of Christ in the last days, what Philip Ziegler is exploring under the heading of biblical apocalyptic in Bonhoeffer's *Ethics*. See Ziegler, "Dietrich Bonhoeffer—An Ethics of God's Apocalypse?"

24. *Christ the Center*, 46–47. Pelikan summarizes this point about the unsteady guarantees of history in the following way: "For the dogma of the Church, therefore, the foundation dare not be the history of Jesus Christ as past, but the presence of Jesus Christ as history" (Jaroslav Pelikan, "Bonhoeffer's *Christologie* of 1933," in Martin, *The Place of Bonhoeffer*, 156).

25. Bonhoeffer, *Christ the Center*, 51–52.

26. Bonhoeffer wrote in the drafts of his work *Ethics*: "From now on we can speak rightly of either God or of the world without speaking of Jesus Christ" (*DBWE* 6:54).

Christ.[27] Such an experience, however, was difficult for even Bonhoeffer to name. In *Sanctorum Communio*, Bonhoeffer suggests a new theological axiom for understanding the community of saints: "Christ existing as community."[28] This formulation held a certain theological and rhetorical potency that at first stirred controversy and continues to captivate those concerned with a theological understanding of community.[29] In essence, Bonhoeffer sought, among many things, to convey a sense of the ongoing power and presence of Christ among his disciples. Specifically, he wants to indicate that a wholly unique and restorative dynamic exists among the community of saints by virtue of Christ's presence there. In this way, Bonhoeffer asserts: "Christian community is not an ideal, but a divine reality."[30] This redemptive movement toward reconciliation, however, is established through the life and ministry of Christ and only maintained by his ongoing mediatory service in exaltation at the right hand of God the Father. In Bonhoeffer's conception, Christ stands *pro me*, and his role as mediator serves to redeem humanity's self-defeating and sinful inwardness and give us a conciliatory relation with one another.[31] In this way, solidarity with the

27. Cf. especially *Life Together*.

28. *DBWE* 1:124.

29. Bethge recalls that the publication of *Sanctorum Communio* caused one colleague to inform Bonhoeffer of the following: "Not many will really grasp and accept your concern: not the Barthians because of your sociology—and not the sociologists because of your Barth." Quoted in Eberhard Bethge, "The Challenge of Dietrich Bonhoeffer's Life and Theology," in Smith and Barth, *World Come of Age*, 33–34. In more recent times, Clifford Green has described the central historic significance of Bonhoeffer's formulation thus: "When he first wrote in 1927 about the Christian community in his doctoral dissertation, Bonhoeffer hardly anticipated the church crisis which would occur when Hitler became Chancellor in January 1933. However, he laid down the foundation which was to be invulnerable to all Nazi co-opting of the church. That was the simple theological axiom the church is *Christus als Gemeinde existierend*, Christ existing as community. This phrase was an adaptation of Hegel's statement, 'God existing as community,' with the alteration of one word. But given the ease with which people project all manner of self-serving ideas into the word 'God,' and the difficulty of doing it so easily with the name of Christ, the Christological concentration of Bonhoeffer's axiom was liberating. Single-minded adherence to Christ was all it took to resist the whole world panoply of National Socialism" (Green, "Human Sociality and Christian Community," in De Gruchy, *The Cambridge Companion to Dietrich Bonhoeffer*, 120. See also Green, *Bonhoeffer*).

30. *DBWE* 5:35.

31. For discussion of Christ's *pro me* stance, see Bonhoeffer, *Christ the Center*, 60. Bonhoeffer states plainly: "It is in being known by God that human beings know God. But to be known by God means to become a new person."

incarnate Christ who has already fully identified with humanity produces a unique solidarity with and for each other in the community of saints.

In contrast to most accounts of Christian fellowship, this sense of community is founded on the spiritual reality of Christ's life with us and not the wisdom or virtues of Christian pragmatism. Such good intentions, Bonhoeffer warns, are the enemy of true community. For his part, only the justification by faith offered us in Christ can free us from self-justification, what Bonhoeffer sees as the great enemy of community. Therefore, rather than merely suggesting some novel or enlightened picture of human sociality, Bonhoeffer's vision of community in Christ seeks to embody Luther's paradoxical maxim from *On Christian Liberty*: "A Christian is a perfectly free lord of all, subject to none. A Christian is a perfectly dutiful servant of all, subject to all."[32] In this way, Bonhoeffer tells us repeatedly that we belong to one another in and through Jesus Christ only, and such solidarity in Christ should send the church into the world to find Christ at work there.

Life in the World with Christ

The last encounter with Christ that defines the church was a particular emphasis of Bonhoeffer's late theology. Remarking on that period of Bonhoeffer's thought, Bethge describes the often-enigmatic themes of *Letters and Papers from Prison* as "a theology of God's solidarity with the world."[33] In this way, Bonhoeffer emphasizes that just as Jesus is "the man for others" the church can only truly be in Christ when it is the "church for others." Principally, this emphasis meant new ethical categories for the church. If self-justification was finally done away with by the gospel, Christians are free to risk themselves for the sake of God's will in the real difficulties and tensions of life.[34] In this way, Christians are called to more fully participate in a life of faith unto God. This notion of an "ethics of free responsibility" became a significant emphasis in the unfinished pieces that were collected

---

32. Luther, *On Christian Liberty*, 2.

33. Bethge, *Bonhoeffer*, 854. Although Bethge labels this segment of Bonhoeffer's thought a "New Theology," he also notes that, "The specific roots of Bonhoeffer's new theology go back to particular ideas from his early period that he in part had retained and in part given new accents" (856). Others provide the same caution.

34. Consider, for example: "There are no acts that are bad in and of themselves; even murder can be sanctified. There is only faithfulness to or deviation from God's will. There is no law with a specific content, but only the law of freedom, that is, bearing responsibility alone before God and oneself" (*DBWE* 10:367).

for Bonhoeffer's *Ethics*, a book that shows that as his time in prison drew on Bonhoeffer was wrestling with the ethical questions in ways he could never have imagined. One letter of July 21, 1944, includes particularly candid insights into the small assurances that were Bonhoeffer's during this time. He writes:

> Later on I discovered, and am still discovering to this day, that one learns to have faith by living in the full this-worldliness of life. If one has completely renounced making something of oneself—whether it be a saint or a converted sinner or a church leader (a so-called priestly figure!), a just or an unjust person, a sick or healthy person—then one throws oneself completely into the arms of God, and this is what I call this-worldliness: living fully in the midst of life's tasks, questions, successes and failures, experiences, and perplexities—then one takes seriously no longer one's own sufferings but rather the suffering of God in the world. Then one stays awake with Christ in Gethsemane. And I think this is faith; this is *metanoia*. And this is how one becomes a human being, a Christian. (cf. Jer 45) How should one become arrogant over successes or shaken by one's failures when one shares in God's suffering in the life of this world?[35]

In the case of Bonhoeffer's life, his ethics of free responsibility led him to conspire with others to assassinate a tyrant, and ultimately he paid for this risk with his own life. Such grand risks, however, need not be the focus for everyone in the church attempting to live the life of faith. For Bonhoeffer, the question is not how much has one risked for God but rather how fully entrusted to Christ one is. Rather than grand risks, such faith is the true witness for Christ before the world.

Conclusion

This brief sketch of Bonhoeffer's ecclesiocentrism reveals three distinct elements of his contribution to ecclesiology: fidelity to the Reformation hope in the gospel of Jesus Christ, an abiding reliance on the spiritual nature of Christian community, and a charge for the church's ethical witness in the world. In their own way, each of these serves to underscore the essential solidarity of Christ with his church and further directs the church into the reality of God. In the end, the most clear and direct way to answer the

---

35. *DBWE* 8:486.

question of "Who is Bonhoeffer for us today?" is to reject the narrow and short-sighted tests of twenty-first-century political theologians and theological politicians. To be sure, these are the wrong questions. If we have learned anything from the last five decades of Bonhoeffer scholarship, it is that looking for our own reflection when we look into the life and thought of Dietrich Bonhoeffer is a problematic venture at best. His life and thought cannot and should not be domesticated to the theological whims and annoyances of our day.

Who is Bonhoeffer for us today? Bonhoeffer remains for us an irrepressibly prophetic voice for the church's theology, and looking ahead, he represents for us a generative *theological* resource, especially on the doctrine of the church.[36] If his legacy is to guide future generations of Christ's church, however, we must not privilege his biography to the exclusion of his theological contributions.[37] Here is one last provocation from the theologian. Hear Bonhoeffer's call to value theology for building up the faith of God's people: "Our time is not poor in experiences but in faith. Only faith creates true experience of the Church. Therefore, we believe that it is more important to lead our time towards faith in the community of God, rather than to manufacture experiences which are useless in themselves but appear of themselves where there is faith in the *sanctorum communion*."[38]

---

36. Kelly and Nelson, *Testament to Freedom*, 472: "'God revealed in the flesh,' the God-man Jesus Christ, is the holy mystery which theology is appointed to guard. What a mistake to think that it is the task of theology to unravel God's mystery, to bring it down to the flat, ordinary human wisdom of experience and reason! It is the task of theology solely to preserve God's wonder as wonder, to understand, to defend, to glorify God's mystery as mystery."

37. Marty, *Bonhoeffer's* Letters and Papers from Prison, 164. Marty, however, remains hopeful: "Clearly many Evangelicals are on the move from frozen positions they held or stereotypes they suffered, and Bonhoeffer, always an inspirer and often an enigma, will continue to be a challenge most will welcome." According to Stephen Plant, "Bonhoeffer was courageous, intelligent; loyal to friends and family and, in the darkest moment of German history, he was on the side of the Angels. Yet these qualities have no necessary bearing on the value of his politics, theology or ethics today. Any theologian, any thinker from the past, serves us best when we resist the urge to domesticate them by our approval and admiration . . . Bonhoeffer's theology and ethics have this classic quality but their potential is only realized when we resist the urge to tame his legacy by assuming that it is easily applied to our own situation" (Plant, *Bonhoeffer*, 139).

38. Quoted in Berger, "Sociology and Ecclesiology," 74–75.

Holy

Sanctified in Christ Jesus and Called to Be Holy

Ontological Union and the Holiness of the Church

—Jim Larsen

Introduction

Despite adamant affirmation of a Nicene-Chalcedonian Christology, ontological considerations underlying early creeds and definitions are foreign to most contemporary Evangelicals. These considerations formed the foundation for ecclesiological reflection during the early and medieval periods, but that foundation was lost with the rise of nominalism in the late Middle Ages and the eclipse of metaphysics by modernity's substitution of epistemology as the foundation for theological reflection. Thus, the ontology of union and its associated ramifications for ecclesiology have faded to near insignificance in many theological discussions today. Contemporary arguments concerning church organization or church functions fail to address the issue from the perspective of what the church *is*. The church *is* holy because it *is* the sum total of all those who are in union with Christ. The church is *called* to be holy, as the manifest presence of Christ in the world in order that God's kingdom agenda may progress through her.

This chapter will argue that, in order to understand the holiness of the church, the ontology of union—believers' union with Christ as well as the divine-human union of the Incarnation—must take center stage in Evangelical theological reflection. This thesis will be developed along the following lines: (1) a brief discussion will be presented regarding ontological considerations which contributed to the formulation of Nicene-Chalcedonian Christology as it bears on questions of ecclesiology; (2) examples of the impact of these ontological considerations will be presented as they relate to premodern ecclesiology; (3) developments of the late Middle Ages and Enlightenment such as nominalism and Scottish Common Sense Realism will be discussed as they relate to the eclipse of the ontology of union in contemporary ecclesiological discussions; and (4) examples of contemporary ecclesiological discussions will be provided which illustrate difficulties and ambiguities which have resulted from the shift away from an ontology of participation, or union with Christ.

One, Holy, Catholic, Apostolic Church?

In his prayer recorded in John 17, after focusing on his current followers, Jesus then prays, "I do not ask for these only, but also for those who will believe in me through their word, that they may all be one, just as you, Father, are in me, and I in you, that they also may be in us, so that the world may believe that you have sent me" (John 17:20–21). That there is an ontological foundation for the unity of the church seems warranted by these verses. Further, the success of the church's testimony regarding Jesus is tied to that unity. Jesus continues, "The glory that you have given me I have given to them, that they may be one even as we are one, I in them and you in me, that they may become perfectly one, so that the world may know that you sent me and loved them even as you loved me" (John 17:22–23). Again, the successful witness of the church is directly related to its unity, and that unity is founded in an ontological reality which is the participation, or union, of believers collectively with Christ. Jesus refutes the charge that it is Satan's power that allows him to cast out demons, stating that "if a kingdom is divided against itself, that kingdom cannot stand. And if a house is divided against itself, that house will not be able to stand" (Mark 3:23–25). The important connection between Jesus' prayer for unity among his followers and the kingdom divided analogy here is emphasized, for me, in the very next verse: "And if Satan has risen up against himself and is divided, he cannot stand, but is coming to an end" (Mark 3:26). How can the church manifest God's love for the world and the truth that he sent his only begotten Son, as Jesus prayed in John 17, when the church is so visibly fractured beyond any credible claim of unity? How can "the church" be seen as "holy" by the world around us when churches and denominations continue to split in the ugliest of manners?

However, schisms such as the Reformation were not about "nothing." For example, in a recent book dealing with the differences between Roman Catholic and Protestant soteriologies, R. C. Sproul states that "the objective content of the gospel is the person and work of Jesus—who He is and what He accomplished in His life. The subjective side is the question of how the benefits of Christ's work are appropriated to the believer. There the doctrine of justification comes to the fore."[1] And as most are aware, the doctrine of justification remains a significant barrier to ecumenical reconciliation. In this regard, Sproul goes on to say, "I think the biggest crisis over the purity of the gospel that I have experienced in my ministerial career was the initiative known as Evangelicals & Catholics Together." For Sproul, the heart of this crisis is the affirmation that "Evangelicals and Roman Catholics have a unity of faith in the gospel."[2] In the eyes of many, then, to take a firm stance in support of ecumenical dialogue and reconciliation, especially with respect to Rome, places one's Evangelical identity into question. How can one possibly seek reconciliation with Rome—or any other "questionable" group—when that church preaches a gospel other than the one affirmed by the Magisterial Reformers and the traditions descending from them?

The problem is that, while there was much good accomplished by the Reformation, the unity prayed for by Christ as well as the "one, holy, apostolic catholic church" proclaimed by the early creeds does not exist as a material manifestation of the presence of Christ in the world, and this is of great concern. Hans Boersma laments that "the Reformation, while focusing on doctrinal issues and abusive practices that certainly needed to be addressed, failed to address appropriately the underlying problems that had given rise to the need for reform."[3] And a crucial "problem" that the Reformers failed to conclusively address was a movement away from a participatory understanding of created reality's relationship with its Creator, and with it the ontological nature of union with Christ as it relates to the church as "the body of Christ." For it is through this union that one must understand the "holiness" of "the church."

1. Sproul, *Are We Together?*, 1.

2. Ibid., 4.

3. Boersma, *Heavenly Participation*, 86–87.

Nicene-Constantinopolitan Christology and One, Holy, Catholic, Apostolic Church

In reflecting on the American culture of our day, Boersma states that "the distrust of human reason, the opposition to Christian morality, and the flattening or immanentizing of human structures" is merely a reflection of or predicated upon a "desacramentalized universe."[4] He laments a near universal perspective that fails to understand that created reality not only points to but participates in eternal, heavenly realities. To be sure, this is a mystery. Nevertheless, he argues that "the created world cannot be reduced to measurable, manageable dimensions."[5]

Though this flattened, desacramentalized perspective seems to be an accurate assessment of our culture—and I would argue by extension the contemporary church—it was not the case for the early church. While the Nicene-Constantinopolitan declaration focuses most of its attention on the essential humanity and deity of Christ, it also affirms the deity of the Holy Spirit ("co-worshipped and co-glorified with Father and Son"), followed by the affirmation of belief in "one, holy, catholic, and apostolic church."[6] The entire statement to this point has been making ontological claims regarding the relationship between Father, Son, and Holy Spirit, as well as ontological claims regarding the relationship between the two essential natures of Christ. Thus, I see no reason to *preclude* the possibility that the following affirmation relating to the church carries ontological weight as well.

Ontology and Premodern Ecclesiology

While there is an abundance of historical evidence regarding specific discussions and debates dealing with the ontology of divine and human union in the Incarnation, as well as the participation of believers in the divine, the historical evidence for an ontological understanding of the church is much more circumstantial. In this regard, Millard Erickson notes that "at no point in the history of Christian thought has the doctrine of the church received the direct and complete attention that other doctrines have received."[7] This is likely because the *nature* of the church, what it *is*, was something

4. Ibid., 97–98.

5. Ibid., 21.

6. Tanner, *Ecumenical Councils* 1:24.

7. Erickson, *Christian Theology*, 3rd ed., 951.

that was taken for granted.[8] Nevertheless, the evidence does indicate that early writers understood the "the church" as more than a collective term describing the total number of believers in a given location (or locations collectively), rather, that there was an ontological reality called the *church*. J. N. D. Kelly notes that "from the outside, primitive Christianity has the appearance of a vast diffusion of local congregations, each leading its separate life with its own constitutional structure and officers." Nevertheless, "all these communities are conscious of being parts of one universal Church."[9] For example, Ignatius (ca. 35–107) wrote to the church in Ephesus that "the Lord accepted the ointment upon his head for this reason: that he might breathe incorruptibility upon the church,"[10] and to the church in Smyrna, "Wherever the bishop appears, there let the congregation be; just as wherever Jesus Christ is, there is the catholic church."[11] Justin Martyr (ca. 100–165) argued that "the word of God speaks to those who believe in Him as being one soul, and one synagogue, and one church."[12] In his discussion on Paul's use of the expression "the body of Christ" in his first letter to the Corinthians, John Chrysostom (ca. 347–407) states that Paul was "bringing the many together into one, and implying that all become some one thing after the image of the body, and that this one thing is made up of the many and is in the many, and that the many by this are held together and are capable of being many." He goes on to say that "the Church amongst you is a part of the Church existing everywhere and of the body which is made up of all the Churches."[13] Refuting the claim that one could be "Christian" apart from the church, Irenaeus (ca. 130–200) argues in relation to the indwelling Spirit that "all those are not partakers who do not join themselves to the Church, but defraud themselves of life through their perverse opinions and infamous behaviour. For where the Church is, there is the Spirit of God; and where the Spirit of God is, there is the Church, and every kind of grace."[14] Kelly states that in spite of the fact that there were a multiplicity

---

8. Ibid. In support, Erickson quotes Colin Williams as stating that "little direct theological attention was ever given to the church itself—probably because it was taken for granted" (Williams, *The Church*, 11).

9. Kelly, *Early Christian Doctrines*, 189.

10. Ignatius, *To the Ephesians* 17.1; Holmes, *Apostolic Fathers*, 197.

11. Ignatius, *To the Smyrnaens* 8.2; Holmes, *Apostolic Fathers*, 255.

12. Justin Martyr, *Dialogue with Trypho* 63; ANF 1:229.

13. John Chrysostom, *Homilies on First Corinthians* 23.1; NPNF1 12:186.

14. Irenaeus, *Against Heresies* 3.24.1; ANF 1:458.

of local *churches*, they nevertheless, *as a whole*, comprised "a holy community within which the divine Spirit lives and operates."[15] In this regard, Kelly goes on to say that "the term 'holy,' the stock epithet of the Church, expresses the conviction that it is God's chosen people and is indwelt by His Spirit."[16] With respect to the Greek-speaking Eastern churches, G. R. Evans describes the undergirding conviction of *unity* in spite of diversity of location and practice as follows: "Whether very local indeed or the size of the patriarchate, [these churches] saw themselves not as parts, but as microcosms of the whole church."[17] Avery Dulles summarizes the early church's understanding of Paul's use of "body of Christ" as follows:

> Many of the Church Fathers, including Augustine, develop the image of the Body of Christ with particular stress on the mystical and invisible communion that binds together all those who are enlivened by the grace of Christ. Augustine speaks of a Church that includes not only the earthly but the heavenly: The angels and the blessed are members of the heavenly part of the Church. Christ as head makes up one totality together with all his members. The Body is not essentially visible, since it includes angels and separated souls. Still less is it societal, since it includes all men who are animated by the spirit of God. All the just from Abel on are the Body of Christ.[18]

All of these examples, from both Latin and Greek traditions, illustrate the early belief that there was an underlying ontology which made the community of faith *the church*. And this church was not confined to one geographic location, nor was it temporally limited. All believers, past and present, comprise the body of Christ, which is a mysterious yet nevertheless ontological reality.

15. Kelly, *Early Christian Doctrines*, 191.

16. Ibid., 190.

17. Evans, *Roots of the Reformation*, 33.

18. Dulles, *Models of the Church*, 43. The belief in the *mystical* nature of "the body of Christ" is also seen in later Western theology, such as that of Thomas Aquinas. Dulles writes, "For Aquinas the Church essentially consists in a *divinizing* communion with God, whether incompletely in this life or completely in the life of glory . . . Aquinas' view of the Church is 'theological' rather than institutional. The Body of Christ for him is not essentially visible or societal, still less hierarchical" (ibid., 43, emphasis mine). Augustine's understanding of the organic unity of the church is seen in his numerous letters dealing with the Donatists. In this regard, Roger Olson notes that Augustine referred to the Donatists as "impure" because they were "destroying the unity of the church and falling into the sin of schism" (Olson, *Story of Christian Theology*, 265).

Modernity and the Eclipse
of Ontological Union

In *Heavenly Participation*, Boersma argues that the premodern understanding of the created order was based on a *sacramental ontology*, that is, the belief that "created objects found their reality and identity in the eternal Word of God."[19] In this view, the realities of the created world, in some mysterious way, participate in the greater eternal realities to which they point.[20] We see this in Ephesians, for example, when Paul compares the unity of a husband and wife to that of Christ and the church. While both relationships are an ontological mystery, the *reality* of the marriage bond points to the *greater* reality which is Christ united to his church (Eph 5:22–33).

However, Boersma notes that signs of a shift away from a participative understanding of reality can be seen as early as the eleventh century. For example, he notes that the Investiture Controversy, resulting from reforms instituted by Pope Gregory VII (1073–1085), contributed to a shift in the understanding of church authority from intrinsic to extrinsic—the church exercised authority because it had been granted it by God, not that God was at work in and through the church in any direct manner.[21] Subsequent philosophical developments took this subtle shift in understanding and forcefully erected a great barrier between material and heavenly realities. Boersma notes that theologians such as Thomas Aquinas (1224–1274) affirmed an analogy of being (*analogia entis*) in which it was recognized that there is, *at the same time*, "a connection between God and his world" and "an otherness of God [which] needs to be preserved."[22] He writes:

> The resulting doctrine of *analogia entis* was the Great Tradition's way of avoiding a mingling of the divine and the human. The relationship between creation and Creator is merely a sacramental or analogous relationship. The sacramentality of the relationship implies that, although God is present in his creation, and though creation participates in the eternal Word of God, the sacramental reality (*res*) of the Word infinitely transcends terrestrial objects. The infinite difference between Creator and creature implies

---

19. Boersma, *Heavenly Participation*, x.

20. Ibid., 1–2.

21. Ibid., 54–55.

22. Ibid., 72.

the rejection of the pantheism that lurks in straightforward Neo-Platonism.[23]

John Duns Scotus (ca. 1266–1308) believed this view made no sense, and thus argued for a univocal character of being. Either things have being, or they do not. According to this view, Boersma states that "to say that God exists and to say created objects exist is to say one and the same thing. All being is being in the same sense."[24] The consequence of this argument, according to James K. A. Smith, is that "being, now, becomes a category that is *unhooked from participation in God* and is a more neutral or abstract qualifier that is applied *to* God and creatures in the same way."[25]

The movement away from a participatory, sacramental understanding of created reality was virtually completed through the contributions of William of Ockham (ca. 1285–1347) to the rise of nominalism.[26] In nominalism, reality is grounded in individual things themselves.[27] Thus, material reality is divorced from any type of participation in universal or heavenly realities. As Michael Gillespie notes, "The nominalist revolution was an ontological revolution that called being itself into question."[28] He affirms the devastating effect of nominalism as follows:

> All or almost all succeeding forms of thought accepted the ontological individualism that nominalism has so forcefully asserted . . . The deepest disagreements in the period between the fourteenth and seventeenth centuries were thus not ontological but ontic, disagreements not about the nature of being but about which of the three realms of being—the human, the divine, or the natural—had priority. To put it simply, post-scholastic thinkers

---

23. Ibid. This way of understanding the relationship between the created and the Creator can also be seen in Gregory of Nyssa, for example, when he writes, "So likewise, as regards the meaning of our terms, though there may be, so far as words go, some likeness between man and the Eternal, yet the gulf between these two worlds is the real measure of the separation of meanings . . . So in almost all the other terms there is a similarity of names between things human and things divine, revealing nevertheless underneath this sameness a wide difference of meanings" (*Against Eunomius* 1.39; NPNF2 5:93).

24. Boersma, *Heavenly Participation*, 74.

25. Smith, *Introducing Radical Orthodoxy*, 97 (emphasis mine).

26. Boersma, *Heavenly Participation*, 79–81.

27. Gillespie, *Theological Origins of Modernity*, 4.

28. Ibid., 16.

disagreed not about being itself but about the hierarchy among the realms of being.[29]

In this regard, Louis Dupré notes that "today we find it hard to imagine a scale of being in which the individual does not occupy the highest echelon. Yet by far the longer and arguably the most consequential part of our tradition did not grant the individual the ultimate importance we do."[30] Unfortunately, while there were attempts to recover a more sacramental understanding of reality during the Reformation, Boersma states that the Reformers "did not succeed in reweaving the tapestry, and as a result some of the problematic late-medieval presuppositions continued in the Reformation tradition as well as in contemporary evangelicalism."[31]

These streams of medieval and modern thought come to fruition in Thomas Reid (1710–1796), the founder of Scottish Realism. *Inquiry into the Human Mind on the Principles of Common Sense* was a reaction against the extreme skepticism of David Hume (1711–1776). This skepticism, which Reid believed could be traced all the way back to René Descartes (1596–1650), was founded on the false belief that ideas formed an intermediary step between the mind and objects of perception. Therefore, according to this view, we cannot have direct knowledge of the world around us, only representations or impressions of it.[32] Reid rejected this view, arguing instead that our senses in fact derive accurate knowledge of things around us, and that this sense data, coupled with intuitive principles, provides us with an accurate understanding of reality.[33] This is so, Reid argued, because God had so constituted our minds as to allow us to gain direct knowledge of reality.[34] Having been wed to Baconian scientific method, this "common

---

29. Ibid.

30. Dupré, *Passage to Modernity*, 37.

31. Boersma, *Heavenly Participation*, 85. In this vein, Peter Harrison notes that many believe Protestantism itself to be a precondition for the ascendency of science. This seems a further affirmation that modernity replaced mystery with man's quest for empirical, rational certainty. Harrison writes, "Skepticism about Catholic miracles, the denial of sacramental magic, the challenging of the special status of priests, saints, and supernatural intermediaries, have also been plausibly proposed as aspects of Reformed theology and ecclesiology which contributed to the emergence of the lawful and deterministic universe which is the prerequisite for scientific investigation" (Harrison, *Bible, Protestantism, and the Rise of Natural Science*, 7).

32. Kelly, "Scottish Realism," 1079.

33. McCall, "Baconian Common Sense Realism," 224.

34. Kelly, "Scottish Realism," 1079.

sense" approach to understanding reality made its way across the water to the United States, where it became the almost universal foundation for biblical interpretation. Concerning the pervasiveness of Baconian common sense in mid-nineteenth-century America and its fundamental role in biblical interpretation, George Marsden writes:

> For most Protestants . . . the rock of ages and the rock of common sense scientific reasoning seemed to support each other. From the liberal Unitarians at Harvard to the conservative Presbyterians at Princeton, among the moderate Calvinists at Yale, to their more radical perfectionist offspring at Oberlin, among Methodists and Baptists, and including the 'gentlemen theologians' of the South, there prevailed a faith in immutable truth seen clearly by inductive scientific reasoning in Scripture and nature alike.[35]

According to Sydney Ahlstrom, because of religious decadence existing during the post-Revolutionary War period, the apologetic value of this Scottish philosophy was such that it became "a vast subterranean influence, a sort of water-table nourishing dogmatics in an age of increasing doubt."[36]

Contemporary Ecclesiology and the Holiness of "the Church"

In *The Church and the Surprising Offense of God's Love*, Jonathan Leeman describes the contemporary "ecclesiological mess" as follows:

> The pragmatism that has reigned in American churches at least since the twentieth century, especially since the advent of (Donald McGavran-like) church growth thinking in the middle of the last century, has left our understanding of the church itself fairly doctrine-less, principle-less, structure-less. It's almost as if the wind currents of pragmatism and the barometric pressure of postmodernism came together with the temperature drop of Evangelical 'essentialism' (the Evangelical knack for discarding any doctrine not regarded as essential for salvation) in order to produce the 'perfect storm,' a storm that left a decimated ability to think seriously and freshly about the local church in its trail.[37]

---

35. Marsden, "Everyone One's Own Interpreter," 82.

36. Ahlstrom, "Scottish Philosophy," 267–68.

37. Leeman, *Church*, 31.

After briefly describing a variety of ecclesiological concerns across the right-to-left Evangelical spectrum, he concludes that "the result is something of a mess, with Evangelicals across the spectrum building their churches based upon a random mix of tradition, pragmatism, and new ideas that have helpful bits but are premised on inadequate conceptions of God and the gospel."[38] In large part I agree with Leeman's assessment, but I think he too quickly dismisses the importance of a reexamination of the early church Fathers and their understanding of "one, holy, catholic, and apostolic" church,[39] because their deliberations were sourced in a belief in what the church *is* as well as what the church ought to be doing. In this regard, Thomas Oden notes that "ecclesiology has often been pragmatically reduced to the praxis of pastoral care, church administration, homiletics, education, and community organization. When administration is reduced to management, evangelism to technique, soul care to therapeutic strategy, and preaching to rhetoric, the *doctrine* of the church has been misplaced."[40] In a 1994 JETS article, Gerry Breshears placed his finger, I believe, exactly where the problem lies:

> The flurry of ecclesial articles and books describe activity rather than define essence. Even theologians reflect on the Church more organizationally and functionally than ontologically and missiologically . . . Our pragmatic preoccupation with the nitty-gritty running of the Church forces our ecclesiology to suffer from a lack of transcendence. We must reflect first on the essence of the Church. The Church is essence taking form.[41]

Unfortunately, having identified the heart of the problem as being ontological in nature, the remainder of the article proceeds to discuss what the church's relation to the world should look like as defined by Christ's three-fold offices of prophet, priest, and king. That is, that we should "understand the Church . . . as the spiritual people of God who carry out the ongoing

---

38. Ibid., 31–32.

39. Leeman writes, "On the evangelical right are careful thinkers who are absolutely scrupulous in other areas of doctrine but tend to flow with the pragmatic stream in how they lead and structure their churches. When conservatives do write about the church, they usually rehash what the Fathers said about the church being one, holy, universal, and apostolic or what the Reformers described as the two marks of the church" (Ibid., 31). While the emphasis of the Reformers in this context may very well be on what the church does, the emphasis of the early Christian fathers was sourced in what the church *is*.

40. Oden, *Systematic Theology* 3:265 (emphasis mine).

41. Breshears, "The Body of Christ," 3.

mission of Jesus."[42] And thus, he defines the church by what it should be doing, and not what it *is*.

In describing the tensions, and I might add roadblocks, between conservative Evangelicals and the "mainline ecumenical establishment," Mark Ellingsen notes that they are in large part the result of differences between underlying philosophical presuppositions which affect theological interpretations.[43] Arguing that mainline ecumenical theological perspectives depend upon Kantian presuppositions that tend to be excessively subjective, he goes on to state that this dependence results in a failure to "be in touch with the basic suppositions of American life," which are predominantly founded upon Common Sense Realism.[44] The problem with each of these perspectives is that the presuppositions that undergird both favor the quantifiable, *phenomenal* attributes of our world at the expense of *essential* nature. This should be no surprise, since both Immanuel Kant's subjectivism and Common Sense Realism's empiricism are sourced in the same Enlightenment stream that favors autonomy and reason over authority and revelation. James Livingston notes that modernity is characterized by "a renewed awareness and trust in humanity's own capacities or initiative and appreciation of, interest in, and hope for human life on this earth. Reason largely supersedes revelation as the supreme court of appeal."[45] He goes on to say that "the ideal of the Enlightenment is, then, the duty of not entertaining any belief that is not warranted by rational evidence, which means by the assent of autonomous reason rather than biblical or ecclesiastical authority."[46] And thus we have Kant's classic definition of Enlightenment as "man's release from his self-incurred tutelage."[47] This empirical, pragmatic approach to theology is reflected in Carl Michalson's charge that "the Being of God-in-himself, his nature and attributes, the nature of the church, the nature of man, the preexistent nature of Christ—all these conjectural topics which have drawn theology into a realm of either physical or meta-

---

42. Ibid., 5.

43. Ellingsen, "Common Sense Realism," 202.

44. Ibid.

45. Livingston, *Modern Christian Thought* 1:6.

46. Ibid. 1:7.

47. Kant, *Philosophical Writings*, 263. He continues, "Tutelage is man's inability to make use of his understanding without direction from another. Self-incurred is this tutelage when its cause lies not in lack of reason but in lack of resolution and courage to use it without direction from another. *Sapere aude!* 'Have the courage to use your own reason!'—that is the motto of enlightenment."

physical speculation remote from the habitation of living men should be abandoned."[48]

In defining the "nature" of the church, Wayne Grudem states that the church is "the community of all believers for all time."[49] He continues by describing the *community* of faith as that collection of true believers, during both Old and New Testament periods, who have been called by God to assemble and worship Him.[50] He does not present the church as an ontological reality, but as a "fellowship" of all those whose spiritual condition is that of true believers. For Grudem, then, "the invisible church is the church as God sees it,"[51] that is, only those *individuals* from within the material, temporal assembly who are truly believers. Norman Geisler refers to "the universal church" as "Christ's spiritual body of believers,"[52] comprised only of those who are in fact saved. [53] And while he states that "the universal church has an unbreakable unity" because it was "God who *made* this unity when by 'one Spirit' we were baptized into 'one body'," (referencing Eph 4:4–5),[54] and also describes the church as a "spiritual entity," [55] he too falls short of discussing the church in clearly ontological terms.

In contrast to this type of ontological ambiguity, Erickson states that "the ecumenical movement in the twentieth century thrust the church to the forefront of discussion," and thus "the issue of the nature of the church cannot be ignored" because "the primary concern of the ecumenical movement is the relationship of churches to one another."[56] Erickson's discussion in his *Christian Theology* is by far one of the most *ontologically robust* discussions to be found in a contemporary systematic theology volume, so much so that he feels compelled to defend himself against charges of presenting a Platonic rather than biblical account of the church. After an examination of biblical terms and texts relevant to the *nature* of the church, he concludes that "we should note that the individual congregation, or group of believers in a specific place, is never regarded as only a part or

---

48. Michalson, *Worldly Theology*, 218.

49. Grudem, *Systematic Theology*, 853.

50. Ibid., 854.

51. Ibid., 855.

52. Geisler, *Systematic Theology* 4:43.

53. Ibid., 4:55.

54. Ibid., 4:51–52.

55. Ibid., 4:63.

56. Erickson, *Christian Theology*, 2nd ed., 1037.

component of the whole church. The church is not a sum or composite of the individual local groups. Instead, the whole is found in each place."[57] He continues:

> At this point some people might accuse theologians of adopting a Platonic perspective, whereby local churches are regarded as instantiations or concrete particular manifestations of the pure Form, the abstract Idea, of church. Note, however, that theologians are not reading this concept into the Bible. The concept is actually present in the thought of Paul and Luke; it is not introduced by their interpreters. There is on this one point a genuine parallel between biblical thought and that of Plato. This is neither good nor bad, and should not be considered an indication of Platonic influence upon the Bible. It is simply a fact.[58]

Conclusion

The church, that is, all those who are united with Christ, is holy because he is holy. As such, the church is the manifest presence of Christ in the world, and thus is intimately involved in God's bringing about his kingdom purposes in the world from Pentecost until Christ's return. While the unity of the church may seem to be an important concern in contemporary discussions, the fact of the extremely fractured condition of Christ's body seems to indicate that unity is not particularly high on the laundry list of theological problems to correct.[59] I do not want to minimize the theological im-

---

57. Erickson, *Christian Theology*, 3rd ed., 956.

58. Ibid., 957. As one who rejected "Platonic conceptions" of the church, Stanley Grenz argued for an understanding of the church which is dependent upon what it is "destined to become" in God's eschatological kingdom. He states that "the church is directed toward the destiny God intends for humankind—participation in the consummated reign of God" (Grenz, *Theology for the Community of God*, 623). To be sure, Grenz is correct in his affirmation that the church is a community of faith called by the Spirit to proclaim Christ's kingdom message and live in light of its expected arrival (Ibid., 622). Nevertheless, one does not need to reject an ontological understanding of the church to affirm a present activity and eschatological expectation. Nor does it preclude understanding that the church will be somehow *different* in the eschaton.

59. For example, in relation to the individualistic perspectives involved in various denomination splits during the early twentieth-century, Marsden states that "the important spiritual unit was the individual. The church existed as a body of sanctified *individuals* united by commitment to Christ and secondarily as a network of *ad hoc* spiritual organizations. The institutional church hence had no particular status. Separation, at least at this time, could be regarded as an individual question rather than an

portance of doctrinal issues that continue to weigh heavily in ecumenical discourse, such as justification by faith. Yet it is my belief that the single most significant issue that is preventing the church from accomplishing its purpose is its lack of unity. And I believe the root cause of this problem is that contemporary Christians do not understand the "church" in terms of an ontological or "organic" reality. Yet it is the *pervasive* focus on the individual in American Christianity, particularly its Evangelical strains, that is antithetical to an organic, ontological understanding of the church.[60]

A friend shared a conversation that he had with an Indian Orthodox priest at a patristics conference not long ago. The priest, who was in the U.S. overseeing a parish, was lamenting a problem encountered when individuals from his communion were sent to the U.S. for training. He said that their time in the U.S. "corrupted" the body. My friend asked if he meant that they learned things here that they took back and taught to those at home. The priest's reply was "no." He meant that by spending time in the U.S., the individuals *themselves* were corrupted, and because *they* were corrupted, the *whole body* was corrupted.[61] This is the type of ontological, organic view of the body of Christ that the Evangelical community lacks, but that the early church assumed. I close with a quote from Kelly which describes the early church's understanding of *the church*, which I believe we must recover:

---

institutional one" (Marsden, *Fundamentalism and American Culture*, 71, emphasis mine). Unfortunately, I see no reason to believe that the situation described here is substantially different today.

60. In this regard, Steve Bruce comments that "individual autonomy, the freedom to choose, competes with the power of the community. To the extent that the former is stressed, the latter is necessarily weakened" (Bruce, *God is Dead*, 93). Although Bruce's comments focus on "New Agers," his conclusions I believe are quite applicable to contemporary Evangelicals. He states that "in so far as New Agers [insert "Evangelicals" here] are bound to each other at all (and many associate only in the sense of coincidentally consuming the same product), those bonds are weak because they are entirely voluntary and their voluntary nature is repeatedly asserted" (Ibid). Mirroring the shift in authority from intrinsic to extrinsic described by Boersma above, Hart states that "by becoming a synonym for conservative Protestantism, through the popularity of evangelical celebrities and their parachurch organizations, the evangelical movement forfeited the authority that the institutional church possesses" (Hart, *Deconstructing Evangelicalism*, 128). He goes on to describe "evangelicalism" as an abstraction that individuals, congregations, whole denominations, and parachurch organizations alike can adopt without having to ascribe to any set collection of beliefs or practices. Thus, what it means to be "evangelical" is in Hart's terms, "fluid" (Ibid., 129).

61. Discussion with Christopher Graham during a PhD seminar at Dallas Theological Seminary. While neither of us recall the exact date of our discussion, the details of the discussion were verified by email, October 25, 2012.

If the Church is one, it is so in virtue of the divine life pulsing through it. Called into existence by God, it is no more a mere man-made agglomerate than was God's ancient people Israel. It is in fact the body of Christ, forming a spiritual unity with Him as close as is His unity with the Father, so that Christians can be called His 'members.' As the incarnation is the union of seen with unseen, flesh with spirit, so Ignatius teaches that the Church is at once flesh and Spirit, its unity being the union of both. And it is a holy community within which the divine Spirit lives and operates.[62]

62. Kelly, *Early Christian Doctrines*, 190–91.

The Splendor of Holiness

The Church as the Theatre of Divine Beauty

—*Taylor Worley*

Introduction

As one of the most intriguing figures of contemporary continental thought, Jean-Luc Nancy has further complicated the so-called "religious turn" in postmodern theory by troubling the simple narratives of secularism. He rejects the standard claim that sees secularism as patently antagonistic to monotheism. Both a critic and commentator on Christianity's ancient faith, he asks probing and poignant questions of religion that neither the faithful nor the faithless should avoid. Like many of his major influences, his discussions of modern life range widely and include economics, aesthetics, and technology alongside deconstruction and ontology. In his brief essay entitled "Art, a fragment," Nancy describes well the tyranny of aesthetic fragmentation that so dominates our cultural life today. He reflects:

> By this time, no doubt, fragmentation, spacing, exposition, piecework, and exhaustion have begun to arrive at their most extreme limit. We have done so much fracturing, fraying, wounding, crumpling, splintering, fragilizing, shattering, and exceeding that we would seem to have begun to exceed excess itself. This is why worldliness may appear to be the reverse, in tiny pieces, of a totalization madly in love with itself.
>
> Today, there is a chagrined, reactive, and vengeful tone in which this is often said. It gives its auditor to understand that our art, thought, and text are in ruin, and that one must call for a

renewal. As in all such cases, this is nothing but a flight from the event and its truth.[1]

Nancy's words, perhaps most importantly, bear the strong medicine of a double indictment; for as he intimates, our accusations against the culture of fragmentation charge us at the same time. It is no longer a viable option for Christians concerned about the state of culture and society to decry its errors and then retreat back into the closed-off conversations about culture among merely ourselves. Such conversations seem the last refuge for any theological account of beauty, but this should not be. Though very much a fragment in its own right, this essay will seek a remedy to the insufficient and insular talk of beauty among Evangelicals by following a brief pursuit of three questions. They are: What is beauty? What is the relationship of beauty to holiness? What is the place of beauty in the life of the church?

What is beauty?

It seems that establishing a theological account of beauty remains for many Christians an essential starting point for any engagement with art, culture, or aesthetics. Most of the interest in establishing a distinctly theological or Christian account of beauty, however, presumes an innocent naiveté on the matter, such that particularly discouraging voices like that of modern and contemporary philosophers of aesthetics are not allowed any opportunity to clarify the issues related to such a quest. Here follows a brief sampling of how difficult such voices can make the question.

The modern disavowal of transcendent beauty in the arts finds no more ardent proponent than Friedrich Nietzsche. In his own caustic way, he acknowledges the undeniable connection between religious and artistic truth, and therefore in pronouncing the demise of one he must pronounce the demise of the other as well. In his work *Human, All Too Human*, Nietzsche engages the issue in a the section entitled "From the Soul of Artists and Writers," and here he brings his forceful conclusions to bear on the fate of transcendence in art and religion. He writes:

> 220 *The Beyond in Art.* – It is not without profound sorrow that one admits to oneself that in their highest flights the artists of all ages have raised to heavenly transfiguration precisely those conceptions which we now recognize as false: they are the glorifiers of

---

1. Nancy, *Sense of the World*, 123.

the religious and philosophical errors of mankind, and they could not have been so without believing in the absolute truth of their errors. If belief in such truth declines in general, if the rainbow-colours at the extreme limits of human knowledge and supposition grow pale; that species of art can never flourish again which, like the *Divina Commedia*, the pictures of Raphael, the frescoes of Michelangelo, the Gothic cathedrals, presupposes not only a cosmic but also a metaphysical significance in the objects of art object. A moving tale will one day be told how there once existed such an art, such an artist's faith.[2]

Perhaps in response to such sentiments, Alexandr Solzhenitsyn took opportunity to repudiate the loss of beauty in the world with his Nobel Prize lecture of 1970. Citing the enigmatic words of his Russian literary forebear Fyodor Dostoevsky, Solzhenitsyn reflects on the future of beauty in the aftermath of a half-century of war, genocide, starvation, and isolation. His own trials and suffering in a Siberian gulag make his hopeful tones that much more startling and worthy of consideration. When the world has lost its sense of human decency and propaganda has triumphed over truth-telling, Solzhenitsyn sees an opening for beauty. He concludes:

> But a work of art bears within itself its own verification: conceptions which are devised or stretched do not stand being portrayed in images, they all come crashing down, appear sickly and pale, convince no one. But those works of art which have scooped up the truth and presented it to us as a living force—they take hold of us, compel us, and nobody ever, not even in ages to come, will appear to refute them. So perhaps that ancient trinity of Truth, Goodness, and Beauty is not simply an empty, faded formula as we thought in the days of our self-confident, materialistic youth? If the tops of these three trees converge, as the scholars maintained, but the too blatant, too direct stems of Truth and Goodness are crushed, cut down, not allowed through—then perhaps the fantastic, unpredictable, unexpected stems of Beauty will push through and soar TO THAT VERY SAME PLACE, and in so doing will fulfil the work of all three?
>
> In that case Dostoevsky's remark, 'Beauty will save the world,' was not a careless phrase but a prophecy? After all HE was granted to see much, a man of fantastic illumination. And in that case art, literature might really be able to help the world today?[3]

2. Nietzsche, *Human, All Too Human*, 102.
3. Solzhenitsyn, "Nobel Lecture," n.p.

Solzhenitsyn's confidence in beauty was certainly hard-won, and few would dispute his hopeful reflections. Once the survivors have died and the memory of their trauma has faded, however, where will we turn for an authoritative voice to discern the beautiful? Which beauty? Whose truth? Such concerns seem to haunt the school of analytic philosophy going back to Ludwig Wittgenstein. He found the designation "beautiful" to be particularly problematic. During his lectures on aesthetics, Wittgenstein imparts to his students a certain wry and cynical distaste for the term. Consider the following warning from Wittgenstein:

> 1. The subject (Aesthetics) is very big and entirely misunderstood as far as I can see. The use of such a word as 'beautiful' is even more apt to be misunderstood if you look at the linguistic form of the sentences in which it occurs than most other words. 'Beautiful' is an adjective, so you are inclined to say: 'This has a certain quality, that of being beautiful' . . .Would it matter if instead of saying 'This is lovely [beautiful],' I just said 'Ah!' and smiled, or just rubbed my stomach? As far as these primitive languages go, problems about what these words are about—what their real subject is, what is 'beautiful' or 'good'—don't come up at all. 8. It is remarkable that in real life, when aesthetic judgments are made, aesthetic adjectives such as 'beautiful,' 'fine,' etc., play hardly any role at all.[4]

Perhaps Wittgenstein's annoyance with the term could be written off or avoided, and that would be an appealing option if not for the fact that his frustrations have served to ground much of what has come after him in the tradition of analytic philosophy of art and aesthetics. Figures like Arthur Danto and George Dickie—the shapers of the institutional theory of art so prevalent in the contemporary art-critical discourse today—share Wittgenstein's quintessential fussiness with "beauty" and reject it outright as well. This particular trajectory away from beauty could be seen then as a profound aberration if not for the fact that two of the most significant voices in recent years on Christian aesthetics confirm the move. Perhaps not so shocking today, Nicholas Wolterstorff's recent classic *Art in Action* gives a correspondingly dismal take on "beauty." Following the lead of contemporary analytic philosophers of art, Wolterstorff affirms the departure and concludes that "Beauty is most emphatically not the necessary and

---

4. Wittgenstein, *Lectures and Conversations on Aesthetics, Psychology and Religious Belief*, 1, 3.

sufficient condition of aesthetic excellence."[5] Both Wolterstorff and Calvin Seerveld acknowledge that engaging well with the arts from the perspective of careful Christian reflection need not require the recovery of a theology or philosophy of beauty as a prerequisite to the project. Seerveld goes so far as to wave the white flag on this issue: "Secular aesthetic theorists by and large have won the war against 'beauty,' as I see it, but are in danger of losing the peace of aesthetic meaning because they have simultaneously excommunicated any (aesthetic) normativity other than various makeshift, subjectivist varieties."[6] Along with Wolterstorff, Seerveld's energies have been directed toward refining new or novel categories of valuation to describe what the term "beauty" once commended. Indeed their thoughtful contributions—"fittingness" and "allusivity" respectively—have offered fresh ways to engage with contemporary developments, but many still see the loss of "beauty" as an unforgivable casualty of the conflict.

With such a fraught history, it is therefore not surprising that many have shied away from any attempt at recovering the term. It seems, however, that partial understanding built upon partial experience leads in two directions, and the ideation of beauty becomes then a desperate quest to either escape the notion altogether (e.g., adopting a posture of wholesale neglect) or descending into ideological obsession. While the first is certainly unhealthy, the second verges on making our idea of beauty the object of epistemic idolatry. While avoiding the temptation to argue anyone out of such an obsession, this essay seeks to entice us toward another starting point.

It seems that the entire force of the term "beauty" as a culturally cohesive and enduring value in traditional Western thinking lingers because it smacks of transcendence, what Peter Berger creatively called "a rumor of angels."[7] It is for this reason that such a long-suffering and much-maligned category as "beauty" has any role to play in our understanding of the Christian life and church. Whether we are interested in sensible and aesthetic beauty or intellectual and moral beauty, any Christian regard for beauty begins from a conceptual foundation that acknowledges God as author or source of such wonder. But beginning with a sense of the transcendent ontology of all beauty is easy enough for most of us. To exercise the imaginative restraint necessary to unite such lofty ideals with the surpris-

---

5. Wolterstorff, *Art in Action*, 163. Cf. 159–63.

6. Seerveld, *Rainbows for the Fallen World*, 124–25.

7. Berger, *A Rumor of Angels*, 52.

ing—if not, scandalous—implications of Christ's Incarnation is not nearly as simple. Let us keep in mind that Christ's earthly life represents one long and protracted journey to Emmaus. In other words, no one ever recognized him—that is, in the fullest aesthetic sense—without his tender help to do so. His true glory or his true beauty remained veiled and hidden throughout the majority of his life.

So, here follows the radical claim of this essay: purely human reasoning, as demonstrated chiefly in the refinement of aesthetic theories and the collection of neuroscientific data, cannot lead in itself to a sense of ultimate beauty. Seeing Christ Jesus as the epitome of beauty is nothing less than a spiritual epiphany of the mind and the heart. Such identification is profoundly theological, but almost completely in spite of theology. It is a "Damascus road" kind of experience. While this claim might seem to offer us the best opportunity to finally end our pursuit of ideas about beauty, it may in fact have the opposite effect. Perhaps, it can force us to pursue "beauty" with greater intensity and hope. Christ is the key, and if we know that, it remains for us to live with or live into the mystery that is the beauty of Christ. The challenge presented now is for us to stop theorizing about beauty and go and meet beauty where it can be found. This means that the comfortable reductionism of Christian accounts of beauty must give way to an unnerving and even wildly maximalist view. Here is where we begin.

What is the relationship of beauty to holiness?

Like Moses reminds the Israelites on the plains of Moab, we Evangelicals have entered a rich and cultured place that we did not ourselves establish. While we are far from anything like a promised land, it is no exaggeration to say that we are nourished on an artistic culture in the Western tradition that we did not sow and even now struggle or refuse to cultivate. In the cultural tradition of the West, a certain set of aesthetic qualities or characteristics have been supremely valued around the term beauty. These are proportion and relation of parts, radiance, integrity, and the ability to grant cognitive pleasure.[8] Whatever produces in us a *longing* for an experience of these qualities is what usually goes under the name beauty, and there

---

8. For a discussion of beauty as an "evolutionary target" and its primary range of experiences (i.e., relation of parts, order amid chaos, utility, and cognitive pleasure), see Ewald and Krentz, "Beauty and Beholders."

exist at least three dominant paths to such experiences.[9] These paths are, in fact, based on three different conceptions of beauty. They include objective, transcendental, and subjective beauty. Let us consider a brief survey of these three modes for beauty. They roughly correspond to three successive periods in the history of the West. The object of discovery and the applications thereof also differ dramatically across these three categories.

The objective account of beauty has the oldest lineage of the three and stretches back to the time of the ancient Greeks and Romans. Greco-Roman Antiquity understood beauty to be found in the natural order and symmetry of our world, and they pursued that sense of natural order in a host of ways. Mathematics dominated in learning, architecture, and the arts. Harmonious proportions and a strong sense of balance and symmetry was prized above all other standards of design. Mathematical philosophers like Pythagoras and Euclid helped to refine this sense of order with the development of "The Golden Ratio," a formula for expressing the sense of balance represented by naturally occurring shapes and patterns in the physical world. Examples of such natural phenomena include the spiral form consistently seen in the nautilus mollusk and the horns of certain sheep. Such ordered patterns were meant to be reproduced in the built forms of Greco-Roman culture, and indeed the Parthenon and other structures display these formulas as well as examples of classical sculpture like Polykleitos's *Doryphoros* (The Spear-Bearer). Often the apparent naturalism of such works gave way to a subtle suggestion of perfection and supra-natural order and symmetry (e.g., Michelangelo's *David* has inexact but visually pleasing proportions and hence bears the most blatant sign of this ancient influence). The tragic poets of ancient Greece and Rome, however, tested the bounds of such order and balance in their dramatic representations of the human experience. All too often, the demand for a reasoned life free from the imbalance of passion and emotion remains beyond the grasp of many of their tragic heroes. The order and balance they seek, however, provide the frame for their downfalls. All such projects in Greco-Roman Antiquity belie the essential quest for beauty as a mastery over the natural order.

As Plato had intimated from the same age, the beauty of the heavenly order must surpass the beauty of the natural order in this world. The pursuit of divine beauty therefore dominated in the transition from Greco-Roman Antiquity to the transcendental traditions of the medieval and Renaissance ages. During the flowering of the arts in Christendom, the beautiful was

9. Cf. Sartwell, *Six Names of Beauty*, 1–18.

seen as a portal from an earthly reality to an eschatological one. The architectural marvels of antiquity that represented the ordered governance of the state gave way to the spiritual portals of monasteries and cathedrals as the new centers for communal and social experience. As a microcosm of the universe, the Gothic cathedral instantiated the believer in a world designed to reflect the majesty and creativity of its Maker, and the Mass performed within this space rehearsed for each congregation the means by which the earthly communicant makes contact with the transcendent realm of the divine. Icons and altarpieces became more than pictures: they were portals of prayer and windows into a new and better world. Visual representations of spiritual presence thus expanded through new imaginative developments, and the primitive and symbolic figuration of the icon eventually found itself alongside the gorgeous naturalism of Renaissance painting and sculpture. New and more realistic forms manifested the ancient spiritual potency of the icons. All art, design, and literature had a metaphysical referent or orientation. No better example of this remains than Dante's magisterial reclamation of antiquity's epic in the spiritual pilgrimage he depicted in *The Divine Comedy*. With the pervasive if not always stable influence of the church in society, the beautiful dwelt secure within an enchanted imaginative landscape of religious authority and order. In other words, beauty was all around in the city of God.

Such peace, however, did not last. Operating as a germ of unrest and doubt even amid the Renaissance, the modern rejection of a supreme and heavenly order for the beautiful eventually won the day, and transcendental accounts of beauty were overwhelmed by what we can only describe through contrast as a thoroughly subjective account of beauty. This third category represents well the state of "beauty" in modern and postmodern accounts. If the ancients pursued the order of the natural world and the medievals pursued the order of heaven, then the moderns have surely taken up the exploration of the self and its order. Rather than pure order or divine design, this age affirms the ontology of difference and the fragmentation of meaning. Nietzsche's comments above are emblematic of this age and its disdain for any order not established by the canons of personal experience. The dissolution of the bond between the arts and the sciences has been accompanied by the rise of psychology and an unending fascination with the social sciences. All around us we see the monuments of church and state replaced by our temples to the self. The human figure is lost to the diametrically distorted worlds of identity politics and pornography. On the whole, the arts either parody the achievements of the past by filling metaphysical forms with utterly mundane content or celebrate the singular perspective of one isolated individual. Either way, the artist's vocation has been reduced to a painful project of poetically collecting and pasting together the detritus of meaning in our fragmented age. One generation of the avant-garde gives way to the next, and the artistic sons continue to rise up and kill their fathers. All of it presses forward in a Hegelian, death-drive pursuit of whatever is next, because each new form of consciousness reserves the right to call "beautiful" what it will. What may then seem like a doomsday scenario for "beauty," however, is not quite that bad. The self eventually ceases to be a secret garden to explore, and as Kierkegaard would caution us, it quickly becomes a cage. Beauty can aid our escape and in the process show us that we are better off for having sought to encompass all three modes of understanding the beautiful.

If we have truly seen that the cardinal sin regarding beauty is identifying the source of beauty with the experience of it, we can, in time, become more responsible and more *receptive* participants. When we lay aside the question of beauty's ideation, we can instead seek to appreciate these pursuits as complementary rather than rival experiences of beauty. This, it seems, is the best way forward. It does, however, demand a great deal of us. We must transition from being passive consumers to active agents. In other words, we provide the synthesis, a synthesis of hope. Let us examine that claim more fully.

The history of aesthetics and its idolizing of beauty testifies to us that beauty cannot be pursued solely for itself. The ancients (e.g., Plato, Augustine, and others) did not even want to speak of beauty without connection to signal values like truth and justice, and we should not either. If beauty creates in us a sense of longing, then that longing, I believe, parallels most significantly the church's longing to be holy. So, we need to think about beauty alongside holiness because of the way in which both order our longings: what we long for and how we long for it. In his 2011 presidential address to the Society for the Study of Theology, Graham Ward took up the topic of "Becoming Holy" and expanded on the theme of Christ's transfigurative work in us through the Spirit as addressing "the heart of our own longing."[10] And he explored there the ways in which the longing to be holy occupies the places within us of greatest humility and shame. On Ward's account, sanctification is the process in which God restores our

10. Ward, "Becoming Holy," 1.

humble state by humbling us further with the humiliation of Christ. And if he is right, we must demonstrate a similar descent in our pursuits of beauty. That means we look for beauty—the hidden beauty of Christ—in the midst of this world and as a means of storing up treasure in the kingdom of God (e.g., valuing the restoration of a broken life much more than we value a great aesthetic achievement). Both of these pursuits, however, represent a goal for life in this world that can only be fulfilled in the next.

What is the place of beauty in the life of the Church?

The beauty of Christ is holy, and the holiness of Christ is his beauty. This beauty does not hold out the hope of leaving the world but rather the promise of redeeming it by pressing in. Holiness is other-worldly but never other-worldliness. Holiness is an alien orientation inside the perfectly mundane. In Christ's Incarnation, we discover again and again what our simple minds cannot master: Eternity has meet us in the here and now. And in this way, the promise of sanctification given to the church has to change *everything*.[11] Jesus tells us that the kingdom of God is within his disciples in Luke 17:20–21: "Being asked by the Pharisees when the kingdom of God would come, he answered them, 'The kingdom of God is not coming in ways that can be observed, nor will they say, "Look, here it is!" or "There!" for behold, the kingdom of God is in the midst of you.'" This startling announcement by Jesus creates the possibility from which Paul envisions the comprehensive restoration of the individual and the community that frames his concluding prayer in 1 Thessalonians: "Now may the God of peace himself sanctify you completely, and may your whole spirit and soul

---

11. In a recent interview with Ginney Mooney at *The Christian Post* entitled "Is 'the Culture' Really the Church's Problem?" Ken Myers relayed his sobering perspective once more. When he was asked about the biggest challenge facing the church today he responded this way: "It's not 'the culture,' as we often hear, that poses the most significant challenge for the church today. It's the culture *of the church*. . . we have reduced the Gospel to an abstract message of salvation that can be believed without having any necessary consequences for how we live. In contrast, the redemption announced in the Bible is clearly understood as restoring human thriving in creation . . . Salvation is about God's restoring our whole life, not just one invisible aspect of our being (our soul), but our life as lived out in the world in ways that are in keeping with how God made us. The goal of salvation is blessedness for us as human beings. In other words, we are saved so that our way of life can be fully in keeping with God's ordering of reality" (Mooney, "Is 'the Culture' Really the Church's Problem?" n.p.).

and body be kept blameless at the coming of our Lord Jesus Christ. He who calls you is faithful; he will surely do it" (1 Thess 5:23–24). Why would Paul pray this prayer with such confidence? It seems that Paul has this immense confidence because his gospel announces a great message of transformation (i.e., the power of God for the redemption and restoration of any life has been given to the church by Christ through the Holy Spirit). So, why is the church *the* place to pursue beauty? Or, as the title of this essay indicates, why "the theatre of divine beauty"?

Simply put, the church, and the church alone, has been given the gifts to image forth the beauty of Christ. Let us identify then just two of the unique resources given to the church for this purpose. Rather than name specific virtues or ministerial agencies that uniquely equip the church, here we will thematize two larger issues. First, the church becomes a theatre for divine beauty because of its restorative sociality. In the Incarnation, we come to recognize that the beauty of Christ emerges through encounter. In the encounter with the other and the interactions between each other, the church constitutes a community of rich encounters, and it is through such encounters that the form of Christ is shaped in us—individually and collectively. As community, the church makes Christ present in the world even as each believer makes Christ present to each other. While the church participates in this spiritual reality both incompletely and falteringly, the role of Christ as mediator both makes possible *any* transformation and guarantees its final consummation. Similarly and secondly, the church bears a redemptive ethic for culture that neither idolizes nor neglects the world. In this way, we can transition from awkward attempts at dominion and seek rather a redemptive stewardship. We do this by taking a certain posture in the church and toward the world—a posture that celebrates imagination over ideology. As Gregory Wolfe is fond of reminding the church, "culture war," as a term, is an oxymoron.[12] Culture is never about conquest but rather cultivation—growing something in the garden of the world.

These promises, however, offer no hope for us if we do not instantiate them in embodied practices. In this way, the church's pursuit of beauty has two specific applications: our inward transformation and outward witness. Let us then hasten to add that our inward transformation is, in fact, vitally linked to our outward witness. Charles Taliaferro explains the connection in this way: "By seeing beauty in the extraordinary sacrifice and resurrection-triumph of Christ, we are led to a profoundly humble, non-aristocratic

12. See Wolfe, *Beauty Will Save the World*.

aesthetics. Rather than finding beauty in fame, reputation, and celebrity, one finds beauty in self-sacrificial love."[13] In other words, love is the place where our inward transformation to beauty and our outward witness are united. And this means that our outward witness is really a bearing witness to the reconciling love of God in the world. Therefore, the church does not need more activism (i.e., world changing activity) but rather more disciplines, practices, and spiritual exercises (i.e., the cultivation the soul). To emphasize the necessity of healthy disciplines for chasing beauty, we should hear from Wendell Berry's recent and perhaps landmark address to the National Endowment for the Humanities. In that lecture, he described well the relationship between affection and imagination. His argument called for the recovery of imagination and its roots in reality:

> The term 'imagination' in what I take to be its truest sense refers to a mental faculty that some people have used and thought about with the utmost seriousness. The sense of the verb 'to imagine' contains the full richness of the verb 'to see.' To imagine is to see most clearly, familiarly, and understandingly with the eyes, but also to see inwardly, with 'the mind's eye.' It is to see, not passively, but with a force of vision and even with visionary force. To take it seriously we must give up at once any notion that imagination is disconnected from reality or truth or knowledge. It has nothing to do either with clever imitation of appearances or with 'dreaming up.' It does not depend upon one's attitude or point of view, but grasps securely the qualities of things seen or envisioned.[14]

Quite plainly, he says "imagination thrives on contact." That contact begins a cycle that grows affection and fosters more contact in the perpetuation of culture. He explains: "As imagination enables sympathy, sympathy enables affection. And it is in affection that we find the possibility of a neighborly, kind, and conserving economy."[15]

The partial (or perhaps prophetic) glimpse of beauty in the church as she leans into the kingdom and its holy eschatological reality will only come about in the places where love lives. Love—the love of Christ—provides the atmosphere, the environment, and the good soil where beauty

---

13. Taliaferro, "Beauty and Aesthetics in Theology," 213.

14. Berry, "It All Turns on Affection," n.p. Cf. Keith Critchlow as quoted in Berry: "The human mind takes apart with its analytic habits of reasoning but the human heart puts things together because it loves them."

15. Ibid. Cf. Scarry, On Beauty and Being Just, 18: "Beauty always takes place in the particular, and if there are no particulars, the chances of seeing it go down."

can grow. Fostering Christ-like affection is the only means of fostering Christ-like beauty. In the end, the cultivation of beauty in and through the church seems less a responsibility of the mind and more a vocation of the heart. In this way, we should draw away from much of what is being said and repeated in the increasingly diverse conversation around theology and the arts or theological aesthetics. While much of what is being done there is good, this essay stands as a protest against the sustained and self-serving discourse there that calls for a greater quantity and quality of concepts to recover a theology of beauty. Evangelicals do not have a great need of concepts concerning beauty. In all honesty, they have a glaring and embarrassing need of practices, practices to train the heart to long for what the mind cannot comprehend, that is the infinite beauty of Christ Jesus.

Concluding Exhortation

Therefore, in the final assessment, it seems that the church cannot ultimately escape the charges of her cultured despisers *and* maintain fidelity to the eschatological hope for beauty. Indeed, some will, no doubt, accuse her of not only a "slave morality" but also a "slave aesthetics" that holds out the promise of eventually reaching beauty without any sure guarantee of its fulfillment. And in this way, the church must decide on what foundation she will rest. To such challenges, she would do well to anchor herself more deeply in the mystery of the gospel—the gospel that exposes our deep and unimaginable ugliness before Christ and at the same time reveals God's desire for us and our renewal, along with all things. This desire has both overcome our ugliness and bound us up in reciprocal desire for itself. This desire in the heart of God for each of us remains a mystery, but it is a mystery that we can grow into even as we embrace these mysterious words of the Apostle Paul: "For you have died, and your life is hidden with Christ in God. When Christ who is your life appears, then you also will appear with him in glory" (Col 3:3–4).

The Church Curved in on Itself

Sin, Holiness, Communion, and Mission

—Matt Jenson

66 "We believe in one holy . . . church"—surely one of the most difficult confessions that Christians make. It is difficult precisely because it belies much of our experience of the church. Ecclesial holiness is too often hidden from view, mocked by the sins of the church that parade in plain sight. Worse, the history of the church is riddled with this effrontery, such that the church's holiness has rarely been obvious, patent. The church of God, the "city on a hill," the "light of the world" whose illumination brings the church's good works into view and moves the nations to glorify God, has seldom shone brightly since the ascension of Jesus (Matt 5:14–16). It is tempting, surely, to back away from describing the church as holy in the face of its heinous sin. The Roman Catholic Church's pastors sexually abuse children over decades, and then *their* pastors smother the voices of the victims. A Baptist congregation refuses to allow a black family to join them in worship, despite the fact that their children play together at school. A Pentecostal leader swindles old women out of their retirement savings, in the promise that God will care for them in return. Who would have the audacity to declare *these* people holy? How could that be anything other than a formal description utterly divorced from the actual people so described? Indeed, what could it possibly mean to call *this* people "holy"?

Recognizing the challenge of confessing a holy church, Martin Luther admits that the church's holiness "cannot be seen. God conceals and covers it with weaknesses, sins, errors, and various offenses and forms of the cross in such a way that it is not evident to the senses anywhere."[1] "The church is

---

1. *LW* 27:84.

indeed holy, but it is a sinner at the same time."[2] Thus "it is faith alone that discerns" the holy church. Luther faces the dilemma squarely:

> If you consult your reason and your eyes, you will judge differently. For in devout people you will see many things that offend you; you will see them fall now and again, see them sin, or be weak in faith, or be troubled by a bad temper, envy, or other evil emotions. 'Therefore the church is not holy.' I deny the conclusion that you draw. If I look at my own person or at that of my neighbor, the church will never be holy. But if I look at Christ, who is the Propitiator and Cleanser of the church, then it is completely holy; for He bore the sins of the entire world.[3]

Because the church's holiness is found in Christ, it is invisible, according to Luther.[4] We might better say that it is only, but really, spiritually visible—that is, there for those with eyes to see.[5] While Luther is right to locate ecclesial holiness in Christ, such a comment runs the risk of eclipsing Paul's call to the church to "put on Christ" by daily dying and rising with him, to echo his holiness in her life (Rom 13:14).

For the sake of our integrity, as well as for the sake of our mission, it is incumbent on us to engage in critical self-reflection, which will lead in many cases to a recognition and confession of ecclesial sin and the bearing of "fruit in keeping with repentance" (Matt 3:8, Luke 3:8). Still, a penitent humility should not cause us to shrink back from a confession of the church as the holy people of God. Even in its sin, the church is God's holy people, those to whom the promise and command is given that they shall be holy even as he is holy (Lev 20:26, 1 Pet 1:16).

Furthermore, it has never been as easy as some would suggest to discern the marks of the church in concrete ecclesial communities. The church's unity, catholicity, and apostolicity present as much of a challenge as its holiness when we seek to identify the church in the world. They cannot be easily read off of our life together, and this lack of transparency throws the marks of the church into question.

---

2. *LW* 26:109.

3. *LW* 26:285.

4. *LW* 27:84.

5. See Webster, *Holiness*, 71. Barth "sought to affirm that the Church has such visible form by virtue of the presence and action of Christ through the Spirit. 'Visibility' is therefore a spiritual event."

One response is flatly to deny that a particular company of people or, more drastically, the universal church itself *is* one, say, or holy, catholic, or apostolic. Too often, almost inevitably when this move is made, when I deny that this group is "holy," I take refuge in the recognition that *my* group is holy. This form of ecclesiology is sectarian, then, and radical in its willingness to reject claims to ecclesial fullness by those other, unholy groups. Or I may despair of the church entirely, retiring to a life of private devotion following the conclusion that the church is not holy and therefore that the church as such is dead in its sin.[6]

Another strategy, more familiar to Evangelicals, involves a punt to invisibility. Here the confession of the church's holiness is unproblematic, in that all sincere believers are spiritually holy in Christ. The problem here lies in the effortlessness of the move, as I take refuge in an abstraction and pass over the concrete, sinful church. Also, I am in danger of positing two churches, one in which true believers blithely rest and another, a church in name only, of which I can only expect division, sin, provinciality, and a departure from "the faith that was once for all delivered to the saints" (Jude 3). By aligning myself with the true, invisible church, I can even make a virtue of abandoning the visible church and construct personal holiness in terms of a being called out of the church. Like the first strategy, here I succumb to a "temptation to distance," preferring the good life of abstraction to the suffering of participation in the broken body of Christ.[7]

In contrast to these two strategies, we must not shrink back—either from a confession that the church of God is holy or from an ascription of holiness to the obviously sinful company of people of whom we are a part. Nor is this a legal fiction. The church really is holy, even as it really is sinful. These dual claims suggest the dialectical character of ecclesial holiness. We cannot rest in our holiness; we cannot even rest in a statement of our holiness. The very grammar of holiness for the *communio sanctorum in via* requires a shuttling back-and-forth between equally robust confessions of holiness and sinfulness. With Luther and Barth, we can speak of the total character of this; the church, like each believer, is *simul totus iustus et totus*

---

6. Ephraim Radner believes that the church is dead and the Spirit gone, but does not conclude that we should retire to private Christianity. Instead, he champions a humble, penitent form of what his friend Rusty Reno describes as life "in the ruins of the church." Reno, it should be noted, has left the building and entered the Roman Catholic church. See Radner, *End of the Church*; Reno, *In the Ruins of the Church*; and Reno, "Out of the Ruins."

7. Craig Keen first suggested to me this evocative description of the church.

peccator (simultaneously wholly just and wholly sinful). Gone is another refuge, that of the *partial* character of our sin, where we might at least claim that that other congregation is more sinful than we are. While we ought to guard against turning this simultaneity into a double bookkeeping that downgrades the threat of sin, its total character serves to caution the church against any sense of having arrived at non-dialectical holiness this side of the return of Christ.[8]

Properly Christian speech about the church, then, requires one to say two things of the same body of people, that this people who is holy is also sinful. And we find Paul doing just this in 1 Corinthians. He addresses his letter to "the church of God that is in Corinth, to those sanctified in Christ Jesus, called to be saints together with all those who in every place call upon the name of the Lord Jesus Christ" (1 Cor 1:2). He reminds them: "Do you not know that you are God's temple and that God's Spirit dwells in you? If anyone destroys God's temple, God will destroy him. For God's temple is holy, and you are that temple" (1 Cor 3:16–17). Yet it is this holy assembly that tolerates sexual immorality that would not be tolerated by pagans (1 Cor 5:1, also possibly chapters 6–7), whose worship is plagued by disorder, division, and competition (chapters 3, 11–14). Instead of flatly calling into question the holiness of the church, though, Paul uses it to agitate the Corinthians. It is precisely because they have been sanctified in Jesus to be the temple of the Holy Spirit that they must conduct themselves in a manner of life that fits the gospel (Phil 1:27). Their holiness is a gift, and so it is a task.[9]

Clearly, belief in the holy church calls for discernment on the part of the people of God as they walk in the Spirit and put on the mind of Christ in ecclesial reflection. As an aid to that reflection, in what follows I will consider a key image of the sinner as *homo incurvatus in se* (humanity curved in on itself) as the obverse of the saint as *homo excurvatus ex se* (humanity curved away from itself) and then ask after its implications for

---

8. Barth worries that the Reformation *simul* might lead to "a stabilization of life under a double bookkeeping" (Busch, *The Great Passion*, 202). On a dialectical account of the marks of the church, see Bender, *Karl Barth's Christological Ecclesiology*, 185.

9. Louis Berkhof is right in pointing out that "it is not correct to think of holiness primarily as a moral or religious quality, as it generally done. Its fundamental idea is that of a *position* or *relationship* existing between God and some person or thing" (*Systematic Theology*, 73). Still, the sanctifying work of the Spirit sets the church in a relationship towards God and the world that implies and requires holiness of life. The indicative precedes the imperative; it also activates it.

the holiness of a church drawn out of itself into worship of the triune God and participation in his mission in the world.

Ecclesia incurvata in se[10]

Despairing of himself and throwing himself on the mercy of Christ, Martin Luther castigated a sinful curving inward and advocated an adherence to that which comes to us from outside of us. In the midst of the 1510s, as he awoke to the unmerited, unparalleled, unanticipated grace of God revealed and given in the death of Christ, Luther came to realize the hopelessly tangled mess of sin. In his lectures on Romans, he writes that

> our nature has been so deeply curved in upon itself because of the viciousness of original sin that it not only turns the finest gifts of God in upon itself and enjoys them (as is evident in the case of legalists and hypocrites), indeed, it even uses God Himself to achieve these aims, but it also seems to be ignorant of this very fact, that in acting so iniquitously, so perversely, and in such a depraved way, it is even seeking God for its own sake. Thus the prophet Jeremiah says in Jeremiah 17:9: 'The heart is perverse above all things, and desperately corrupt; who can understand it?' that is, it is so curved in on itself that no man, no matter how holy (if a testing is kept from him) can understand it.[11]

Sin transcends understanding, not least because it compromises the very faculties by which we understand. We are hopelessly self-serving, and we are helplessly self-deceived about it. Keep in mind that this comes from the quill of Luther the monk, who plumbed the depths of religious egoism more relentlessly than perhaps anyone in the tradition. Luther did more than canvass the church's sin; he subjected even its purported holiness to withering critique.

> It is easy, I say to understand how in these things [i.e., sensual evils] we seek our fulfillment and love ourselves, how we are turned in upon ourselves and become ingrown at least in our heart, even when we cannot sense it in our actions.
>
> In spiritual matters, however (that is, in our understanding, our righteousness, our chastity, our piety), it is most difficult to

---

10. For what follows, see Jenson, *The Gravity of Sin*. The application to the church is new.

11. *LW* 25:291.

see whether we are seeking only ourselves in them. For the love of
these things, since it is honorable and good, often becomes an end
in itself for us and does not permit us to regulate them in accord
with God and refer them to Him, so that as a result we do them
not because they are pleasing to God but because they delight us
and quiet the fears of our heart, because we are praised by men,
and thus we do them not for the sake of God but for ourselves.[12]

It is not difficult to conjure an image of the proud cleric sanctimoniously
bestowing absolution on the dirty sinners under his care. As he does so, he
curves inward, ungratefully and idolatrously denying his reliance upon the
triune God for holiness and help and refusing the return of friendship and
love from the forgiven sinners in his midst. God and neighbor represent a
threat to his flourishing in a zero-sum game where there are only so many
pieces of the pie to go around. Like Garcin in Sartre's *No Exit*, he exclaims,
"Hell is—other people!"[13] He would speak more truthfully in echoing Satan's
line in *Paradise Lost*, "Myself am hell."[14] Luther insists that this proud,
isolated, disdainful man curved in on himself is all of us—in more sophisticated,
more subtle forms, perhaps, but none the better for that.

Daphne Hampson begs to differ.[15] Hampson is a post-Christian
feminist—"post-Christian" because, on her read, one must choose between
Christianity and heteronomy or feminism and autonomy. Because she
believes that women should be *self*-ruled, she rejects Christianity, with its
confession that Jesus is Lord.[16] Women *should* be self-ruled, according to
Hampson, but they have not been historically; they have been systematically
used and abused by men. She agrees with Luther's diagnosis of the human
condition *in its application to men*; they are indeed proud, isolated, and disdainfully
curved inward. But women are precisely the opposite. They suffer
from slothful self-denigration and tend to lose themselves in relationships.
Far from being a world to themselves, they have lost any sense of self at all.
Different diagnoses of sin suggest different prescriptions for holiness. If a
man grows in holiness by humbly taking up his cross and dying, a woman
becomes holy by learning to speak in her own voice and take responsibility

---

12. *LW* 25:245.

13. Sartre, *No Exit*, 47.

14. Milton, *Paradise Lost* 4.75.

15. See, *inter alia*, Hampson, "Luther on the Self."

16. Hampson, *After Christianity*, vii; also see Hampson, "On Autonomy and Heteronomy," 1–16.

for her life. Pride needs humiliation; the humiliated, on the other hand, need exaltation, need lifting up.

Despite its pastoral merits, Hampson's account finally fails in its inability to name women's self-evacuation as sin. Rightly alert to centuries of diminishment and degradation under the thumb of men, Hampson has trouble identifying women's failure to speak for themselves as sin. She thus offers therapy and healing, but avoids a call to repentance. Ironically, Hampson misses an opportunity to empower chronically self-less women to speak in their own voices by engaging in Christian practices of repentance and forgiveness, beginning with confession of sin. I hasten to add that this must be handled with care; one could pervert this pastoral opportunity and insist that sinful women be put in their place, thus perpetuating patriarchal cycles. But rightly understood, confession of sin ennobles. Still, while Hampson cannot coherently name women's self-evacuation as sin, her critique demonstrates the need for a flexible account of the variety of ways in which one might curve in on oneself. Prometheus cannot be our only model for sin.

In his threefold discussion of humanity curved in on itself as proud, slothful, and false, Karl Barth expands the explanatory range of the metaphor.[17] Each form of sin represents a counter-movement to the movement of God in Christ in which he is with and for us. Where the Son of God is humiliated, we in our pride exalt ourselves. Where the Son of Man is exalted, we in our sloth remain mired in our humiliation. Where the God-man is the one true witness, we bear false witness. We see the familiar Promethean character in pride. But in sloth, Barth describes something closer to Hampson's self-denigration. (Note that feminist theologians often speak of this uniquely feminine form of sin as "sloth.") Here is Barth:

> The sin of man is not merely heroic in its perversion. It is also
> . . . ordinary, trivial and mediocre. The sinner is not merely Prometheus or Lucifer. He is also—and for the sake of clarity, and
> to match the grossness of the matter, we will use rather popular
> expressions—a lazy-bones, a sluggard, a good-for-nothing, a slow-
> coach, and a loafer.[18]

Sloth is not simply, say, an unwillingness to get off one's butt and get a job; it is a fearful, stubborn refusal of the exaltation that has come to humanity as Jesus has sat down at the right hand of the Father and been given the name

17. See Karl Barth, *CD* IV/1–IV/3.

18. *CD* IV/2, 404.

above every name. It is a despairing stagnancy resistant to the agitating hope of the risen Christ. It is the craven preference for mediocrity over a participation in the royal office of Christ (even as pride seeks to avoid participation in his priestly office). Finally, in its falsehood, sinful humanity turns away from the truth of Emmanuel, that God and humanity have been united in Christ. Here we evade any encounters with the One who is the truth and reject his calling to serve as witnesses to the gospel. We may do this through an out-and-out lie, though we may as easily bear false witness by preferring to speak *of* God than to speak and listen *to* him.[19]

The church between whence and whither

With perfect consistency, Luther applied the remedy of eccentricity to the sin of incurvature. If the sinful church's problem is its tendency to curve inward and distort, manipulate, block, or reject relationship with others, it can only be helped as it goes out of itself and finds life in another. But given our abiding habit of collapsing inward, that move outward cannot be self-generated or self-sustained. We must be drawn out of ourselves by the Spirit as he unites us to Christ by faith and our neighbor by love. "But when they are gathered in Christ, from no people they really become the people of God," Calvin writes.[20] The Spirit sanctifies the church by uniting her to Christ, turning dead and isolated sinners into the people of God who find their lives not in themselves but in Christ and one another.

Thus is ecclesial life radically eccentric, as the church's locus shifts from self to Christ and neighbor.[21] What Luther says of the individual Christian is true of the church as a whole:

A Christian lives not in himself, but in Christ and in his neighbor. Otherwise he is not a Christian. He lives in Christ through faith, in

19. Job is the model of a true witness here, as opposed to his false friends, whose fault lay more in their refusal of encounter with the living God than it did in incorrect theology. See Barth, *CD* IV/3.1, 457–60.

20. John Calvin, *Commentaries on the Catholic Epistles,* 76–77 (commenting on 1 Pet 2:10).

21. Lesslie Newbigin says it perfectly: "That which constitutes the Church is the act of God in Christ by which men are reborn in him and made sharers through the Holy Spirit in that divine life which the Son shares with the Father. But it is this same fact which gives to those who have been so reborn into him their mission to the world" (Newbigin, *The Reunion of the Church,* 18–19).

his neighbor through love. By faith he is caught up beyond himself into God. By love he descends beneath himself into his neighbor. Yet he always remains in God and in his love . . . [22]

The church as Christ's bride has everything it needs by virtue of its marriage to him. All that Christ has belongs to the church, and all that the church has now belongs to Christ.[23] Wedded to Christ, the church's beauty surpasses all others: "Christ adorns the Church his bride with holiness as a proof of his regard."[24] Because the Lord is its shepherd, the church does not want. Sinful self-protection is superfluous, as our lives are "hidden with Christ in God" (Col 3:3). We are thereby freed to give our lives away, even as Jesus gave his life away. Ascending with Christ to God, the church joyfully and self-forgetfully descends with him to the world.

The church finds its being in the activity of listening to the voice of the good shepherd and witnessing to him in the world: "It is in this, in its whence [the Word of God] and whither [the world], that it has its specific basis of existence."[25] The Word the church hears is the Word of promise: "You shall be holy for I am holy . . . " David Willis describes a "declarative ontology" in light of the fact that "creaturely holiness is the work of God's word which is efficacious declaration." God does what he says, and so his declaration of his people's holiness *is* his making them holy.[26] In this sense, the Word of God is the chief means of grace, the site of God's making and molding of his people. In speaking his Word, God sets his people apart and puts them in the way of holiness.

To be opened to the Word, to receive the divine vocation, is to enter into the Word's way in the world, the mission of the church. Because the church is *ecstatic*, it is *missional*. In fact, the church "can exist only as it points beyond itself."[27] Whenever it curves in on itself, it risks its very being, "denying and suppressing its witness by witnessing only to itself."[28] The

---

22. *LW* 31:371.

23. *LW* 31:351–52. Luther can even call Christ "the highest, the greatest, and the only sinner" (*LW* 26:281).

24. John Calvin, *Commentaries on the Epistles of Paul*, 321 (commenting on Eph 5:27). Barth is clear that the church's holiness can only ever be "the reflection of the holiness of Jesus Christ as its heavenly Head, falling upon it as He enters into and remains in fellowship with it by his Holy Spirit" (*CD* IV/1, 686).

25. *CD* IV/3.2, 830.

26. Willis, *Notes on the Holiness of God*, 102, 103.

27. *CD* IV/2, 623.

28. *CD* IV/1, 670.

church curved in on itself seeks to deny its whence or whither and to live from itself or for its own sake. It refuses to worship God, trading the living God who bears it from birth for idols who must themselves be carried; and it refuses to follow the way of its Lord, self-complacently grasping at glory rather than giving itself away in mission.[29] The holy church recognizes and rejoices in its being called out of the world by God that it might be a blessing to the nations. In its devotion to the Lord, it lives a "peculiar" life, one whose character marks it as other than the world, but one whose momentum, in service to its Lord, is ever with and for the world.[30] The *communio sanctorum* is a fellowship caught up in the *missio Dei*. As it lives in Christ by the Spirit, the church is driven by the same Spirit, and joyfully goes, into the world.

> As his community it points beyond itself. At bottom it can never consider its own security, let alone its appearance. As his community it is always free from itself. In its deepest and most proper tendency it is not churchly, but worldly—the Church with open doors and great windows, behind which it does better not to close itself in upon itself again by putting in pious stained-glass windows. It is holy in its openness to the street and even the alley, in its turning to the profanity of all human life—the holiness which, according to Romans 12:5, does not scorn to rejoice with them that do rejoice and to weep with them that weep. Its mission is not additional to its being. It is, as it is sent and active in its mission. It builds up itself for the sake of its mission and in relation to it.[31]

Building on Barth's threefold account of sin and an eccentric account of the church, in what follows I will consider the shape of the church's holiness as it is drawn out of itself by the Spirit into Christ and becomes conformed

---

29. Isa 46:1–4; Phil 2:5–11.

30. "Peculiar" is the delightful KJV rendering of ecclesial uniqueness as God's people in 1 Peter 2:9.

31. *CD* IV/1, 725. This means that withdrawal may only ever be a tactical move, never a strategic one: "The true Church may sometimes engage in tactical withdrawal, but never in strategic. It can never cease wholly or basically from activity in the world . . . In every respect, even in what seems to be purely inner activity like prayer and the liturgy and the cure of souls and biblical exegesis and theology, its activity is always *ad extra*. It is always directed *extra muros* to those who are not, or not yet, within, and visibly perhaps never will be . . . The world exists in self-orientation; the Church in visible contrast cannot do so" (*CD* IV/3.2, 780). This suggests a fruitful lens for a Protestant consideration of monasticism in light of the church's mission. On Protestants and monasticism, see Peters, *Reforming the Monastery*.

to the image of Christ by living in correspondence to his holy humiliation, exaltation, and true witness.

The holy church

The holy church seeks and finds its life not in itself, but in Christ and neighbor. It does so, according to the first form of ecclesial holiness, as the church lives humbly in correspondence to the humiliation of the Son of God. But before speaking of correspondence, we need to register the one contradiction between the church and its Lord in their respective humiliations. The church sins. In its humiliation, it confesses its belief in the forgiveness of sins. Indeed, the church never ceases to be a penitential people. Like Augustine, who asked that the penitential Psalms be tacked to the wall in large letters that he might pray them in his dying days, the church knows itself to be the publican who can only cry, "God, be merciful to me, a sinner" (Luke 18:13).[32] It knows the fellowship of Jesus, friend of sinners, and so knows this greatest of contradictions overcome at the cross; but unlike Jesus, the church knows its humiliation is *deserved*. As such, it knows its own fallibility and thus corrigibility and, rather than being surprised at revelations of its poverty, gratefully receives them, confident that the kingdom of heaven belongs to the poor in spirit.

The church does only what it sees the Father and his Son doing and speaks only the Word the Father speaks in the Son (John 5:19, John 12:49–50; Heb 1:2). Its entire being is deferential, and its life takes the form of doxology. The humble church is a worshipping church, ever singing the *Non nobis*—"Not to us, O Lord, not to us, but to your name give glory" (Ps 115:1). The worshipping church is also a serving church, following the lead of its Lord who washed its feet. It knows that it is no better than its Master and joyfully takes on the form of a servant (John 13:16, Phil 2:7). Thérèse of Lisieux evokes the abandon of the church in its humble self-offering:

> For some time I had been accustomed to offer myself as a plaything to the Child Jesus. I told him not to treat me like an expensive toy which children look at but dare not touch. I was a cheap little ball which He could fling on the ground or kick or pierce or leave neglected in a corner or even press to His Heart if it gave him pleasure.[33]

32. Brown, *Augustine of Hippo*, 436.
33. Thérèse of Lisieux, *Autobiography of Saint Thérèse of Lisieux*, 85.

The humble church gives no thought to itself, but only seeks to give him pleasure. Nor is it surprised when it suffers persecution, as the world "has hated me before it hated you" (John 15:18).

Losing (but finding) its life in worship and service, the church recognizes its ministerial role in the economy of salvation. In two ways it is merely a means to an end. The church is the theatre in which the gospel is proclaimed and performed, the means of evangelical grace by which the Spirit draws people to Christ. He, then, not the church, is the end. And, the church is a servant to the kingdom. It is the first fruits of the kingdom as it is united to Christ and filled by the Spirit. The church is the people of God on the way to the kingdom in its fullness and exists for the kingdom's sake. It is that peculiar company of people called out of the world by God to be a blessing to the nations by witnessing to the kingdom come in the life, death, and resurrection of Jesus as it sees and seeks the kingdom come in its midst by the presence and power of the Spirit. With John the Baptist, the church recognizes that it is not worthy to untie the strap of Jesus' sandal. Also like John, the church can only be a voice, eager to herald the coming of the King and perfectly happy to fade into the crowd that joyfully receives him.

In the second form of ecclesial holiness, the church receives its exaltation in correspondence to that of the Son of Man. Where the proud church seeks to justify itself, the humble church knows that it is justified by grace through faith.[34] Where the slothful church shirks its calling to maturity, the exalted church seeks to "grow up in every way into him who is the head, into Christ" (Eph 4:15). Exhortations to humility are common enough, but calls for the church to be strong and courageous in light of its exaltation in Christ are less so (cf. Josh 1:9). Since it finds its life not in itself, but in Christ and its neighbor, the exalted church may never, but also need never, make a name for itself. It is not Babel, but the new Jerusalem, taking its very name from the Lord who is present in its midst. Precisely in that it is the city of God, it is dignified and glorious.

There is a proper confidence flowing from its exaltation in Christ, by virtue of which the exalted church proceeds with its mission as Christ's royal representative in the world. Confidence is not presumption, though, and the church recognizes that it is a pilgrim people on the way to meet its Lord. It sets a brisk pace along the way, and refuses temptations to lethargy

---

34. See the discussion of justification by faith as the basis for the (re)union of the church in Newbigin, *The Reunion of the Church*.

or premature declarations of arrival.[35] The church is active, having been exalted to partnership with God in his mission in the world. It seeks first the kingdom (Matt 6:33). The active and confident church is a risky church, and risky because utterly without fear.

Such a glorious freedom from fear coincides with a freedom for service to Christ in the world. It is for freedom that Christ set the church free, and the holy church is a church that stands firm in its freedom (Gal 5:1). The joyfully free church knows the victory won by Christ in his death and resurrection and ventures forth in bold proclamation and presence in the world. The church exalted in Christ to the right hand of the Father need not worry about its acceptance by the world, but regally represents Christ to the world as its King. In light of Christ's triumph, Barth scoffs at Christian apologetics, with its desperate attempts to beg a hearing for the gospel, as "anxiety concerning the victory of the gospel"—a joyless, burdensome, and utterly unnecessary posture in light of the resurrection.[36] Christ, and in him the church, has won the victory; so the church's ministry must never imply that the outcome in the world is in doubt. Because Jesus is victor, the church is "anxious for nothing" (Phil 4:6). It never apologizes for itself, never begs for attention. The exalted church finds self-justification a petty waste of time and is if anything regally self-forgetful in its confidence. It knows it has something to say, and no worldly animosity can move it to shrink back from its work of witness.

In the third form of ecclesial holiness, the church tells the truth and demonstrates its truthfulness in its life, thereby corresponding to Jesus, the one faithful truth-teller who is himself the Truth. The church called out of itself tells the truth to God as it confesses its sins, worships him, prays to him on behalf of the world, and declares its readiness to follow him. In all this, the basic form of Christian speech to God is a grateful "Here I am." Thus its speech occurs in direct encounter with the God who calls it into existence and sends it into the world as his representative.

The holy church tells the truth about God in the world by proclaiming the "strange new world within the Bible" to be the world's own story.[37]

---

35. Jesus' "holiness is not given to it as a kind of umbrella under which it can rest or walk up and down at will, but as a pillar of cloud and fire like that which determined the way of the Israelites in the wilderness, as the mystery by which it has to direct itself in its human Church work" (Barth, *CD* IV/1, 701).

36. Barth, *Epistle to the Romans*, 35.

37. See Barth, "The Strange New World within the Bible," in *The Word of God and the Word of Man*, trans. Douglas Horton (London: Hodder & Stoughton, 1935), 28–50;

In this story, God is the primary actor whose loving freedom is the condition for creaturely agency; here humanity is open to God and radically non-self-sufficient, even as it remains the object of God's humbling and exalting grace. When the church tells the world the truth, it refuses any self-enclosed account of the world, instead proclaiming God the creator of the world out of nothing, who enters into covenant fellowship with humanity, fulfills the covenant in Christ and the Spirit and promises the renewal of the world at the last day.

As witness to this God, the church's truthful speech concerns Father, Son, and Spirit first, and only then the world. It is least of all interested in talking about itself. The truthful church is deferential rather than self-referential. Even in telling of the mighty acts of God in its midst, the church is not engaged in autobiography so much as testimony.[38] The church, we might even say, is shy.

The church's call to speak truthfully does not presuppose its infallibility. In fact, insofar as it is a *call* it recognizes the church's liability—even at times its penchant—to veer into falsehood. At the same time, in that Jesus calls the church to truthful speech, it really may speak the truth. In the realm of the Spirit, the Kantian maxim holds: "ought" does imply "can." So the church need and may not despair of the truth. If it can only speak the truth in humble recognition of its frailty, it must speak the truth in the confidence of its Spirit-enabled vocation.

The truth of the church's proclamation demands a truthful form. In a nearly post-Christian American context, we are left with linguistic husks. People remain familiar with the vocabulary of the Christian faith but show little evidence of having grasped the kernel. Many believe they intelligently reject a known account of God and the world. Truth in such a context falls on deaf ears, and familiarity breeds contempt. In its truthful life together, the church demonstrates the surprising intelligibility of evangelical truth.[39]

---

now published as "The New World in the Bible." See also Frei, *The Eclipse of Biblical Narrative*.

38. John Webster refers to a "rhetoric of indication" in *Word and Church*, 124. Webster elsewhere describes testimony as "astonished indication" (*Confessing God*, 185).

39. This sentence might well summarize Stanley Hauerwas's *corpus*. As he puts it in his Gifford Lectures, "Witnesses must exist if Christians are to be intelligible to themselves and hopefully to those who are not Christians, just as the intelligibility of science depends in the end on the success of experiments" (Hauerwas, *With the Grain of the Universe*, 212).

"The truth is finally known in the showing."[40] Perhaps our situation in the decline of an empire approaches that of the church's first few centuries, one in which the truthfulness of God's people serves to elucidate the truth. Rowan Williams writes that

> we make the best sense of doctrine in the historical context of the early Church if we see it as an exegesis of martyrdom; with martyrdom itself being an exegesis, a lived exposition, of taking Christ seriously as the one through whom the definition of God's people has been changed.[41]

Martyrs make no sense apart from the death and resurrection of Jesus Christ.[42] The happy self-possession of Christian martyrs was unintelligible to Rome, and gospel proclamation became a way of making sense of those seemingly absurd deaths. Similarly today, the church finds itself on the margins, where its truthfulness suggests at best a holy folly whose very strangeness opens up space for the proclamation of the truth.

Conclusion

Let me conclude with two comments. The first comes from Jonathan Edwards:

> Holiness is in a peculiar manner the beauty of the divine nature . . . This renders all his other attributes glorious and lovely. 'Tis the glory of God's wisdom, that 'tis a holy wisdom, and not a wicked subtlety and craftiness. This makes his majesty lovely, and not merely dreadful and horrible, that it is a holy majesty. 'Tis the glory of God's immutability, that it is a holy immutability, and not an inflexible obstinacy in wickedness.
>
> A true love to God must begin with a delight in his holiness, and not with delight in any other attribute; for no other attribute is truly lovely without this.[43]

The holiness of the Lord is beautiful, turning attributes that, in anyone else, would threaten into occasions for delight. There is none like him. Truly, he

---

40. Hauerwas, *Sanctify Them in the Truth*, 43.

41. Williams, *Why Study the Past?*, 53.

42. This is why Athanasius can describe martyrdom as a proof of the Godhead of the Savior (*De incarnatione*, 52).

43. Edwards, *Works of Jonathan Edwards* 2:257.

is the Lord; and there is no other.[44] The holy one in our midst is beautiful, and he is beatifying. For Edwards, God is a communicative being, giving his people a share in the beauty of his holiness and making them happy.

The second comment comes from Eberhard Busch:

> What God's holiness is, is defined by his will to enter into a covenant: 'I will be your God, and you will be my people.' Here an understanding of holiness as mere separation from others is transcended . . . God's holiness itself contains the freedom to 'go beyond' oneself (without doing away with oneself) in order to form a bond with someone who is totally different from oneself, someone who is holy.[45]

The triune God gives humanity a share in his holiness by going out of himself in the incarnation of the Word and the descent of the Spirit, gathering a people to himself and sending them out into the world. They are "a holy nation, a people for his own possession, that [they] may proclaim the excellencies of him who called [them] out of darkness into his marvelous light" (1 Pet 2:9). Holiness, it turns out, takes its form in communion and mission.

44. Jer 10:6; Isa 45:5.

45. Eberhard Busch, *Karl Barth and the Pietists: The Young Karl Barth's Critique of Pietism and Its Response,* trans. Daniel W. Bloesch (Downers Grove, IL: IVP Academic, 2004), 299–300. In the Scripture citation, Busch cites *KD* IV/2, 565, in which Barth cites Jer 7:23, 31:33; Ezek 36:28.

Embodying Faithfulness

New Monastic Retrieval and the Christian Imagination

—Kent Eilers[1]

In the closing lines of Alistair MacIntyre's *After Virtue,* he cryptically suggests that the moral revitalization of the post-Christian West requires the witness of another "doubtless very different" St. Benedict.[2] The figure of St. Benedict embodied for MacIntyre the ideal of local communities of virtue "within which civility and the intellectual and moral life can be sustained through the dark ages which are already upon us." Three decades on from MacIntyre's remark we are, perhaps, witnessing St. Benedict's return.

This essay explores the possibility of that return among new monastics, most specifically as it is represented in the work of Jonathan Wilson-Hartgrove. I hope to show that the ecclesial renewal sought by new monastics necessitates *not merely* the formation of monastic-like communities who perform monastic-like practices, but the cultivation and maintenance of a distinctly *theological* imagination sufficient to fund the meaning of its forms of life. In other words, new monastic retrieval requires a community whose shared theological imagination makes its practices intelligible, sensible, and livable.[3] Retrieval such as this is social in orientation, and, as I

1. Portions of this essay are published elsewhere, and I am grateful to the editors of *American Theological Inquiry* and *InterVarsity Press* for granting permission to republish them here (respectively, Kent Eilers "New Monastic Social Imaginary: Theological Retrieval for Ecclesial Renewal," 45–57; W. David Buschart and Kent Eilers, *Theology as Retrieval,* chapter 5).

2. MacIntyre, *After Virtue,* 263; see also, 199.

3. This necessitates skirting the origins and ongoing significance of new monasticism. On the origins of new monasticism see the following: Howard, "Introducing New Monasticism"; Wilson-Hartgrove, *New Monasticism*; Wilson, "Introduction"; and

will argue in what follows, necessarily theological, though for reasons that might not be apparent at first.

The essay proceeds in five parts. The first is largely descriptive. I begin by tracing the object new monastics seek to retrieve in order to show it as a past they believe one *inhabits*. I fill out this sketch in the second part by focusing on two books by Jonathan Wilson-Hartgrove, and in the third part I bring him into conversation with Charles Taylor. Taylor's social theory offers a useful conceptual angle to better understand the interplay between imagination and practices in new monastic retrieval. In the fourth part, I introduce Etienne Wenger's social theory of learning to sharpen my primary contention: new monastic retrieval requires the formation and maintenance of a distinct *theological* imagination in order to fund the meaning of its shared practices.[4] This insight is relevant not only for new monastics but for the church more broadly, a point briefly developed in the conclusion.

The Monastic Impulse

For new monastics the Christian tradition is a resource.[5] In this sense new monasticism is a form of retrieval. They look *back* to various monas-

---

Harrold, "New Monasticism," 182–93.

4. Jonathan R. Wilson emphasizes the importance of theology for new monastics, but not from the cultural formation perspective I present here (see Wilson, *Living Faithfully*, 70; Wilson, "Introduction," 1–9).

5. There are at least five related but nonetheless separate contemporary expressions of new monasticism (Harrold identifies four [Harrold, "New Monasticism"]). (1) The first expression is voiced by Scott Bessenecker, director of global projects for InterVarsity Christian Fellowship. He applies the term "new friars" to describe a swell of young people who leave North America to serve people around the world in extreme poverty (see Bessenecker, *New Friars*; Bessenecker, *Living Mission*; see also, Annan, "Chaos and Grace in the Slums of the Earth"; Moll, "New Monasticism"); (2) The second expression focuses specifically on the Rule of Benedict. Michel Casey, Dennis Okholm, and Benet Tveldten share no formal relationship, but each commends the wisdom of the Benedictine way for contemporary Christians (see Casey, *Strangers to the City*; Okholm, *Monk Habits for Everyday People*; Tveldten, *How to Be Monastic and Not Leave your Day Job*; (3) The third expression is expressed by Aaron Milavec who presents the *Didache* as a "life-transforming training program" for Gentile converts. It is not so much the *Didache* that Milavec seeks but the Christian perception of the world that living according to the *Didache* fosters (see Milavec, *Didache*); (4) The fourth expression is The Boiler Room Network that originated in Great Britain and spread to the United States. Taking inspiration from Celtic, Franciscan, Benedictine, and Moravian spirituality and figures like

tic movements and practices in order to discern how the church should faithfully inhabit the present and live into her future. However, while their attention to the Christian tradition and more narrowly to the traditions of monasticism is obvious, it is not immediately apparent *how* these are resources.

When new monastics view the Christian past they do so through a particular set of lenses, ones through which certain communities stand out because their lifestyle is judged to be most faithful to the Christian witness. Some of these communities are patently monastic, but others like the Catholic Worker movement are clearly not. The faithfulness of their lifestyle is variously named and then sought after. Some describe it as an "attitude of life" (Freeman and Grieg), a "long-established pattern" (Bessenecker), a "training program" (Milavec), a "flexible hermeneutic" (Okholm), or, as Jonathan Wilson-Hartgrove calls it, the "monastic impulse."[6] However it is named, and regardless of the historical, geographical, or cultural differences that separate new monastics from the object of their retrieval, they strive to recover an identifiable *form of life* that entails locating themselves within it.[7] Harrold writes, "It is as if history itself becomes a form of con-

---

Dietrich Bonhoeffer, Francis Schaeffer, and Lesslie Newbigin, they apply the term "monastic" to describe how the Christian faith is taking shape in their communities (in the United States, see "Communities," *24–7 Prayer USA*, 24-7prayer.us/communities; and in the United Kingdom, "Boiler Rooms and Communities," *24–7 Prayer UK*, uk.24-7prayer. com/boiler-rooms-and-communities/; Freeman and Grieg, *Punk Monk*; Grieg and Roberts, *Red Moon Rising*); (5) The fifth is Jonathan Wilson-Hartgrove who occupies our attention below. Evan Howard suggests that at least three *other* forms of new monasticism exist whose relationship to these five expressions is difficult to discern: Northumbria, Missional Wisdom Foundation/Elaine Heath, and Raven's Bread (email correspondence, 5/11/2013). Further, Ray Simpson and Bernadette Flanagan offer frameworks for the emergence of recent new monasticisms—Flanagan's being the more exhaustive (Simpson, *High Street Monasteries*; Flanagan, *Embracing Solitude*). Flanagan's framework also names several emerging monasticisms that overlap my list: "monasticism without walls," "invisible monasticism," "portable monasticism," "secular monasticism," "lay monasticism," and "everyday monasticism" (17–18).

6. See previous note. Wilson-Hartgrove adopts the term "monastic impulse" from Capps, *Monastic Impulse*. The monastic impulse is "a form of human awareness consonant with a specific way of life" (8). See Wilson-Hartgrove, *New Monasticism*, 43.

7. Giorgio Agamben argues that the syntagma "form of life" (*forma vivendi*) names the basic instinct of Western monasticism in which life and rule come together indistinguishably within communal life. He writes, "What is in question in the monastic rules is thus a transformation that seems to bear on the very way in which human action is conceived, so that one shifts from the level of practice and acting to that of form of life and living. This dis-location of ethics and politics from the sphere of action to that of

sciousness that involves not only rational thought and action, but a sense of real participation through 're-enactment.'" [8] As Wilson-Hartgrove describes it, new monastics attempt to join a "river of faithfulness . . . as it finds its way to the future God has for us."[9] The "river of faithfulness" they seek is a past you can *inhabit*, one you can creatively re-enact.

Thus, participating in the monastic impulse through reenactment requires the creative transposition of both a distinct imagination and fitting, appropriate practices.[10] Ideas and actions, doctrines and practices are involved in a dynamic interplay. New monastic retrieval (at its best) is not narrowly doctrinal, the attempt to recover a lost or underemphasized belief. Recovering the monastic impulse requires more than comprehension: it must be lived, or reenacted. Nor is it an effort to only retrieve ancient or distinctly monastic practices.[11] Merely pulling forward an attitude or activity from the past would be inadequate.[12] And the same can be said for any wise, theological retrieval.[13] The "livable past" new monastics seek is a particular way of both expressing the Christian faith—*practices*—and seeing the world in light of the Christian confession—*imagination*.

form of life represents the demanding legacy of monasticism, which modernity has failed to recognize. How should one understand this figure of a living and a life that—while affirming itself as 'form of life'—cannot be brought back to either law or morals, to a precept or advice, to labor or contemplation, and that nonetheless appears explicitly as the canon of a perfect community?" (Agamben, *Highest Poverty*, 60; see also, 86–88).

8. Harrold, "New Monasticism," 190. Interestingly, Alan Hirsch deploys the term "apostolic genius" similarly to how new monastics deploy "monastic impulse" (Hirsch, *The Forgotten Ways*). For example, Hirsch describes "apostolic genius" as a "potent inheritance" (22), "movement ethos" (62), "life force" (77), and "alternative imagination" (67–68). In each case he argues that the apostolic genius was inherent to the post-apostolic movement and must be retrieved or "cultivated." Hirsch's retrieval is not of methods or sources but of a paradigm and mindset.

9. Wilson-Hartgrove, *New Monasticism*, 33–34.

10. Alan Jacobs reviewed several recent retrievals including new monasticism and critiqued them for their lack of historical consciousness and overbearing pragmatism. They are "bricoleurs" who pick and choose what is readily on hand for their own purposes. However, he argues that Wilson-Hartgrove's *New Monasticism* offers the best promise, because it puts monastic-like practices in the context of an entire way of life (Jacobs, "Do-It-Yourself Tradition").

11. An unfortunate example is McLaren, *Finding Our Way Again*.

12. David Hardy calls this a "discourse of 'intimate identification,' a 'kinship,' constituted by a diverse array of epistemic practices and ethical structures and norms" (Hardy, "Sociality, Rationality, and Culture," 1–19; quoted in Harrold, "Ancient-Future Belonging," 190).

13. See, Buschart and Eilers, *Theology as Retrieval*.

These terms, "imagination" and "practices," should be unpacked as I am using them here. "Imagination" names the capacity for perception that takes place without having to consciously think about the act of perception. This is similar to what Walter Capps refers to when he describes the monastic impulse: "a form of human awareness consonant with a specific way of life"[14] In this sense imagination is not one's creativity or fancy—the ability to "make things up"—but the capacity for *sense-making*.

James K. A. Smith describes the imagination as a "quasi-faculty whereby we construe the world on a precognitive level . . . a kind of mid-level organizing faculty that constitutes the world for us in a primarily *affective* mode." [15] Through the imagination we "navigate and make sense of our world, but in ways and on a register that flies below the radar of conscious reflection."[16] The imagination renders our perception of ourselves and our world, but it is not only "constructive" but also "receptive."[17] In other words, the imagination is not disembodied or disconnected from the environment it perceives; rather, it is in constant negotiation with its setting. For example, Alasdair MacIntyre emphasizes the receptive character of the imagination in narrative terms: "I can only answer the question 'What am I to do?' if I can answer the prior question 'Of what story or stories do I find myself a part?'"[18] As the normative narrative for Christians, the Bible has a role of obvious importance for shaping the Christian imagination. The Bible has the "productive power of redescribing reality in a way that can engage and lead our imaginations."[19] In other words, the Bible shapes the imagination and therefore how Christians "see."

I am employing the term "practice" in roughly the same manner as MacIntyre which, although cumbersome, is massively influential.[20] A practice is

---

14. Capps, *Monastic Impulse*, 8.

15. Smith, *Imagining the Kingdom*, 17–18 (emphasis added).

16. Ibid., 19.

17. Bryant, *Faith and the Play of the Imagination*, 5.

18. MacIntyre, *After Virtue*, 216. cf. Bryant: "Its receptivity takes the form of being shaped by the past in a way that attunes it to the interplay between life and world" (*Faith and the Play of Imagination*, 5).

19. Bryant, *Faith and the Play of Imagination*, 6.

20. For example, Jonathan R. Wilson laments that many in the church do not understand their shared activities (such as worship, studying the Bible, or service) along the lines of MacIntyre's definition. They either do not see the connection between practices and the Christian conception of the common good, or importance of achieving the

any coherent and complex form of socially established coopera-
tive human activity through which goods internal to that form of
activity are realized in the course of trying to achieve those standards of excellence which are appropriate to, and partially definitive of, that form of activity, with the result that human powers to
achieve excellence, and human conceptions of the ends and goods
involved, are systematically extended.[21]

More compactly: practices are "routines and rituals that inscribe particular
ongoing habits into our character, such that they become second nature
to us."[22] For example, the contributors to School(s) for Conversion develop
twelve marks that "name the unique witness" of new monastic communities.[23] These practices include relocation to the abandoned places of empire
(Mark 1), sharing economic resources with fellow community members
and the needy (Mark 2), nurturing common life among members of intentional community (Mark 7), and commitment to a disciplined contemplative life (Mark 12).

With terms in hand, I can summarize: the monastic impulse is a livable past in which a particular imagination (way of viewing, perceiving)
is wedded to and intertwined with distinctive, fitting practices (ways of
expressing). One cannot be separated from the other. Simply trying to pull
forward an attitude or ideal from the past would be inadequate. More than
an idea or ideal, it is a social consciousness that new monastics seek to
reenact and in which to participate.

Wayne Meeks has something like this in mind with the term "hermeneutics of social embodiment." For Meeks, social practices are necessary
for communities to effectively interpret the meaning of texts. Interpretation
requires, Meeks explains, a "community competent to understand, and that
means a community whose ethos, worldview, and sacred symbols . . . can
be tuned" to the way particular texts "worked in the time past."[24] In other

---

"goods" that are "internal" to the practice, or the formative power of practices in partnership with the Holy Spirit to shape individuals toward Christlikeness (Living Faithfully,
52–53). The essays in School(s) for Conversion seem to generally follow suit.

21. MacIntyre, After Virtue, 187.

22. Smith, Desiring the Kingdom, 80.

23. Rutba House, School(s) for Conversion.

24. Meeks, "Hermeneutics of Social Embodiment," 192–93. See also Lindbeck, Nature of Doctrine, 128–35: "The grammar of religion, like that of any language, cannot
be explicated or learned by analysis of experience, but only by practice" (129); Placher,
Unapologetic Theology, 167; Wood, Formation of Christian Understanding, chapter 1.

words, forms of life are required that "correspond to the symbolic universe rendered or signaled" by a text.[25]

Extending a social hermeneutic such as this to new monastic retrieval provides two immediate insights. First, as a "text" of sorts, comprehending and appropriating the "monastic impulse" in an entirely new geographic, cultural and temporal location requires the embodiment of its forms of life. Not surprisingly, new monastics are generally recognizable by their appropriation of monastic-like practices in more or less sophisticated ways. Second, and this is the nub, such embodiment requires a community whose collective *imagination*—ethos, worldview, and sacred symbols[26]—is tuned to the way the monastic impulse was embodied *in the past*. In other words, new monastic retrieval necessitates a particular interplay between imagination and practices, an interplay found implicitly throughout new monastic literature and, perhaps, most clearly seen in the work of Jonathan Wilson-Hartgrove.

Jonathan Wilson-Hartgrove: Cultivating the New Monastic Theological Imagination

Wilson-Hartgrove is one of the leading exponents of new monasticism in North America,[27] the director of School for Conversion,[28] cofounder of the new monastic community Rutba House, and the author of numerous books and articles on new monasticism. [29] Two books by Wilson-Hartgrove are sufficient to illustrate the relationship between imagination and practices.

His first book on new monasticism was *New Monasticism: What It Has to Say to Today's Church* (hereafter *NM*). The order of presentation in

25. Meeks, "Hermeneutics," 193.

26. See Geertz, "Ethos, World-View and the Analysis of Sacred Symbols," 421–37.

27. North American new monastics that loosely associate themselves with Wilson-Hartgrove's influence are broadly identifiable by their association with the Community of Communities network (communityofcommunities.info/) and their resemblance to the "twelve marks" of new monasticism described in Rutba House, *School(s) for Conversion*.

28. Schoolforconversion.org/.

29. For example, *The Awakening of Hope*; "Liturgy for Our Whole Life," with Claiborne; *Wisdom of Stability*; *Common Prayer*, with Claiborne and Okoro; "Money Enough/Rediscovering our Values"; *God's Economy*; "Advent 2009"; "New Monasticism and the Resurrection of American Christianity"; "Economics for Disciples"; "Together on the Ark"; *New Monasticism; Becoming the Answer to Our Prayers*, with Claiborne; and *Inhabiting the Church*, with Otto and Stock.

this book suggests that the imagination dimension of the monastic impulse is required to bring forth particular, fitting practices. On one hand, the monastic impulse is presented in chapters one through four as a hermeneutic for reading the Bible, history, and culture. On the other hand, the practices that occupy the second half of the book are said to fund, generate, and build the new monastic imagination: relocation to urban areas, financial stewardship, peacemaking, and ecumenism. Wilson-Hartgrove describes them as means for "living into the story of the people of God" and "catalysts for imagination."[30] While the texture of the interplay and its implications are never developed, the traffic appears to run both ways. On a different metaphor, the gears of imagination and practices are clearly turning together, but their causal relationship is never clear.

In Wilson-Hartgrove's subsequent book, *The Awakening of Hope: Why We Practice a Common Faith* (*AH*), the interplay between imagination and practice is more explicit. *Awakening* is a catechism with a twist. Rather than progress from questions to what Christians believe, it moves from questions to the practices that reveal and shape underlying convictions. "Instead of saying what we believe and how we might apply that to our lives" the book focuses on "practices that inspire hope in our time and ask what convictions undergird a way of life that makes such witness possible."[31] Each chapter elaborates the back-and-forth between a selected practice and the new monastic imagination in order to demonstrate how, on one hand, practices do not merely *flow out from* particular convictions, but *shape* and *form* the Christian imagination. On the other hand, Christian practices are shown to *reveal* underlying, supporting, sense-making Christian convictions: "a gospel that *makes sense* of a peculiar way of living."[32]

An example will illustrate. The second chapter in *AH* focuses on shared meals. Following a story of Sojourners Community in San Francisco, Wilson-Hartgrove argues that the practice forms our self-perception:

> Subtle as it might seem at first, eating together is an interruption to business as usual—a constant reminder that God's movement goes against the grain of the status quo, calling us ever deeper into a new reality beyond the available options of this world's systems

---

30. Wilson-Hartgrove, *New Monasticism*, 70.

31. Wilson-Hartgrove, *Awakening of Hope*, 15.

32. Ibid., 27.

> . . . As creatures in communion, *we learn the habits that make it possible to know what it means to say Jesus Christ is Lord.*[33]

Wilson-Hartgrove concedes that shared meals are traceable to Jesus and the earliest Christians, but argues for a rationale other than a desire to follow an historical pattern or repristinate a lost activity. Rather, the practice shapes our perception of our alliance to Christ and inclusion in the community of Christians. Eating together "remind[s] us of our connections that tie us to the soil," but more than this, it "should also *point us toward* our source (and end) in the Trinitarian God."[34]

On this manner of conceiving the interplay between practices and imagination, practices do not merely *spring out* from theological commitments such as "God's grace sustains and redeems," but they in fact contribute to one's perception of and ability to live out from such convictions.[35] Wilson-Hartgrove works to counterbalance what he sees as an overemphasis on doctrine to galvanize the renewal of the church by focusing, instead, on the formative potential of practices.[36] However, his approach assumes an imagination that, as he says, "makes sense of a peculiar way of living." Although Wilson-Hartgrove takes for granted the prior background of one's allegiance to Jesus Christ as Lord, he emphasizes the influence this practice has in helping one to "know what it means" to do so.

In these two books there are clear hints about the interplay between imagination and practices, even if they are not explicitly drawn out. At this turn, Charles Taylor's concept of "social imaginary" is helpful. It offers a conceptual angle for interpreting Wilson-Hartgrove's retrieval, and, more broadly, the concept of social imaginary helps us to think about the interplay between imagination and practices in the life and ministry of churches.

---

33. Ibid., 36 (emphasis added).

34. Ibid., 43 (emphasis added). Jonathan R. Wilson makes a similar move in the introduction to *School(s) for Conversion*. "The simple task of providing for daily sustenance of life . . . *reminds us of our dependence.* The tasks of praying, worshipping, fasting, and discerning together also *open the community to God's grace*, though of course they can also be distorted by acts of heroism. Continual openness to others through the central practice of hospitality *makes clear the community's dependence upon grace.* Finally, the monastic vows of poverty, chastity, and obedience, whatever form they take in the discernment of new monastic communities, are best understood as *commitment to a way of life made possible only by God's sustaining and redeeming grace*" ("Introduction," 8–9, emphasis added).

35. Wilson, "Introduction," 9.

36. Wilson-Hartgrove, "Introduction," in *Awakening of Hope*.

Taylor's model also helps us address a pressing question: what is the *causal* relationship between ideas and practices? In other words, do doctrines and ideas cause or produce particular practices, or do the practices generate particular ways of thinking, believing, and perceiving? It is not a new question but certainly one relevant for retrieving the monastic impulse. It is also a relevant question for the church: should churches invest in changing the ways people think or the ways people behave? Which comes first? Which holds priority?

Charles Taylor: The Monastic Impulse as Social Imaginary

By "social imaginary" Taylor works to coordinate two elements of communal life.

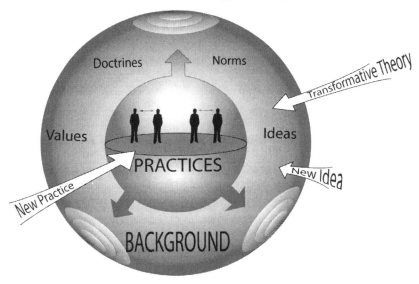

The first is a community's ideas, doctrines, and beliefs that orient their way of interpreting the world and understanding their place within it. This is what Taylor calls the "background" (a communal rendering of one's imagination). The features of a community's background are what they take for granted. It is their "lived understanding" about which they do not give a second thought.[37] The background is like an intuitive map of one's home-town. Without even remembering the street names, one knows how to get around without having to think which way to turn. The second dimension of a social imaginary entails all the practices one finds sensible and fitting as they are understood within the fabric, or against the backdrop, of their "background." Taken together, the collective participation in social life that comes about through the interplay of background and practices is a social imaginary. [38]

Within the fabric of one's particular background certain practices are simply taken for granted as the way to act, the most sensible and fitting way to live one's life. Social imaginaries render "the ways in which [people] imagine their social existence, how they fit together with others, how things go on between them and their fellows, the expectations which are normally met, and the deeper normative notions and images which underlie these expectations." [39] In other words, one's practices only make sense, or fit, because they are embedded within a particular background.

Do practices form and shape the imagination, or does the imagination lead to fitting practices? Taylor suspects that the causal interplay runs *both ways*. "If the understanding makes the practice possible, it is also true that it is the practice which largely carries the understanding."[40] "In fact," Taylor continues,

> . . . what we see in human history is ranges in human practices that are both at once, that is, material practices carried out by human beings in space and time, and very often coercively maintained, and at the same time, self-conceptions, modes of understanding. These are often inseparable . . . Because human practices are the kind of thing that makes sense, certain ideas are internal to them; one cannot distinguish the two in order to ask the question Which causes which?[41]

---

37. Taylor, *Secular Age*, 30–31 (also 173).

38. Taylor first articulated this in *Modern Social Imaginaries* (2004), and developed it further in *Secular Age* (2007).

39. Taylor, *Secular Age*, 171.

40. Ibid., 173.

41. Taylor, *Social Imaginaries*, 31.

Taylor summarizes: "Ideas always come in history wrapped up in certain practices . . . even if these are only discursive practices."[42] A transformative theory might enter a social imagination to unsettle and shift its "seeing" of the way things are, or practices might affect slow but nonetheless dramatic changes to the social imaginary.[43]

Adopting Taylor's terms, the monastic impulse is a distinct social imaginary that comprises the complex relationship between imagination and practices found in various new monastic expressions as seen in Wilson-Hartgrove's *NM* and *AH*. The imagination Wilson-Hartgrove profiles in the first half of *NM* satisfies each component of Taylor's description of the "background" element of a social imaginary: biblical imagination— "grasp of our whole predicament, how we stand to each other"; historical imagination—"how we got where we are"; cultural imagination—"how we relate to other groups." The discussion of practices in the second half of the book is nested within a biblical, historical, and cultural imagination provided in the first half.[44]

The foregoing exploration in new monastic retrieval suggests the following insight: the cultivation and maintenance of a community's shared imagination is fundamental for practices to carry their intended meaning. Said differently, a collective imagination is required to make "sense" of practices ("background" on Taylor's terms), and without sufficient attention to its cultivation and maintenance it will simply drop out. Or, an imagination of a different sort will take its place and provide its own, and quite different, sense-making function. Such a challenge calls for the new monastic communities to discover and invest in fitting avenues through which to *theologically* imagine, name, and embrace the practices that constitute the monastic social imaginary.[45]

It is worth pausing to emphasize this point. In order for new monastic retrieval to succeed on its own terms—to recover the monastic impulse

---

42. Ibid., 33.

43. Taylor, *Secular Age*, 175. James K. A. Smith takes the opposite view, arguing for the directive influence of practices on understanding (Smith, *Desiring the Kingdom*, 67 n. 53).

44. Wilson provides a more thoroughly eschatological vision of this ("Introduction," 5–7).

45. Similarly, in the afterword to the second edition to *Living Faithfully in A Fragmented World*, Jonathan R. Wilson observes the importance of discovering and expositing "a theology native to NMC's [new monastic communities]" (Wilson, *Living Faithfully*, 70; see also Wilson, "Introduction," 1–9).

from past Christian, monastic movements—new monastic imagination must be distinctly theological. That is, some imagination, Christian or otherwise, will invest the practices of new monastics with meaning(s); the issue is whether that imagination will be theological. This is not to say anything of the actual efficacy of such practices, in other words whether or not they achieve the "ends" or telos they are believed to serve (e.g., spiritual transformation, ecological stewardship, community formation). Rather, the issue at stake is the cultivation and maintenance of a theological imagination sufficient for the task of investing their practices with meanings broadly consistent with the Christian tradition and more narrowly with the monastic-like movements in which they see the monastic impulse and seek to retrieve it.

This insight is confirmed by Taylor's idea of social imaginary. Taylor contends that the practices of a social imaginary are "made sense of" by the background elements of theory, doctrine or ideas, what he terms the "new outlook." This "new outlook" is the "context that gives sense to the practices."[46] The "sense-making" function of the social imaginary registers the importance of painting a rich, textured theological vision for communal practices ("theological vision" renders Taylor's phrase "new outlook" in religious terms). Thus, without the cultivation and maintenance of a theological imagination capable of forming the background of new monastic retrieval, their practices have potential, over time, to lose their sensibility.

While theological reflection is necessary to nurture a compelling, rich, evocative, theological frame ("new outlook"), borrowing Taylor's model also suggests that retrieval of the monastic social imaginary requires practices (monastic or otherwise) that are consonant with the monastic impulse. The new outlook "comes to be accessible" through practices! "It begins to define the contours of one's world, and can eventually come to count as the taken-for-granted shape of things, too obvious to mention." Taylor is clear that theories by themselves are incapable of transforming the social imaginary but require practices to give them "shape" in the "dense sphere of common practice."[47]

---

46. Taylor, *Secular Age*, 175.
47. Ibid., 176.

Etienne Wenger: Imagination, Practices, Reification, and Repertoire

I will sharpen the point further with Etienne Wenger's social theory of learning.[48] On Wenger's theory, certain forms of *participation* are available to members of a community at any given time.[49] Some practices are sensible and fitting while others are not, although one might not be consciously aware why this is the case.[50] For example, a first grade teacher might expect her students to raise a hand to speak in class, but their parents might not expect them to do so at their dinner tables. Raising a hand and being called on is a practice in which student and teacher participate during classroom interaction, but the practice rarely fits the repertoire of practices at home. If a child blushes after raising their hand at the dinner table, this signals their awareness that the action is unfitting to the setting; they instinctively know they are participating in the wrong repertoire of practices.

Reification names the process whereby shared ideas, values, and concepts are turned into "material things," such as objects, gestures, or sounds. A child's practice of gaining their teacher's attention is a classroom practice because the values of respect and attentiveness have been reified into the gesture of raising a hand and waiting to be called on.[51] In Wenger's theory, the processes of participation and reification are always interacting as members of a group "negotiate the meaning of their actions with one another."[52]

Over time the processes of participation and reification lead to a *repertoire* of acceptable and meaningful shared practices.[53] "Repertoire (like

48. Wenger, *Communities of Practice*.

49. Ibid., 55–57.

50. Wenger defines "practice" as "doing, but not just doing in and of itself. It is doing in a historical context that gives structure and meaning to what we do. In this sense, practice is always social practice" (Ibid., 47. See also 102).

51. Reification includes more than gestures. Wenger illustrates with the concept of "justice" as it is sometimes reified in the form of a blindfolded maid holding a scale (Ibid., 58–71).

52. Smith and Smith, "Introduction: Practices, Faith, and Pedagogy," 13.

53. Wenger, *Communities*, 82–84. Taylor describes a similar set of practices he calls "repertory": "At any given time, we can speak of the 'repertory' of collective actions at the disposal of a given group in society. These are the common actions which they know how to undertake" (Taylor, *Secular Age*, 173). Pierre Bourdieu describes the term habitus as "a system of durable, transposable dispositions, structured structures predisposed to function as structuring structures, that is, as principles which generate and organize

habitus) is a way of naming the patterns inscribed in the way we do things together, and helps to define the boundaries that form between the different communities of practice of which any given individual is a part."[54] The repertoire of fitting practices in a child's home are often different than their classroom repertoire because teachers and students have reified a different set of acceptable practices. To summarize: when a group participates together in meaningful practices (such as teaching and learning or eating together) they are actively reifying their beliefs and intentions into a repertoire of acceptable actions.

The background for the entire process is *imagination*. Wenger illustrates with two stonecutters who are asked about *what* they are doing:

> One responds: 'I am cutting this stone into a perfectly square shape.' The other responds: 'I am building a cathedral.' Both answers are correct and meaningful, but they reflect different relations to the world. The difference between these answers does not imply that one is a better stonecutter than the other, as far as holding a chisel is concerned. At the level of engagement, they may well be doing exactly the same thing. But it does suggest that their experiences of what they are doing and their sense of self in doing it are rather different. This difference is a function of imagination.[55]

It is the element of imagination that generates the perspective and sense of *telos* which limits one stonecutter but enables another to "see" the cathedral.

Similar to Taylor, Wenger describes the imagination as a *collective* possession formed through a *collective* process. The practices in which a group participates forms the imagination and, in the reverse, the imagination provides the perspective that provides meaning and *telos* to their repertoire of actions. "Over time, imagination becomes embodied in repertoire, and repertoire at the same time shapes imagination. Shared imagination

---

practices and representations" (Bourdieu, *Outline of a Theory of Practice*, 72). Habitus is the dialectical relationship between "positions and dispositions" (Bourdieu, *Pascalian Meditations*, 155). More simply, habitus names second-nature behavior that arises without conscious rule following. According to Michel de Certeau, the term habitus does not actually originate with Bourdieu but goes back to Marcel Mauss, and more directly to Panofsky's demonstration of the practical and theoretical importance of habitus in medieval society (Certeau, *Practice of Everyday Life*, 57 n. 29).

54. Smith and Smith, "Introduction," 13.

55. "Imagination is this sense of looking at an apple seed and seeing a tree" or "reading a biography and recognizing yourself in the struggles of a character" (Wenger, *Communities*, 176).

is manifest as much in what we do as in what we say."[56] In short, shared imagination sustains the meaning of practices and, in turn, is sustained by them.

Wenger's model elaborates the necessity for new monastic communities to cultivate and maintain the theological imagination which generates the sensibility of their communal practices. This necessity is made especially apparent when considering the challenges to new monastic retrieval. One such challenge is the dissimilarity between the cultures *from which* new monastics seek to retrieve practices and the culture of the recipients *for whom* they are being recovered. For example, North American Christianity is historically individualistic, but monastic communities have entailed a distinctly *communal* element.[57] Or, prosperity-Gospel Christians understand wealth as blessing, but some monastic communities have historically taken vows of poverty or relocated to abandoned city centers. More deeply still, the sacramental ontology present in most, if not all, patristic and medieval monastic movements is scarcely present in most (all?) late modern, North American, Protestant communities.[58] Thus, while new monastics attempt to recover various practices they find integral to the monastic impulse (e.g., communal living, relocation), those practices risk the attachment of divergent meanings if they lack a theological imagination capable of providing the appropriate "sense-making" function.[59]

This could also be said on Wenger's terms. Practices such as communal living or relocation are made meaningful, in part, because they are part of the *repertoire* of actions made sensible by the monastic social imaginary. Thus, for instance, while a prosperity-Gospel Christian may value care for the poor, that value is not reified into the practice of relocation as it is for new monastics because it is not part of that particular Christian's repertoire of sensible actions. Or, some new monastics recommend ecological stewardship, but they do so without the sacramental ontology of medieval monastics which elevated the value of the terrestrial order by "anchoring [it] in the eternal Logos."[60] In both cases, we might perform the practice but its

---

56. Smith and Smith, "Introduction: Practices, Faith, and Pedagogy," 14.

57. See, Sheridan, "The Origins of Monasticism in the Eastern Church" (3–41) and Peifer, "Pre-Benedictine Monasticism in the Western Church" (42–64) in *RB 1980*.

58. See, Boersma, *Heavenly Participation*, 17–67.

59. The most robust appreciation and development of this dynamic among new monastics is found in Stock, Otto, and Wilson-Hartgrove, *Inhabiting the Church*.

60. Boersma, *Heavenly Participation*, 52.

meaning(s) depend upon the repertoire of practice in which it is nested and the collective imagination which makes those practices sensible.

Conclusion

Whatever effort new monastics expend to recover monastic-like practices (some place the majority of their emphasis here), the foregoing considerations recommend that such efforts are matched by sustained, creative, deliberate attention to the cultivation and maintenance of a theological imagination capable of making such practices sensible and fitting. To repeat my contention: the marks of new monastic communities will carry whatever meaning(s) their theological imagination provides. Thus, like stonecutters who may or may not "see" the cathedral, retrieving a monastic social imaginary necessitates that all *see* a shared theological vision.[61] Without such attention, new monastic practices risk floating free from their theological moorings in the Christian confession.

In fact, the same challenge persists for any church practice. The insights that become available through pressing new monastic retrieval apply well beyond it. Any church practice risks floating free from its moorings if sustained attention is not given to nurturing the community's theological imagination. The traditional venues for such attention are many and varied: catechesis, preaching, spiritual direction, parochial education, etc. Among these and a host of others, the potential of one in particular should not be overlooked: liturgy. "It is in and through the worshipping community," Geoffrey Wainwright suggests, "that most believers *catch* the Christian vision."[62] It is also the case that in the liturgy the full trinitarian weight of the Christian confession is found present, at least tacitly. New monastics will find no more thoroughly *theological* venue for the cultivation and maintenance of theological imagination—nor will any church—than a liturgy which intentionally and forthrightly celebrates the trinitarian shape of the Christian confession.[63]

---

61. Craig Van Gelder offers a similar critique (Van Gelder, "How We Hear Mission in North America," 51–60).

62. Wainwright, *Doxology*, 435 (emphasis added). See also, Torrance, *God and Rationality*, 204. Walter Brueggemann's definition of preaching as "re-texting" is remarkably similar: "the task of re-texting, or scribal refraction, is to let the text itself be the resource for offering an alternative imagination, energy, and identity for the community" (Brueggemann, "Preacher as Scribe," 14).

63. For altogether encouraging signs among new monastics consider, Jonathan

Second, the breadth of such trinitarian theological imagination would also remind new monastics that the *efficacy* of church practices do *not* derive from the material process of habituation but from the agency of the Holy Spirit.[64] While church practices are never less than natural, Christians will always want to insist that they are surely *more* than natural.[65] The intention is not to dichotomize God's agency and church practice, rather to emphasize the gracious character of divine initiative to which our embodied practices are always *graced responses.*

A theological account of church practices can be given any number of ways. The issue is complex, and, at least in the modern West, it is complicated by competitive views of divine and human agency.[66] Yet examples abound that seek to transcend those complications. For example, Buckley and Yeago identify a mode of theological reflection that is both Evangelical and Catholic. It holds to the unity of divine and human action through the agency of the Spirit: "Such a mode or style of theological reflection must begin *both* from God's always-precedent action and grace (Evangelical emphasis) *and* from the holy catholic church, the communion of saints, which is likewise also always prior to the thinking and pondering of the individual theologian (Catholic emphasis)."[67] Sarah Coakley's trinitarian account of practice falls into this category. Describing Paul's portrayal of prayer in Romans 8, she writes, "the 'Father' . . . is both source and ultimate object of divine longing in us; the 'Spirit' is that irreducibly—though obscurely— distinct enabler and incorporator of that longing in creation—that which makes the creation divine; and the 'Son' is that divine and perfected creation, into whose life I, as prayer, am caught up."[68] On the same trajectory, but from a Wesleyan perspective, L. Roger Owens writes, "The church's participation in God is none other than Christ's practicing himself as the embodied practices of the church, in the Spirit, on behalf of the world."[69]

Wilson-Hartgrove and Shane Claiborne, "Liturgy for our Whole Life," 46–52; Wilson-Hartgrove, *Common Prayer.*

64. Nicholas Healy argues similarly concerning the "new ecclesiology" (Healy, "Practices and the New Ecclesiology," 285–308).

65. Smith and Smith, "Introduction: Practices, Faith, and Pedagogy," 15.

66. See, Placher, *Domestication of Transcendence.*

67. Buckley and Yeago, *Knowing the Triune God,* 17.

68. Coakley, "Living into the Mystery of the Holy Trinity," 224.

69. Owens, *Shape of Participation,* 183.

The point is this: for new monastics heavily invested in practices, a trinitarian liturgy would remind them through the practice of worship that the *efficacy* of participation derives not solely (or even primarily) from the one practicing but from the triune God into whose life the redeemed community is being drawn through the agency of his Spirit. What is true of original creation is likewise true for Providence, Redemption, Sanctification, and Consummation: all are gracious gifts of divine love. Each indicates the character of divine grace which always precedes, always initiates, always perfects. This is no less true of church practices, monastic or otherwise.

Catholic

The "C" in Catholic

–John Halsey Wood Jr.

I must begin with a small confession, that the title by my name on the list of contributors, "Independent Scholar," is a bit of an exaggeration. It is not that I have not done scholarly work in the past, but it is no longer my day job, and my comments here are not as disciplined as I would normally wish. Of course, understanding can be impeded by too much information as much as by too little, and at least I have avoided Scylla if not Charybdis. I am now a businessman in the wholesale food business. I buy frozen pizza and potato chips in 42,000lb truckloads. If you like, you can think of me as the Lex Luthor to Wendell Berry's Superman. For that I have no excuse, except to say that it puts food—using the term loosely—on the table. In these reflections I have started mainly with my own experience and then gone hunting for answers. In more exalted terms, this is ecclesiology from below, and only with that caveat can I accept the esteemed title of "Independent Scholar."

With that apology out of the way, let me get to the matter at hand. I begin with just the kind of anecdotal evidence that characterizes these reflections. It is hardly substantial evidence. In fact it is a mere asterisk, a literal tittle in the liturgy of a church service. This asterisk stood at the end of the word "catholic" in the creed, one, holy, *catholic*, and apostolic church, and it pointed to a footnote at the bottom of the page. I had seen these kinds of footnotes before, and at times I have diligently sought them out. The note at the bottom explained that the term "catholic" actually meant "universal," a qualification meant to set us Protestants at ease but which I am sure that any *Roman* Catholic would happily agree to. One cannot be too careful in these days of celebrity priests like Marcelo Rossi of Sao Paulo.[1]

---

1. Mac Margolis, "Brazil's Celebrity Priest"; Simon Romero, "Laboratory for Revitalizing Catholicism."

Stadium seating and business casual are no longer distinguishing marks of Protestant worship, and one might walk into a *Roman* Catholic church unwittingly were it not for such asterisks that guard Protestant orthodoxy.

Of more importance, the "c" in this particular "catholic" was carefully lower case, and this is the specific "c" in catholic that I have in mind in this essay. This "c" has become a pea under the mattress for me, literarily and theologically. Literarily, I learned from Strunk and White that I am supposed to write with nouns and verbs, not adjectives. The lower case "c" turns the word catholic from a proper noun into an adjective. In our present context, the adjectival, lowercase "catholic" bespeaks to me the mire of "spiritual but not religious." It lacks the firmness that makes for easy going. Theologically, I am pricked by fathers like Augustine who, when they speak of one, holy, Catholic church, do so in a capital "C" sort of way. I long to be part of the church of Augustine, Irenaeus, and Cyprian, as much as that of Calvin, the Westminster Confession, and Charles Hodge, not just in some ethereal way or in sympathy but in flesh and blood, and bricks and mortar, that is, the visible, Catholic church. To make matters more complicated for myself, I am not convinced that that visible Catholic church of Augustine is the sole inheritance of the Roman Catholic Church. Otherwise, I could simply make the jump to Rome as other discomfited Evangelicals have done. These are the frustrations that have prompted my reflections on the catholicity of the church, and my thoughts fall into roughly three parts: the nature of catholicity, the challenges to catholicity, and finally the promises of catholicity.

When we say that the church is catholic, we must first of all ask what we mean by it, if we do not mean by it that the church is *Roman* Catholic. If we are not Roman Catholics, are we any kind of catholics at all? Or is this perhaps just a keepsake in our creed, retained not so much out of theological concern but from a respect for the past? The Westminster Confession of Faith says this about the catholicity of the church: under the gospel the church is catholic in so far as it is "not confined to one nation, as before under the law" (23.2). Similarly Augustine says that the catholicity of the "Catholic Church" derives from "from the unity of all nations," and the sin of the Donatists is a sin against catholicity.[2] Catholicity, therefore, refers to universality, the comprehensiveness, and the wholeness of the church. The church is catholic in so far as it comprehends all peoples, all families, and all nations of the world. Contrast this to, say, the modern nation-state

2. Augustine, "Treatise on the Correction of the Donatists," 209.

which aims for one state for one people. The logic of catholicity, in contrast, is Paul's logic: "The mystery is that the Gentiles are fellow heirs, members of the same body, and partakers of the promise [to Abraham] in Christ Jesus through the gospel" (Eph 3:6). Indeed we might say that from Paul's first call to preach to the Gentiles, to his polemics at the Jerusalem council, to this unveiling of the mystery of the gospel in Ephesians, that the catholicity of the church is the ecclesiological cornerstone of Paul's message. Of course, catholicity is more than an ethnic or national designation. In Christ there is neither slave nor free, as Paul says (Gal 3:28). The church is also "intergenerational," as one church leader recently explained to me, though the fact that this needed explaining at all signals the challenges that face catholicity. I will come to those presently. In any case, catholicity has socio-economic, generational, ethnic, and other implications.

Protestants nowadays commonly ascribe catholicity to the invisible church. For Abraham Kuyper, the diversity of the visible church need not trouble anyone. It was the natural consequence of the variegated course of human history, and anyway an underlying "organic" unity persisted.[3] More recently Amos Yong provides a Pentecostal account for the unity and catholicity of the church that locates these ecclesial marks in the Pentecostal experience of the Spirit.[4] One Evangelical institution handles it this way in their statement of faith: "All believers are spiritually united in the Lord Jesus Christ, the Head of the church. Every believer is a member of the body of Christ."[5] This is no doubt true, and as long as catholicity pertains to the invisible church, it need not trouble us too much. The shoe begins to pinch, however, when we inquire into the catholicity of the visible church, and yet Westminster asserts just that. The visible church "is also catholic or universal under the gospel" (23.2). It is good and well to talk about such things in confessional statements and in conference papers, but we hardly experience this catholicity as a fact of everyday life.

Besides catholicity, Westminster also claims unity for this visible church. Unity is a necessary correlate of catholicity. It makes no more sense to speak of two catholic churches than it does to speak of, say, two peoples of God, two kingdoms of God, or two Israels. Consequently Westminster

---

3. Kuyper, *De Gemeene Gratie* 3.291.

4. Yong, "Spirit Poured out on All Flesh." Also see Meilaender, "Catholic That I Am."

5. Westminster School at Oak Mountain, "Our Beliefs: Statement of Faith," http://westminsterknights.org/about/our-mission/our-beliefs/, accessed October 21, 2013.

speaks of this church in the singular. The practical consequences of this are easy to spot. Charles Hodge, for example, argued for the validity of Roman Catholic baptism, that the Roman Catholic church was part of the visible church, and—surprisingly perhaps—that the Presbyterian church was "the most catholic of Churches."[6] Certainly Luther and Calvin were not rebaptized (*ana-baptized*) when they became Protestants. One baptism for the forgiveness of sins means one visible catholic church.

Finally, the catholicity of the visible church is both synchronic and diachronic. The church is catholic at every moment *in time*, and it is catholic *through time*. These features of catholicity are not explicit in the theology of Westminster that I have been expositing, but they seem to be the necessary implications of catholicity, and they are upheld by the best examples in Protestantism. As a student of church history, let me speak specifically to the catholicity of the church with the past and by implication with the future, what Philip Schaff elegantly called the "catholic union with the past."[7] Against Bishop Sadoleto, John Calvin defended the Protestant church's unity with the patristic church not only in doctrine but in its institutional forms. The church of Geneva not only believed what the fathers believed, it carried on the "ancient *form of the Church*, such as [the fathers'] writings prove it to have been in the age of Chrysostom and Basil, among the Greeks, and of Cyprian, Ambrose, and Augustine, among the Latins."[8] A presumption of catholicity with the past underwrites Calvin's defense of the Protestant church just as a presumption of catholicity with the present underwrites Charles Hodge's account of Roman Catholic baptism.

But catholicity is on the rocks these days. The first and I think most formidable theological challenge to catholicity is Lockeanism. John Locke, author of *A Letter Concerning Toleration*, does not get the credit he deserves as an ecclesiologist. The new Routledge *Reader in Ecclesiology*, an otherwise excellent primer on the history of ecclesiology, leaves out Locke entirely. I know it is pedantic to point out omissions, but I think this is an important one. When I refer to Locke's ecclesiology I mean his doctrine of the nature and origin of the church. With regard to Locke's *Letter Concerning*

---

6. Hodge, "Validity of Romish Baptism," 198. Also see Hodge, "Is the Church of Rome Part of the Visible Church?"

7. Schaff, *Principle of Protestantism*, 59.

8. Calvin, "Calvin's Reply to Sadoleto," 64 (emphasis mine). Cp. Sadoleto, who charged that the Genevan church "had turned the faithful people of Christ aside from the way of their fathers and ancestors, and from the perpetual sentiments of the Catholic church" (30).

Toleration, Locke's account of the church in relation to the wider civil society is most often in view. Let us call that Locke's social ethics. His social ethics depend, however, on a particular construal of the church. Locke's church is not a divine institution. It is not a society constituted by the work of God. Neither is the church an inheritance. No one is born into a church, "than which nothing can be imagined more absurd." [9] It is a voluntary society constituted by the active participation of its members. How this ecclesiology relates to Locke's social ethics is an important question but one I want to bracket for the time being.

The remarkable thing about Locke's ecclesiology is that you need not have a particularly well-developed Christology or a very sophisticated soteriology to be a Lockean in your ecclesiology. In fact you do not have to be a trained theologian or even a Christian at all. You will find Christians and atheists equal champions of Locke's voluntarist doctrine of the church. Recently I found it haunting the comments of a Huffington Post article on prayer in an Alabama government function. The comment read, "SEXUALITY is inborn. Religion is a CHOICE. So are bigotry, hatred, and ignorance," and it had earned 402 fans the last time I checked.[10] As to whether ignorance is inborn, let us admit that there is some strong evidence to the contrary. As to whether religion and membership in a religious community is a choice, that notion belongs to John Locke, and the remarkable thing about this comment is that it could have as easily come from a Southern Baptist or an Evangelical Presbyterian as from Christopher Hitchens or a HuffPo super fan.

Perhaps even more impressive than his intellectual influence is Locke's influence over Evangelical Protestants' functional theology. Whatever we may believe on paper, in practice we act like catechumens of Locke. We Evangelicals, clergy and laity alike, trade churches as casually as the fall fashions. We even have a term for this, "church shopping." A Sunday school student once told me that, in fact, she had been a member of her bridge club longer than she had been a member of any one church. I suspect that we are all guilty of this. I confess that I am. The problem with Locke's voluntarism is not that it prevents the being together of Christians, but it changes the nature of our being together. It individualizes and immanentizes our being together. The church becomes not the body of Christ but a box of body

9. Locke, "Letter Concerning Toleration," 132.

10. Stuart, "Alabama Government Agency Holds Prayer against Abortion, Gay Marriage."

parts. The wholeness of the church is lost. The small group movement in American Christianity, rooted as it is in a voluntarist spirituality, evidences this diminished sociality. "Their weakness," says Robert Wuthnow, "lies in their inability to forge the more enduring bonds that many of us would like or to strongly resist the fragmenting forces in our society."[11] We ought to be more wary of this Americanized, Lockean form of Christianity. Augustine described the Donatist principle in a way that anticipated Locke: "Man is at liberty to believe or not to believe."[12] Moreover, this voluntarism is difficult to reconcile with biblical notions that speak to the logic of the Christian society, notions like adoption, inheritance, heirs, children of God, and grace.

The catholicity of the church is also beset by a common Whig interpretation of theology, which like its cousin in history, operates with a progressive, newer-is-better optimism.[13] If Locke's voluntarism dissolves the catholicity of the present, Whig interpretation severs the "catholic unity with the past." Perhaps someone can correct my next assertion (I admit that my scientific evidence here is dangerously thin), but it seems to me that biblical studies, academic and popular, is especially prone to Whig interpretation. Peruse the footnotes of nearly any article in the field of biblical studies in any academic journal, and you will find few if any secondary sources from before the nineteenth century. More than likely you will find none dating before World War II.[14] Popularly, the constant stream of Bible translations, versions, and commentaries from *The Green Bible*, to the *Teen Life Application Study Bible*, to Jimmy Carter's *NIV Lessons from Life Bible*, and yes, even the new *ESV Study Bible*, which has now been thoroughly commercialized, commodified, and marketed (a search at wtsbooks.com turns up 78 different products), every "all new" Bible that rolls off the presses nurtures a Whig ethic.

Herbert Butterfield attributed this tendency especially to Protestants,[15] and perhaps it is especially tempting to Protestants, but is not equally distributed among Protestants. The burden of Calvin's response to Sadoleto was precisely to combat the charge of innovation.[16] I

11. Wuthnow, *Sharing the Journey*, 16.

12. Augustine, "Treatise on the Correction of the Donatists," 216.

13. Cf. Butterfield, *Whig Interpretation of History*.

14. I have not been immune to this myself. See Wood Jr., "New Testament Gospels and the Gospel of Thomas."

15. Butterfield, *Whig Interpretation of History*, 3–4.

16. Calvin, "Calvin's Reply to Sadoleto," 57.

am inclined to think that today Whig interpretation owes more to consumer capitalism and some very capable marketing departments than anything inherent in Protestantism. In fact, Whig interpretation, its faith in progress and change, is probably not unique to the theological and historical disciplines but to our modern mind in all its facets. A more sober Augustinian realism may be of help.

As you can see I have borrowed a lot from others, and with more space, I would like to discuss Protestant resources on the catholicity of the church. These include St. Augustine, Westminster, and Philip Schaff, and as far as I can tell, a host of Lutherans like Gilbert Meilaender, George Lindbeck, and the obscure Carl Piepkorn. Lacking space for that, I would like to conclude on a happier note regarding some of the promises of the catholicity of the church. Without a doubt the most glorious promise given to the visible catholic church is the promise of friendship with God and membership in His people. In Westminster's words, it is "the kingdom of the Lord Jesus Christ, the house and family of God, out of which there is no ordinary possibility of salvation" (25.2). George Lindbeck goes so far as to say that in Scripture the "people of God" is always an empirical community.[17] *Extra ecclesiam nulla salus* (there is no salvation outside the church). This was the judgment of Cyprian and, if memory serves, of Calvin also. Stated in more positive terms, the church is God's plan *for the world*. That our salvation should be joined to such visible forms seems to me a natural corollary of the fact that Christ is not only savior of our souls but of our bodies as well.

Another promise is for the recently popular theological interpretation of the Bible. Theological interpretation promises to correct Whig interpretation by returning biblical interpretation to the Christian community, present *and past*. Theological interpretation acknowledges that all biblical interpretation is guided by theological presuppositions. The proper context for the formation of these presuppositions is the Christian tradition, that is, the church through history.[18] Naturally this raises the question, who or what belongs to the tradition and what does not? That is a question of the catholicity of the visible church. A spiritual ecclesiology, like Amos Yong's perhaps, whatever its other virtues, is of little help since individual mystical experiences of the Spirit are not available to future generations. Theological interpretation depends on a community with concrete boundaries, a visible church and a catholic one.

17. Lindbeck, "Church."
18. Billings, *Word of God for the People of God*.

A final promise occurs to me as a lay person and illustrates the practical importance of this doctrine. In a common communion practice today, we the laity are invited to the table so long as we have been duly baptized in a Christian church. Often there is little more instruction than this. This practice requires the laity to discern our own fittingness for participation in the Supper, and in so doing it devolves upon us to determine what counts as a Christian church and what does not. This is a practical application of Locke's voluntarist ecclesiology, and it is a judgment which some of us (me, at least) feel ill at ease making on our own. Implicit in this practice, nonetheless, is a notion of the catholicity of the visible church. If this particular kind of open communion practice continues, we the laity would benefit from a more careful and open discussion of catholicity.

The attractiveness of ascribing catholicity to some form of invisible church is obvious. Besides the truth of it, there is the ease of it. The invisible church offers a convenient explanation of our catholicity without having to face the fractiousness and multiplicity of our churches.[19] But the church is not only one in spirit; it is one body (Eph 4:4, 1 Cor 12:12, N.B., "body" is another biblical image that excludes voluntarism). In order to explain our predicament, I would like to offer a simple image, that of a wine glass, one lying on the floor in pieces. I like this image because it captures the wholeness and unity of the glass, without permitting any simple justification for our present situation. The pieces do indeed form one glass, not several. There is unity. The pieces also form a whole glass of differing, complementary parts, not a partial one, a catholic glass, if you will. Yet, clearly the pieces as pieces are not the best or intended end for the glass.

This is surely the "heap of broken images" that T.S. Eliot spoke of in *The Waste Land*. The church is fragmented, like the poem; the whole is difficult to discern. The heap of images, our so-called denominations, may be irreparable. Some hope to rise above them; others try to hide from them,[20] but if we are going to discuss catholicity, I think we cannot avoid speaking of them. By now, you have no doubt guessed that I am a Presbyterian, so as a final thought let me frame my proposal in terms of Presbyterianism. The Presbyterian church is not different than the church of Augustine; it is the church of Augustine, at least a fragment of it and not less than that.

19. N.B., the fathers of the church regarded this as a sin. Locke himself offered it as justification for his voluntarist ecclesiology (Locke, "Letter Concerning Toleration," 133).

20. E.g., Bass, *Christianity after Religion*. And the Evangelical blogger at Marc5Solas. com will not name his denomination for fear of tribalism, a grave sin in a cosmopolitan age, "Marc5solas," http://marc5solas.com/about-marc5solas/, Jan 23, 2016.

My proposal is not that the Presbyterian church is an alternative to the catholic church. Rather Presbyterianism is a way of being catholic, and not in a lowercase, but in a capital "C" kind of way.[21]

21. Cf. Meilaender, "Catholic That I Am."

The Search for Visible Catholicity and the Danger of Boundary-Drawing

Lessons from John Nevin and Richard Hooker[1]

—W. Bradford Littlejohn

Protestantism and the "Marks of the Church"

Protestants have always struggled with the tension between the visibility and invisibility of the church. By their emphasis on the gospel of justification by faith, they are committed, it would seem, to the priority of the invisible features of the church: salvation is by grace alone, through faith alone, in Christ alone, and grace, faith, and Christ are all alike beyond the direct reach of our senses. So whatever visible features the gathered

1. In addition to the version of this essay presented at the Evangelical Theological Society Annual Meeting in 2013, later versions were presented in June 2014 at All Saints Presbyterian Church and at the Mercersburg Society Convocation, both in Lancaster, PA. I am grateful to Rev. Gregg Strawbridge and to the officers of the Mercersburg Society for these opportunities. A version, very similar to the present version aside from the final pages, was published as "Sectarianism and the search for visible catholicity: Lessons from John Nevin and Richard Hooker" in *Theology Today* 71:4 (2014): 404–15; thanks to Gordon Mikoski for that opportunity and the permission to re-use the text here. I would also like to thank Bill Evans for helpful comments at the original presentation of this paper and particularly Lee Barrett for his comments at the Mercersburg Society Convocation, which helped stimulate the expanded reflections in the final pages of the essay as it appears here.

congregation of the church may present to our senses, they ought not to be, it would seem, the locus of our attention.

And yet, creatures of sense that we are, we can hardly prevent ourselves from such preoccupation with the visible. From its beginning, Protestantism had to defend itself against the charge that its church was nothing but a "Platonic form," and also against the charge that the myriad of Anabaptist and radical sects unleashed by the Reformation were truly part of the Protestant churches. Both the solution, and an intensification of the problem, emerged in the form of the Reformers' doctrine of the *notae ecclesiae*, the "marks of the church."

While making a distinction between the church invisible and visible, the church in Christ and the church in the world, the Reformers insisted on affirming their ontological continuity.[2] Luther's concept of the justified sinner, *simul justus et peccator* (simultaneously just and sinner), sometimes provided a framework for ecclesiology. The church was at the same time perfectly righteous by virtue of its union with Christ, but this union, and this righteous identity, were hidden; as manifest in the world, in history, it was still sinful and failing, a *corpus permixtum* composed of wheat and tares, gradually being sanctified. And yet there remained certain "notes" or "marks" by which the true church could be visibly recognized in history. The Augsburg Confession of 1530 established two marks: "The Church is the congregation of saints, in which the Gospel is rightly taught and the Sacraments are rightly administered,"[3] but some over the next couple decades, wanting to emphasize that just as true Christians must be characterized by godly life, so must the true church, added a third, "discipline," which initially had quite a broad sense, rather than simply designating excommunication and its precursors.[4]

Now, these were all fairly useful in giving you a decent idea of where the church *was* (although they obviously could not stand alone; they presupposed a Protestant understanding of what the Gospel and sacraments were): if you saw a minister faithfully expounding the text of Scripture, and administering baptism and the Lord's Supper, well then you could assume that there was a manifestation of Christ's body; imperfect, perhaps,

2. For a good sketch of the Reformers' doctrine of the invisible and visible church, the *notae ecclesiae*, and other aspects of their ecclesiology, see Avis, *Church in the Theology of the Reformers*.

3. Art. VII (http://bookofconcord.org/augsburgconfession.php, accessed May 27, 2014).

4. See Avis, "True Church"; Ballor and Littlejohn, "European Calvinism."

but in communion with the Head. But they were not so good at telling you where the church *wasn't*.[5] How false did a church's preaching have to be before it could no longer count as part of the body of Christ? How distorted or rationalistic or superstitious did its sacramental practice have to be? How lax did its discipline have to be? In response to Catholic polemic and persecution, many Protestants in the latter half of the 16th century, particularly among the Reformed, increasingly deployed the *notae ecclesiae* to brand Rome as a wholly false church, and in the process, felt the need to lay increasing stress on the adverbs "rightly." Some also tended to redefine "discipline" specifically in terms of a structure of church government, namely presbyterianism, without which, it was suggested, a minister could not *rightly* preach or administer the sacraments.[6] Such a sharp blade of division, wielded zealously, could quickly be turned upon other Protestants, as it was in Elizabethan England. The militant presbyterians suggested that the Church of England was not in fact a true church, despite its Protestant confession, due to the deficiencies in its preaching, sacraments, and discipline.[7] Although most equivocated and held back from quite following through on the implications of this charge, others did not, and broke away into separatism. The separatists, in turn, by application of the same principles, divided and divided still further, particularly once transplanted into America, thus bequeathing to our country the sectarianism that John Nevin and Philip Schaff were to lament 250 years later.[8]

At the same time, many English critics of these Puritans, not content to point out their unhealthy divisiveness, decided to make similarly exclusive claims for the superiority of their own episcopal order. By this means, they could claim that these Puritan sectarians were an unhistorical mutation that did not share in the historic life of the church. By the 1630s, this trend had resulted in a theology of episcopal apostolic succession that threatened

5. Avis, "True Church," 334: "The *notae ecclesiae* is a qualitative concept; theoretically one can say whether a certain ecclesial body possesses the marks or not. But in practice it was found to need supplementing by a quantitative one, such as Calvin's concept that Rome contained the *vestigia* of the church."

6. Theodore Beza was important in this shift (see Maruyama, *Ecclesiology of Theodore Beza*); yet the decisive moves were taken by Scots such as Andrew Melville and Englishmen such as Thomas Cartwright and John Field (see Milton, "Puritanism and the Continental Reformed Churches," 116).

7. Avis, "True Church," 337–39.

8. See Winship, *Godly Republicanism* for a chronicle of the separatists' obsession with distinguishing true from false churches, and their influence on early America.

to unchurch all the non-episcopal Reformed churches (although it was another two centuries before the Oxford Movement Anglicans finally took this drastic step).[9]

Mercersburg's Critique of Sectarianism

All of this backstory is instructive for a consideration of the ecclesiology of the Mercersburg movement, since history has a tendency to repeat itself. In what follows, I will suggest that what began for the Mercersburg theologians as a critique of the scandal of sectarianism (much like the Reformers' attempt to distance themselves from the Anabaptists) risked becoming somewhat sectarian itself, as the pressure increased for a visible definition of the historical church.

Philip Schaff's 1844 *The Principle of Protestantism* set the tone for Mercersburg's stinging rebukes of the biblicist sects that dominated America (then and now):

> Any one [sic] who has, or fancies that he has, some inward experience and a ready tongue, may persuade himself that he is called to be a reformer; and so proceed at once, in his spiritual vanity and pride, to a revolutionary rupture with the historical life of the Church, to which he holds himself immeasurably superior.[10]

Schaff's critique of sectarianism resonated deeply with his new colleague Nevin, who had already published some of his own initial polemics on this score, notably his 1843 *The Anxious Bench*. In a series of writings through the second half of the 1840s, Nevin was to elaborate this critique, targeting what he saw as the individualistic, subjective, rationalistic, unchurchly, and anti-sacramental root of American sectarianism. Many of these critiques were devastatingly effective, such as his essays on "The Sect System" in 1849, where he lampooned how all American Protestants proclaimed their sole fidelity to Scripture, while differing radically from one another and slavishly following the pet teachings of their various micro-traditions. At the same time, however, Nevin was seeking to elaborate a

---

9. For a good survey of the High Church Anglican view of the continental Reformed churches, and the departure marked by the Oxford Movement, see Sykes, *Old Priest and New Presbyter*.

10. Schaff, *Principle of Protestantism*, 149.

positive vision of the church, to answer what he called "the Church question," the great question of the age, as he saw it. The goal of this positive vision was twofold. On the one hand, Nevin sought to articulate the unity of the church as subsisting inwardly in its union with the incarnate Christ—the church was one because it was one body, mystically united to one head. On the other hand, though, this union must not be merely inward, since otherwise what was to prevent all sects from laying claim to it? It must be visible and historical, the sacraments serving as the outward instruments of the inward union.

Nevin, however, was rather ambivalent regarding the concept of the "outward," due in part to his heavy investment in the philosophical and theological categories of German romanticism. Such romanticism made extensive use of "organic" metaphors drawn from the sphere of nature, in contrast to what they saw as the mechanistic metaphors and concepts which the scientific and industrial religions had injected into theology. Accordingly, one of Nevin's favorite critiques of the reigning models of Christology, soteriology, ecclesiology, and sacramentology in American Protestantism was that they remained "external" and "mechanical" and therefore "abstract" rather than "inward" and "vital."[11] Any kind of outward or mechanical conception of the unity of the church, therefore, could not be the solution to sectarianism—indeed, both Schaff and Nevin would often, at this point in their polemics, explain that this was where both Roman Catholicism and Anglo-Catholicism (which was just getting into full swing over in Oxford at this time) went wrong.[12] And yet the "inward" and "organic" conception must be at the same time "concrete" and "objective." Nevin was thus not about to take refuge in the standard Protestantism notion of the "invisible church," as this seemed to him to float free, above history.[13] Accordingly, we find him in an 1846 sermon (really something of a theological essay), "The Church," wrestling his way toward a new articulation of the church's visibility and invisibility.

The sermon begins in a way that substantially resembles the magisterial Protestant doctrine: the one church has two aspects, which Nevin names "ideal" and "actual" rather than "invisible" and "visible." In the first aspect, it is complete already in Christ, perfect, and unspotted, and it will

11. See for instance Nevin, "Sect System, Article 1," 504, 506.

12. Nevin, "Church," 63, 64; Schaff, *Principle of Protestantism*, Pt. II, ch. 2.

13. See especially his later critique of this notion in Nevin, "Hodge on the Ephesians," 46–82.

be revealed in this form at the last day. In the latter aspect, it is revealed in history, incomplete, and imperfect, and yet a true and necessary manifestation, without which the Church would have no reality at all.[14] But as the sermon progresses, it becomes increasingly ambiguous. The church's unity subsists in Christ, yes, but how are we united to Christ? Calvin would have answered in a flash: "through the Spirit," but the Spirit is almost never mentioned in Nevin's exposition. But if the Spirit is not the bond of unity, what is? The question is inescapable. Perhaps we might adapt the Lutheran doctrine of ubiquity, in which Christ's body is everywhere diffused, and thus say that the Church, wherever it is, is united to him, and thus one and catholic.[15] Otherwise we must answer, as the Reformed quite clearly did, "through the Spirit," or else, as the Catholics did, through the Church—that is to say, that the church today is united to Christ through the church of yesterday. Nevin's picture is uncomfortably like the latter: the church is a stream flowing through history, bearing the life of Christ from age to age, and by union with this stream, we have union with the one, holy, catholic, and apostolic church.[16]

It might seem that such an emphasis on the outward historical continuity of the church would exclude sects entirely from membership in it; since they err not merely by a bad theology of the church, but by outright separation from it and willful exclusivism. However, at this point in his career, Nevin does not quite want to take that step. He clarifies that the "actual" church, while subsisting in the "ideal" and growing toward conformity with it, remains imperfect in history, so that "we cannot allow that visible unity of organization and worship is indispensable to the truth of the Church, in the view now under consideration . . . Allow our divisions to be a great and sore defect, they are still not necessarily such a defect as is inconsistent with the conception of the actual Church."[17] Here again he critiques the Catholic and Anglo-Catholic conceptions of visible unity as being too wooden. However, as his polemic against sectarianism intensifies over the ensuing years, we begin to wonder how much he is still willing to sustain this charitable judgment. The whole thrust of his 1848 *Antichrist*,

14. Nevin, "Church," 57–65.

15. It should be noted, of course, that classical Lutheran dogmatics did not deploy the doctrine in this way, but tended to confine it to the specific context of Eucharistic theology. Nonetheless, the application of the idea in an ecclesiological direction was certainly a live option.

16. See ibid., 70–71.

17. Ibid., 63.

for instance, is to elevate the sect system's aberrant ecclesiology to the level of fundamental credal heresy.[18] In it, he goes so far as to say, "A Sect, on the other hand, stands in no such organic connection with the Church as a whole. It is the creature in full of private willfulness [*sic*] and caprice, not the growth of the true Church life itself . . . According to this distinction, Sects as such are always evil, and very man is bound to shun them, as he values his own salvation."[19]

Such judgments, however, necessarily invite the question, "how much separation from the 'organic connection' with the historical church *disqualifies* one from being part of it?"; and conversely, "just how much union with it *qualifies* one to be part of the historic church?" In other words, we must define the visible boundaries of the invisible life of Christ. Nevin manages to hold off seriously facing this question for several years, holding it at arm's length with token denunciations of Catholicism and Anglo-Catholicism, and distracting himself with his work on the Eucharist and Christology, which largely absorbed him from 1846 through 1851.

Indeed, to begin to give an answer to the question might seem to risk implicating himself in the sect spirit as well. For in his 1849 "The Sect Spirit," Nevin identifies as one of the problems of the sect spirit an exclusivity which claims for a particular visible body the attributes of the whole catholic church, which claims the full authority of Christ. "The sect," he said,

> calls on all men, as they value their salvation, to take refuge in her communion. She does not simply offer them the Bible, but along with it her own tradition also, her sacraments, her ministrations of grace . . . This same feeling she tries to infuse into every soul, that falls within the range of her ecclesiastical domain; and she exacts from them accordingly, at the same time, full faith in her separate sufficiency for all church purposes and ends. She assumes in regard to them the full stewardship of Christ's house. She makes herself responsible for their souls, engaging if they do but trust her guidance and care to see them safe into heaven. She carries the

18. See also Nevin, "Thoughts on the Church," 169–98.

19. Nevin, *Anxious Bench, Antichrist, and the Sermon Catholic Unity*, 55. Although he distinguishes here between legitimate interimistic denominations and full-blown sects, he goes on to include most of American Christianity under the condemnation of sectarianism: "Our denominational Christianity is fairly responsible for all the mischief of our Sectarian Christianity. We have full right to speak of the whole indiscriminately, as the *Sect plague* of our age and nation" (57).

keys of the kingdoms of heaven, to bind and to loose, to open and shut, at her own pleasure.[20]

In short, Nevin contends that, in the midst of fervent opposition to Roman Catholicism, the sect system tends to replicate its form in miniature. This sketch may be overdrawn as regards many of the sects and micro-denominations of Nevin's day—certainly nowadays, many have become much less exclusive in their claims—but it was a tendency that certainly did come to fruition in many sects of that era.

Nevin's Vision of Visible Catholicity

Nevin, then, has argued himself into a bit of a corner by the late 1840s. He is determined to find a basis for the unity and catholicity of the church that will provide an answer to the rampant sectarianism and individualism of the age and will draw people back to the traditions, liturgy, and sacraments of the historical institutional church. Mere profession of faith in Christ is not sufficient for the catholicity of the church; for then what need is there for the sects to renounce their ways and pursue visible unity? Likewise, organic union with Christ by the power of the Spirit is not sufficient, for again, any sect or even lone Christian could claim this, and who could deny it? The Spirit is invisible. Nor, however, does Nevin want to define the catholicity of the church in terms of a shared institutional structure, which would exclude from the body of Christ all who are not within it; this, he thinks, would itself be sectarian, not to mention Catholic. He hopes for a while that, by the use of the categories of German romanticism, he can set a course between all of these alternatives, and perhaps, if he were not so eager to find a formula that would *exclude* sects, he might have succeeded. But eventually, the need to provide some concrete visible definition to this objective, concrete, historical body called "the catholic" led him to take a decisively anti-Protestant step.[21]

---

20. Nevin, "Sect System, Article 2," 533.

21. The specific occasion for this step was above all his study of Cyprian's ecclesiology, unfolded in four lengthy articles of *The Mercersburg Review* in 1852 (although we may well wonder how much of what he found in Cyprian, he was already looking to find). See especially Nevin, "Cyprian: Second Article," 359–63 for an unequivocal statement of the vision of apostolic succession that was to later appear in his sermon on "Christian Ministry."

This emerges with vivid clarity in his 1854 sermon (again, as much a treatise as a sermon) on "The Christian Ministry." Interestingly, and promisingly, this sermon begins with an extended discussion of the Spirit, as the means by which the gift of Christ's presence and power is made available to the church in history.[22] Nevin then, however, proceeds to evacuate this appeal to the Spirit of all its traditionally Reformed meaning, confining the Spirit's presence and power in the human agency of the ordained ministry. Strikingly, Nevin makes the establishment of the ministry to be essentially equivalent with the establishment of the Church: "It is, by the terms of this commission, identified with the institution of the Church itself . . . The Church is a much wider conception than the ministry. But still they are so joined together that the one cannot be severed from the other."[23] Obviously, this is a decisive step toward providing visible definition to the church catholic, but it is also a decisive step away from the Protestant doctrine of the priesthood of all believers. But Nevin then goes considerably further: "The idea of the Church is made to involve the idea of the ministry. The first is in truth constituted by the commission that creates the second; for it has its whole existence conditioned by an act of faith in the reality of this commission, and this tested again by an act of real outward homage to its authority."[24] That is to say, the church does not constitute the clergy, the clergy constitute the church.

Lest we imagine that Nevin has for a moment carelessly overspoken, he returns a few pages later to sound this theme again, scored now for full orchestra:

> the Church [is] to be considered as starting in the Apostles, and extending itself out from them in the way of implicit submission to their embassy and proclamation. They were to stand between Christ and the world, to be his witnesses, his legates, the representatives of his authority, the mediators of his grace among men. They were to preach in his name, not merely a doctrine for the nations to hear, but a constitution to which they were required to surrender themselves, in order that they might be saved. The new organization was to be formed, and held together, by those who were thus authorized and empowered to carry into effect officially its conditions and terms . . . The law of derivation is downwards

22. Nevin, "Christian Ministry," 350–54.
23. Ibid., 354.
24. Ibid.

and not upwards, from the few to the many, and not from the many to the few.[25]

In fact, he goes so far as to call the alternate view heresy.

This would appear to be little different from Tridentine Catholicism: defining the *esse* of the church in terms of a juridical constitution of mediating clergy who dispense or withhold grace. Moreover, since the church is to be one, so the ministry must be one; indeed, no minister has authority on his own, only as part of the clerical corporation:

> the office itself could be of force only as it retained always the character of a single body bound together, and in union with itself. As there can be, by the very conception of Christianity, but one faith, one baptism, and one Church, so can there be also but one ministry, and this unity must be taken to extend to all times and ages, as well as to all lands.[26]

Thus we have, he grants, the concept of "apostolical succession" and the conception of ordination "as the veritable channel through which is transmitted mystically, from age to age, the supernatural authority in which this succession consists."[27] Whether Nevin is himself aware of the irony that he has now embraced an "outward" and "mechanical" conception of the church's unity and catholicity, in contradiction to his earlier polemics, I am not sure.[28] But he does go on to attempt to answer the "sneer" against such a concept of "tactual communication" by insisting that this is how God always works: outward, natural signs are always the means for the transmission of grace. Again, though, mere reception of such ordination is not sufficient; one must remain in communion with the whole organization of the ministry in order to validly bear its authority. The logical step from here, and the step that would bring this ecclesiology wholly onto Roman Catholic ground, would be to insist on a single visible authority as the locus of this communion, lest divergent claims arise amongst the clergy as to which party bears the authority of the whole.

25. Ibid., 359. See Nevin, "Cyprian: Second Article," 361–62 for very similar statements.

26. Nevin, "Christian Ministry," 360. Cf. Nevin, "Cyprian: Second Article," 365–66.

27. Nevin, "Christian Ministry," 361.

28. It is indeed quite striking to compare the frequency with which the word "outward" is used in a negative context in Nevin's writings of 1846 to 1850, versus the predominantly—even overwhelmingly—positive connotation it assumes in his articles on Cyprian.

Nevin, in fact, does not take this step. Indeed, this sermon was preached as he was deciding *not* to convert to Roman Catholicism, as he had been considering for some time. The concept of the ministry that Nevin has advanced requires that it be undivided, which it has not been since the Reformation, or indeed since AD 1054, or possibly earlier. Accordingly, neither the Roman Catholic Church nor any church can lay claim to actually having a valid ministry, and thus being the church, based on the criteria of this sermon. Nevin's posture in this sermon then resembles that of many modern Anglo-Catholics, clinging to an ideal fantasy church rather than any actually concretely existing church. It is perhaps no surprise that while Nevin continued to do some excellent theological work after this date, his thought turned more and more in a mystical, inward direction. Thus we have the supreme irony that Nevin's ecclesiology, beginning in polemic against, on the one hand, an "outward and mechanical" concept of church unity, and on the other hand, a subjective "abstraction," ends up with a fair measure of both.

Richard Hooker and the Sanctification of the Visible Church

Given the continuing urgency of the problem of sectarianism in American Protestantism, is there a better way to proceed, a way to champion "Reformed catholicity" against sectarianism without becoming sectarian, or Roman Catholic? One place to look for such a way forward would certainly be the career of Nevin's colleague Philip Schaff, who while excoriating the proliferation of sects, never seemed to become as pre-occupied with them as Nevin grew to be—largely a difference of temperament, perhaps. In his later writing and remarkable ecumenical initiatives, Philip Schaff was able to champion visible forms of unity as testaments to and safeguards of the church's unity in Christ, rather than *sine qua nons* of ecclesial identity. However, I would like here to turn back to the sixteenth century with which we began and draw attention to the admirably clear approach offered by English Reformed theologian Richard Hooker. Though perhaps little known today, particularly to American readers, his fervent ecumenical vision stands as a beacon for today's advocates of "Reformed catholicity" to follow.

Hooker, though certainly himself an advocate of a liturgical, sacramental, historically-rooted church, constructed his ecclesiology carefully in response to a similar sort of turn to that which had shipwrecked Nevin. As we saw, many English Puritans and separatists strikingly resembled the virulently anti-Catholic sects that dominated American revivalist Protestantism in the mid-1800s, and like these, their search for visible purity led them to sometimes make absurdly exclusive claims about how they alone had recovered the true form of the church as it had been laid down by the apostles. In response, some English conformists responded by laying stress on their own visible continuity with the historic church and developing a theology of apostolic succession, much as Nevin was to find himself doing in the 1840s and 1850s. Hooker, however, while a strong proponent of episcopacy, firmly rejected the ecclesiological principles that both ends of the spectrum shared: the quest for an outward visible boundary that could identify the extent of Christ's mystical body, excluding from it other professing believers.

Hooker's ecclesiology starts with the rejection of this false quest for certainty, and indeed of the whole *notae* approach to ecclesiology—although it could be used rightly, it had become so overused and abused that it was better abandoned, he deemed.[29] Hooker begins instead with quite a rigorous assertion of the invisible (or "mystical") and visible church distinction: "That Church of Christ which we properly term his body mystical, can be but one, neither can that one be sensibly discerned by any man . . . Only our minds by intellectual conceit are able to apprehend, that such a real body there is . . . a body mystical, because the mystery of their conjunction is removed altogether from sense."[30] The visible church, on the other hand, is a "sensibly known company," identified by the "outward profession of those things, which supernaturally appertain to the very essence of Christianity, and are necessarily required in every particular Christian man."[31]

When it comes to the church in its invisible identity, hidden in God with Christ, the Lord knows those who are his, and we do not. Sure, we can make some pretty decent guesses based on outward behavior, but in the end, only God knows the heart. There is simply nothing to be gained, Hooker contends, from going around trying to determine with any level of

---

29. Avis, "True Church," 339–43.

30. Richard Hooker, *Of the Lawes of Ecclesiastical Polity* III.1.2; reprinted in Hill and Edelen, eds., *Works* 1:194–95. See also the free online version of Hooker's *Lawes* (digitized from the 19th-century Keble edition) at http://oll.libertyfund.org/titles/hooker-the-works-of-that-learned-and-judicious-divine-mr-richard-hooker. Note that I have modernized all spellings and punctuation for ease of reading.

31. Hooker, *Lawes*, III.1.3, 4; *Works*, 1:195, 196.

certainty who is genuinely invisibly united to Christ and who is not. And just so, although the visible church is the outward, social manifestation of the life in Christ, there is nothing to be gained in trying to determine with any level of certainty when it is obeying Him faithfully enough to count as part of his Body and when it is not. From our human standpoint, all we have to go on is "do they profess faith in Christ the Son of God, and have they affirmed this profession through baptism?" If so, then they are to be counted part of the one visible church of God. They may be unsound members, dead members even, but if so, they will be cut off at the last day:

> If by external profession they be Christians, then are they of the visible Church of Christ: and Christians by external profession they are all, whose mark of recognizance hath in it those things which we have mentioned, yea, although they be impious idolaters, wicked heretics, persons excommunicable, yea, and cast out for notorious improbity. Such withal we deny not to be the imps and limbs of Satan, even as long as they continue such.[32]

Accordingly, Hooker includes not only Rome, but heretics and schismatics, so long as they profess Christ and receive baptism, within the bounds of the visible church. It is not for nothing, on Hooker's account, that we profess in the Creed that the unity and catholicity of the church are matters of *belief*, only dimly perceived this side of the eschaton—we walk by faith, and not by sight.

This conviction has quite practical consequences for Hooker's theory of church discipline; while he accepts excommunication as a useful tool of pastoral rebuke, he does not consider it to actually have the effect of cutting someone off from the visible church.[33] Moreover, he does not agree with the Puritan program of meticulously examining all would-be communicants to see if their faith is genuine or if they are closet papists. Accordingly, the fullest defense of his minimalist ecclesiology comes in the section of the *Laws* where he defends the Eucharistic practice of the Church of England. There he insists that:

> We must define the Church which is a religious society by such differences as do properly explain the essence of such things, that is to say, by the object or matter whereabout the contemplations

---

32. Hooker, *Lawes*, III.1.7; *Works* 1:198.
33. See further my essay, "The Use and Abuse of John Jewel."

and actions of the Church are properly conversant . . . The *only object* which separates ours from other religions is Jesus Christ.[34]

If we go beyond this essential attribute, he says, "we shall but add unto this certain casual and variable accidents, which are not properly of the being, but make only for the happier and better being of the Church of God, either in deed, or in men's opinions and conceits." Such confusion of the features of *esse* of the church with those of the *bene esse*, as we saw with Nevin, tends to lead back toward a Roman Catholic ecclesiology (or its miniature, sectarian form), as Hooker also goes on to point out, remarking sarcastically that "They define not the Church by that which the Church essentially is, but by that wherein they imagine their own more perfect than the rest are." The danger of this approach is that it has no obvious stopping point; the things that make up the *bene esse* of the church are "infinite," and every form of "contention and variance . . . blemishes somewhat the unity that ought to be in the Church of Christ," so that if we begin trying to define the visible church by its lack of such blemishes, we may end with a very small church indeed. Therefore, he concludes, only a credible profession of faith in Jesus Christ is necessary to count one as a member of the visible church, just as only true faith in Jesus Christ is necessary to make one a member of the invisible. Not that the two are equated; no, "to eternal life our profession is not enough. Many things exclude from the kingdom of God although from the Church they separate not." [35] The judgment of charity whereby we treat all *professing* believers as members of the visible church is not a judgment of naiveté whereby we assume that they are all actually united to Christ.

Nevertheless, this minimalist approach might seem to baptize all forms of sectarianism, dismissing the importance of any of the visible markers of historic ecclesial continuity in favor of bare profession of faith. Hooker, however, balances this minimalism with his doctrine of *correspondences*, his insistence that the church outwardly ought to seek to correspond to its inward reality. "Signs must resemble the things they signify," he declares, and we might legitimately speak of the visible church, in his theology, as a sign which signifies the presence of the invisible. Accordingly, it must strive to manifest outwardly the qualities which it has antecedently in Christ:

> That which inwardly each man should be, the Church outwardly ought to testifie. And therefore the duties of our religion which

34. Hooker, *Lawes*, V.68.6; *Works* 2:349.
35. Hooker, *Lawes*, V.68.6; *Works* 2:349–50.

are seen must be such as that affection which is unseen ought to be. Signs must resemble the things they signify. If religion bear the greatest sway in our hartes, our outward religious duties must show it, as far as the Church hath outward ability . . . Yea then are the public duties of religion best ordered, when the militant Church doth resemble by sensible means, as it my in such cases, the hidden dignity and glory wherewith the Church triumphant in heaven is beautified.[36]

This includes, of course, unity. But like all outward manifestations, such unity is to be treated under the heading of the doctrine of sanctification.[37] In Hooker's theology, as in Luther's, the justification/sanctification distinction maps pretty well onto the invisible/visible church distinction: as the mystical body, the church is fully righteous in Christ; as the visible body, it is stained and spotted, urgently needing growth in righteousness. Hooker, accordingly, is well-prepared to argue at length for the importance of historical structures of authority, visible forms of unity, diligent observance of the sacraments, and submission to credal and confessional norms as the signs and seals of the church's catholicity, crucial to its sanctification and well-being.[38] And we must work to restore them to our churches. But these things do not constitute the church's being, the basis of its recognition before God. That is hidden with Christ in God, and our first task is ensure that we, and those in our own churches, are sharing in this life, not to obsess over the criteria for other churches to share in it. Meanwhile, we extend them whatever fellowship we can, and exhort them to grow in truth, unity, and holiness.

Of course, part of that exhortation may include hard words, and strategic withholding of various forms of fellowship. Hooker's own recommended pastoral strategy, in which the bounds of Eucharistic table fellowship were extremely broad and excommunication used very sparsely, is not the only strategy that fits within his general ecclesiological principles. After all, his was a context where the church's disciplinary authority was backed up in many ways by the laws and punishments of a Christian state. Moreover, even if early modern England was no golden age of purity and piety, one could still expect social norms to informally enforce certain broad

36. Hooker, *Lawes*, V.6.1–2; *Works* 2:33–34.

37. Harrison, "Powers of Nature," notes that Hooker's chief concern in the *Lawes* is with the visible church, engaged in the process of sanctification.

38. For more on these elements in Hooker's ecclesiology, and their relationship to his key distinctions of the visible and invisible church, see my *Richard Hooker*, chs. 10–11.

Christian commitments in both faith and morals. Today the church in the Western world cannot count on such supports, and the radical divergence in lifestyles, moral commitments, and even basic conceptions of Christian faith that characterize today's professing Christians has posed deep challenges to any simplistic call to open table fellowship. Can we join in sacramental fellowship with those who hold different views (and act on those views) on women's ordination? On same-sex relationships? On abortion? On the just use of violence? These are no easy questions, and they do not admit of one-size-fits-all solutions, so I cannot attempt to tackle them here as I close this essay. But what does bear emphasizing is that these questions must be addressed in terms of strategic attempts to achieve sanctification *within the visible church*, not as attempts to neatly sketch out its ontological boundaries—always with ourselves well within those boundaries, mind you, and those we just do not want to deal with conveniently outside them. Such a boundary-drawing exercise, as Hooker perceived clearly (and Nevin clearly enough at times, if inconsistently), often begins as and nearly always ends as an attempt at self-justification, in both the idiomatic and theologically precise sense of that term. Our only comfort in life and in death must come not from the prayer of the Pharisee—" God, I thank you that I am not like other men" (Luke 18:11)—but from a resting in our faithful Savior Jesus Christ, and the knowledge of his deliverance.

An Instrumental Explication of George Hunsinger's Eucharistic Real Predication

–James M. Arcadi

Jesus Christ gave theologians, charged with explicating and making clear the words of Scripture, a challenging project when he instituted his Supper. On the night before he was to be crucified, Christ uttered some difficult words. He took bread, drew his disciples' attention to it and said, "Take, eat; this is my body." Then, he took a cup of wine and said similarly, "This is my blood." Christ could have said any number of words to his disciples: "Think about me when you get together and eat" or "keep me in mind when you eat bread and drink wine." Instead, he told his disciples that bread was his body and wine was his blood. What did Christ mean when he predicated his body of bread and his blood of wine? Further, subsequently, what do Christian ministers mean when they do the same? This is what theologians have since attempted to make clear.

This explication and clarification project has been no easy task in the history of theological reflection and Christian practice. In fact, we find ourselves presently divided by this practice that was to be a sign of unity. As Stanley Hauerwas comments, "We Christians are a people divided by what unites us. We believe that God has, through the body and blood of Jesus Christ, made us one people, but how the Eucharist works to make us one with God and one another has been one of the most divisive points of conflict between Christians, particularly since the Reformation."[1] In many cases, our inability to participate in the Eucharist together, is in fact due to

1. Hauerwas, Review of *Eucharist and Ecumenism*, 36.

varying explications of those difficult words, "This is my body" and "This is my blood."

George Hunsinger has executed one of the most thorough and ambitious attempts at explicating and clarifying these difficult Eucharistic words. In his text, *The Eucharist and Ecumenism*, Hunsinger presents a possible route for Christian unity, a route for ecumenical convergence to the point of Eucharistic sharing. This text is certainly not the final word on Eucharistic sharing, but it does present a possible prelude for a great ecumenical Eucharistic feast.

In this chapter, I will offer some clarifications and advancement of one aspect of Hunsinger's project. First, I will re-present some of the main claims that Hunsinger makes with respect to an ecumenical "irreducible minimum" for understanding the dominical words in the context of the liturgy. This will be followed by an attempt to add some greater linguistic clarity to Hunsinger's analysis. The next section will then build on these linguistic reflections by recourse to some recent and traditional work on the metaphysics of the Incarnation. The Incarnation has long served as an analogue for the Eucharist and Hunsinger himself has indicated that Eucharistic theology ought to take incarnational dynamics as its theological North Star. Finally, I will apply the Christological work to the Eucharist before attempting to echo Hunsinger's ecumenical optimism by showing how all this Eucharistic work might serve as an invitation to all Christians to "keep the feast."

Preliminary analyses of the dominical words

There have been various attempts by theologians to analyze the sentence "This is my body." A specific linguistic difficulty for the analysis is the relation between the various components of the sentence and the relation that these components have to the physical and metaphysical reality encountered in the Eucharistic liturgy. Hunsinger presents an analysis of three of the prominent families of answers to the question of the relation of the terms "this" to "my body." It must be noted that there are likely variations and nuances within these families of exegesis, but Hunsinger intends his analysis to present the major characteristics of these families.

Roman Catholic

The traditional Roman Catholic answer to the question of the linguistic relation of "this" to "my body" cannot be addressed without first describing the Roman Catholic position on the metaphysical dynamics of the consecrated elements. On the metaphysical theory of transubstantiation, the bread is no longer metaphysically present at the location where it once was, even if its empirical features remain present there. In conjunction, the body of Christ comes to occupy the place where the bread once was, and where the bread's empirical features continue. This theory requires that at the arrival of the body of Christ none of the empirical features of that body come along with it. Thus, it might seem, as Hunsinger states, that syntactically "this" stands in a relation of identity with "body."[2]

However, as Hunsinger continues, the relation seems to be less like identity and more like that of "container and contained."[3] He goes on, "In the eucharist the bread kept its local dimensionality while losing its substance, whereas the body kept its substance while losing its local dimensionality."[4] What this amounts to is that "this" and "body" both refer to one and the same object, the body of Christ that is contained within the empirical features of bread.

Luther

If we conceive of explications of the metaphysics of the Eucharist as on a spectrum with transubstantiation on one end and something like pure memorialism on the other, then the next step on the spectrum might be the Lutheran view. On Hunsinger's analysis of the linguistic features of Luther's view, the relation of "this" to "body" in the dominical words would be akin to synecdoche. Hunsinger comments, "'This' would apparently be related to 'my body' as . . . a part can be put for the whole in which it is included."[5] For an example of synecdoche, suppose I said, "Check out my wheels!" when I wished to draw someone's attention to my car; the part stands in for the whole. However, Hunsinger thinks that Luther wants to go beyond a "part for whole" locution and instead hold to a "dialectical identity." Dialec-

---

2. Hunsinger, *Eucharist and Ecumenism*, 57.
3. Ibid.
4. Ibid.
5. Ibid., 54.

tical identity is the relation of identity and difference between two complete wholes. "'Bread' and 'body' [or 'this' and 'body'] would be two ways of looking at one integral reality."[6]

Calvin

A third option for understanding the relation between the terms "this" and "body" in the dominical sentence is that which is offered by Calvin. According to Calvin's explication the sentence is a metonymy: "A metonymy uses the name of one thing for something else with which it is associated."[7] For instance, this linguistic phenomenon occurs when one refers to the President of the United States' administration as "the White House." On this construal, according to Hunsinger's presentation, "the word *this* would be related to the word 'body' by a process of association . . . 'bread' and 'body' would in some sense be external to one another."[8]

Metonymy is a slippery linguistic category, and Hunsinger notes that at times it is possible to read a more intimate relation of participation, not just association, into the term. For instance, suppose when the sheriff walks into the saloon in the old West, someone might say, "It's the law!" because the sheriff participates in the legal system of the town.

Real predication

With these three traditional linguistic options on the table, Hunsinger enters his own contribution to understanding the dominical words. I quote him here at length:

> There is arguably an irreducible minimum . . . that pertains to the liturgical use of the statement 'This is my body.' Ecumenically it is not enough to interpret it either as 'This signifies my body' or as 'This contains my body' . . . it must be possible for all traditions to assert—without equivocation—at the level of first-order discourse

---

6. Ibid., 54. Although Lutherans tend to cringe when one uses the term, we might see how "consubstantiation" would be aptly applied to a view wherein there are two complete wholes maintained in the Eucharist.

7. Ibid., 55.

8. Ibid., 55.

as found in the liturgy, that the relation of 'This bread' to 'my body' is actually one of real predication.[9]

Real predication works something like this. When the minister refers to a consecrated piece of bread, he can aptly say "this is the body of Christ," and he must do so really. That is, on this proposal, we cannot use the dominical words with scare quotes, this is not the "body of Christ," Christ did not say this is my "body" (and by "body" I mean, "not my body"). So, we have to ask the faithful, when holding a piece of communion bread, "Is this the body of Christ?" If the answer is "no" then real predication has not obtained and Eucharistic sharing is not possible. If, however, the catechizing minister points to the piece of communion bread and asks, "Is this the body of Christ?" and the respondent says, "Yes," then real predication has obtained and a step toward Eucharistic sharing has been taken.

Now, so Christians from more Free church traditions do not feel as though they are getting the brunt of the assault, know that real predication pushes against Roman Catholic explications of the Eucharist as well. If Protestants at times put scare quotes around the "body" of Christ, Roman Catholic put scare quotes around "this bread." On the official Roman Catholic doctrine, after the consecration the bread is no longer present on the altar. This is in fact just what John Wycliffe was posthumously condemned for holding at the Council of Constance in 1418. But if real predication is to obtain, if the bread is real so is the body, if the body is real so is the bread. Both extremes of the Eucharistic linguistic spectrum are challenged to find a more mediating position such that "this bread" and "my body" are granted reality by real predication.

Real predication

Here in this next section I want to try to add some greater clarity to Hunsinger's theory (or ecumenical "irreducible minimum") of real predication. It seems to me that there are a few possible ways of giving a further account of real predication. I call these routes the *identity* route, the *epiphany* route, and the *equivalence* route. Let us follow these routes a bit to see which path leads us to our desired destination, a greater understanding of Hunsinger's proposal.

9. Ibid., 60.

Identity

This first route proceeds as follows. It might seem that Hunsinger wants to maintain that in the dominical words Christ, and ministers standing *in persona Christi*, make an identity statement: "This bread *is* my body" or "This bread *is* the body of Christ." But first, a caveat, this is a different identity statement than is made in the Roman Catholic explication. Recall on the linguistic analysis of that view the identity statement is between "this" and "the body of Christ." The bread is no longer a part of the sentence. Real predication as identity statement is such that "this bread" is identical with "the body of Christ."

On the simplest explanations of identity, an object is only identical with itself, a=a. But strict identity of this sort is usually neither illuminating nor interesting. However, we language users make identity statements that are interesting and occasionally illuminating, as in the sentence: "Hesperus is Phosphorous" or "Samuel Clemens is Mark Twain." It might not have been clear to the ancients that the first star visible in the evening and the last start visible in the morning were in fact the same star, and thus once one learns that "Hesperus is Phosphorous" and "Phosphorous is Hesperus" one is in fact illuminated by this interesting sentence.

When a speaker predicates "Hesperus" of Venus and "Phosphorous" of Venus, one is able to achieve the sentence "Hesperus is Phosphorous." But one is only able to do so because the object in question is self-identical, and so the different terms *refer* to one and the same object. As philosopher W. V. O. Quine once observed, "What are identical are the objects with themselves and not the names with one another; the names stand in the statement of identity, but it is the named objects that are identified."[10] So when we have a sentence in the form of a statement of identity like "This bread *is* the body of Christ," are we to suppose that we simply have one object that is referred to by two names?

If an identity statement read of real predication is accurate, then we are only talking about one object. "This bread" and "the body of Christ" both refer to one and only one object in the cosmos. But, it is unclear to me how an identity read of real predication is possible; for this would entail that the predicates of one side of the identity statement are apt of the other. Yet, to say of the body of Christ "it is in heaven" does not seem to be proper of "this bread" which is so very clearly right there on the altar. Likewise, to

10. Quine, *Methods of Logic*, 209.

say of the bread "it is two inches tall and weighs 1 ounce" does not seem to be an apt predication of "the body of Christ." Therefore, a strict identity of the predications "this bread" and "the body of Christ" does not seem a plausible explication of real predication.

Epiphany

The second possible route for understanding real predication I call the epiphany route in honor of Alexander Schmemann.[11] With respect to this possible explication of real predication, let me just quote Schmemann from his article "Sacrament and Symbol" contained as an appendix to his *For the Life of the World*:

> In the early tradition . . . the relationship between the sign in the symbol (A) and that which it 'signifies' (B) is neither a merely semantic one (A *means* B), nor causal (A *is the cause of* B), nor representative (A *represents* B). We called this relationship an *epiphany*. 'A *is* B' means that the whole of A expresses, communicates, reveals, manifests the 'reality' of B (although not necessarily the whole of it) without, however, losing its own ontological reality.[12]

Hear also Hans Boersma, "Unlike mere symbols, sacraments actually *participate* in the mysterious reality to which they point. Sacrament *X* and reality *Y* co-inhere: the sacrament participates in the reality to which it points."[13] This seems a more plausible read of real predication, than simple identification. We still have two things, "this bread" and "the body of Christ"; but the bread *participates* in the body of Christ. The whole of the bread, maintaining its ontological reality, expresses, manifests, and participates in the body of Christ. However, a trouble I have with this view is that it is not entirely clear what this participation relation is. Do we need to "universalize" the body of Christ so that it can be multiply instantiated in various particulars? Need we divide Christ's body into non-empirical universal properties that can be instantiated in bread particulars without the body being empirically present? This view might save us the bread, but it is not clear how it *really* gets us the body that makes the predication "the

11. I think Schmemann's thought lingers behind Hunsinger's theology more than his footnotes convey. I think we can also see some of this line of thinking in Hans Boersma's recent *Heavenly Participation*.

12. Schmemann, *For the Life of the World*, 141.

13. Boersma, *Heavenly Participation*, 23.

body of Christ" real. If we can find a more plausible understanding of real predication, that would be preferable.

Equivalence

Finally, the third manner of explicating real predication is one that Hunsinger suggests himself. He writes, "a real predication of syntactical equivalence must be possible regardless of how it is explained."[14] The notion here is that both terms play a similar syntactical role of picking out the object of the predication. "This is bread" and "This is the body of Christ," where "bread" and "the body of Christ" both serve as apt predicates of "this." And further that the terms "this," "bread," and "the body of Christ" all refer to one thing. The distinction between this view and the "identity statement" view is that on that view "this bread" and "the body of Christ" were identical and identical in all their predicates. The syntactical equivalence view merely says that these terms are real predicates of one thing, but not that those predicates themselves are strictly identical.

At this point, I will attempt to clarify and shore up the notion of real predication as syntactical equivalence by recourse to some Chalcedonian Christology. In fact, Hunsinger describes his own Eucharistic proposal as "an analogy between the Incarnation and the Eucharist. This analogy is nothing new, and is in fact a standard item in the ancient, authoritative sources of the undivided church."[15] However, I am here going to be departing from Hunsinger's specific line of reasoning, yet I do so in hopes that the explication of real predication that I offer give a firmer theological and semantic footing than his explanation. In what follows, I will describe an "Incarnation-like" model of the Eucharist. This is not the route that Hunsinger takes in this discussion of the metaphysics of transelementation, his favorite term for describing the metaphysics of Christ's presence in the Eucharist. But I think that the view I expound more closely follows the paradigm of Chalcedonian Christology, and thus may be preferred.

14. Hunsinger, *Eucharist and Ecumenism*, 60.

15. Ibid., 23.

Incarnation as instrumental union

Patristic fathers such as Cyril of Alexandria and Gregory Nazianzus used the phrase "the iron in the fire" to describe both the Eucharistic and Christological state of affairs. One reason for the affinity between reflection on the Eucharist and that on Christology is that one runs into similarly abnormal predications in both situations. On an orthodox Nicene/Chalcedonian explication of Christ's two natures in one person, one can properly point to Christ and aptly utter "This is God," but one can also point to Christ and aptly utter "This is a man." The predicates "is God" and "is a man" are both aptly uttered of Christ, and yet they seem quite contradictory—just as the predicates "is bread" and "is the body of Christ" seem flatly contradictory. Therefore, if we accept the invitation of the phrase "the iron in the fire" to take incarnational dynamics as our theological North Star, perhaps we might further guide our Eucharistic ship to a safe harbor.

The components of Christ, his person, his divine nature, his human nature, and the various predicates of each, are all related to one another in some fashion or other. Numerous models have been adumbrated to explicate these dynamics. One model of these relational dynamics that has been popular both in the tradition and in the recent Christological literature is what might be termed an *instrumental model* of the Incarnation. Simply stated, the state of affairs that underwrites the aptness of the utterance "This is a man" when spoken of the divine person of the Word, is the fact that the human nature of Christ is used by God the Son as an instrument to act in the human sphere.

Let me first offer a traditional explication of this notion given by Thomas Aquinas. In his discussion of the two natures of Christ, Thomas seeks a relation between two things that are as robust as the sort of relation that in the Incarnation the hypostatic union brings about. He looks to the relation between the body and soul as a potential analogy for the hypostatic union. In fact, this relation is noted in the Athanasian Creed, "as the rational soul and flesh are one man, so God and man are one Christ."[16] Thomas then states, "the rational soul is united to the body both as to matter and as to an instrument."[17] Of course, the hypostatic union cannot be an instance of the first kind of relation (that of matter and form), so Thomas looks to the second relation, the instrumental relation, as a possible explication of

---

16. Thomas Aquinas, *Summa contra Gentiles* IV.41.9.

17. Ibid., IV.41.10.

the hypostatic union that is in the spirit of the natural union between the body and the soul.

Thomas then analyzes the relation between a part of the body and the soul. He states, "[a hand] is the soul's very own instrument . . . this hand is deputy to this soul in its very own operation . . . the hand is an instrument of the soul united to it and its very own."[18] So, the soul moves the hand as its very own instrument. In fact, it is in virtue of the fact that the hand is moved by the soul that there is a unity between hand and soul. Thomas then goes on to apply this to the union that obtains between the divine and human natures of Christ:

> But the human nature in Christ is assumed with the result that in-strumentally He performs the things which are the proper operation of God alone: to wash away sins, for example, to enlighten minds by grace, to lead into the perfection of eternal life. The human nature of Christ, then, is compared to God as a proper and conjoined instru-ment is compared, as the hand is compared to the soul.[19]

So the human nature of Christ is used by God to operate humanly and this causal union forms a basis for understanding the hypostatic union.

This instrumental or causal unity that obtains between the human na-ture of Christ and the divine person of the Word underwrites the seeming contradictory predicates that are uttered about Christ. For it might seem im-proper to point to Christ and utter, "This is God." However, because the hu-man nature is an integrally-related instrument of the Word, in virtue of this instrumental relation one can point to Christ and aptly utter, "This is God."

The analogy is such that when one points to my arm and says, "This is James," one speaks aptly, for my arm is an integral, instrumental part of me. It is no more accurate to stand a few feet away, gesture in my general vicinity and say, "This is James." Both are apt predications. It is of course inaccurate to point to my arm and say, "This is the leg of James," just as it is inaccurate to point to my foot and say, "This is James's head." Likewise, if we could reference Christ's divine nature (we cannot point to that), we could not say, "This is the body of Christ," or, "This is the human nature of Christ." We can, however, point to the human nature of Christ and say, "This is the human nature of God the Son." The point of our real predications of Christ are such that, as with the diagram appended to this chapter, when we point to Christ and say, "This is a man," we are able to do so because the instance

18. Ibid., IV.41.11.
19. Ibid.

of human nature to which we point has been "put on," as it were, by God the Son and has become the instrument of God the Son.

Eucharist as instrumental union

Now, let us make the move to apply this to the Eucharist as a possible explication for the "syntactical equivalence" explanation of real predication. And the move is this, Christ uses the consecrated bread and wine as his very own instruments. In so doing, a similar kind of causal unity is formed between the consecrated elements and the body of Christ. As the human nature (and human body) became parts of the second person of the Trinity, so too do the elements become parts of Christ's body. The parts of Christ's body are integrated due to their causal unity. As Christ uses the consecrated bread and wine as his very own they are integrated into the whole of his body. This construal even seems to resonate with some of Hunsinger's comments, for instance, "The bread is the instrument by which Christ bestows himself. Through having joined it to his life-giving flesh, the two are one."[20] Because of this causal union, the predicates "is bread" and "is the body of Christ" both refer to the same object, Christ's body, but not the same aspect of Christ's body, thus the predicates are not identical.

I think this arrangement helps Hunsinger achieve the kinds of consequences of real predication for which he hopes. For instance, "The bread would be identical with the body in one way while remaining different from it in another."[21] One way the bread is identical with the body of Christ is the way that my arm is identical with my body. One way the bread remains different from the body of Christ, is the way that my arm is different from my torso, or my leg, or the sum total of all the parts that compose my body. And this is just the same manner as certain component parts of Christ are both identical and different from one another. "Jesus Christ is God"—Christ is identical to God, but Christ is not the Father or the Spirit. "Jesus Christ is a man"—Christ is an instance of a human nature, but his human nature is not his divine nature. Thus, we have identity and differentiation.

Let us push the incarnation analogy further. The Word, the divine *person*, is the proximate assumer of the human nature. The Word now has another part, a human part, which is referenced by the predication "is a man." Likewise, the body of Christ is the proximate assumer of the bread,

---

20. Hunsinger, *The Eucharist and Ecumenism*, 63.
21. Ibid.

such that the body now has another part, a bread part, which is referenced by the predication "is bread." I think this is important for Hunsinger's notion of syntactical equivalence; it is specifically the body of Christ that is the proximate assumer of the bread. This is why Hunsinger wants to say, "The body, not the bread, would emerge more clearly as the primary reality. The bread would be assimilated into Christ's real, transcendent body more than the other way around."[22] The bread becomes a part of Christ's body, not that Christ's body becomes a part of the bread.

If we were to return to the linguistic analysis, it seems to me that real predication by syntactical equivalence turns out to be a synecdoche. When one says of the consecrated bread, "This is the body of Christ," one has uttered a "whole for part" locution, just as if one pointed to Christ's arm and said, "This is the body of Christ." However, when one says of the consecrated bread, "This is bread," one has not made a "part for whole" synecdoche. Rather one is uttering a simple "part for part" locution, on the order of pointing to Christ's arm and saying, "This is the arm of Christ." Thus, the body is the primary linguistic and ontological reality.

Conclusion

George Hunsinger wants us to be able to refer to the consecrated bread as "this bread" and "the body of Christ." A linguistic explanation of real predication as syntactical equivalence can be construed to be similar to the predications made of Christ, on Nicene/Chalcedonian Christology. An instrumental model of Christ has been used in the tradition to make sense of Chalcedonian Christology, and an instrumental model of the Eucharist can do similar work in underwriting real predication.

Here then is the invitation to ecumenical convergence: Does Christ use the bread and wine as his "very own"? If not, if the bread and wine are mere human tools, then we have reached an ecumenical impasse. But I suspect that ecumenically-minded Christians of even Free church persuasions might be inclined to agree that Christ does use the communion elements. And if he does use them, he uses them as his very own, uses them in the manner that he uses his natural body, uses them in the manner that the divine Word uses his human nature. Then it might just be possible, for the sake of ecumenical convergence to utter, without equivocation, "This bread is the body of Christ."

22. Ibid.

Appendix

"Iron in the fire": *real predication* in Christological and Eucharistic predications

An instrumental model of the Incarnation (à la Thomas Aquinas)

"But the human nature in Christ is assumed with the result that instrumentally He performs the things which are the proper operation of God alone: to wash away sins, for example, to enlighten minds by grace, to lead into the perfection of eternal life. The human nature of Christ, then, is compared to God as a proper and conjoined instrument is compared, as the hand is compared to the soul." (*Summa contra Gentiles* IV.41.11)

An instrumental model of the Eucharist (an Arcadian variation on a Hunsingerian theme)

Apostolic

The Pool Whose Name Means "Sent"

John and the Apostolic Destiny of the Church

—Joseph L. Mangina

Apostolicity is among the most primitive of Christian notions. In the book of Revelation we read that the names of the twelve apostles of the Lamb are written on the walls of the heavenly city, while Paul,[1] in Ephesians, writes that the household of God is "built on the foundation of the apostles and prophets, Christ Jesus himself being the cornerstone" (Rev 21:14, Eph 2:20). And of course the narrative portions of the New Testament are replete with stories concerning the apostles, that elect company who accompanied Jesus throughout his earthly ministry, bore witness to the resurrection, and carried the gospel to the ends of the earth. The apostles loom large in the historic Christian imagination—one thinks of all those medieval cathedrals whose portals are carved with statues of the Twelve, stone-faced, solemn, purposeful.

Apostolicity, I think all would agree, is central to the "Christian thing." But what is it? In histories of the early church and in theological treatises the story is told, with many variations and emphases, but always with the same cast of characters: Ignatius of Antioch, Justin Martyr, Marcion, Origen, Tertullian. Towering above them all is the great Irenaeus of Lyons, whose *Against Heresies* made apostolic continuity central to his case against those local, sectarian, and un-apostolic deviations we call "Gnosticism." Early Christianity is a complex landscape in which both the content of apostolic teaching (canon, rule of faith, creed) and its forms of transmission

1. Or his disciple.

(tradition, episcopal succession, councils) remained deeply contested for centuries; although for all that, a certain clarity emerged—enough for the church to "go on."[2] Whatever else apostolicity may be, it surely points to the church's ineluctably temporal character—as the church moves through time, it is borne along by the life and witness of the apostles. Apostolicity is the church's memory, its self-identity displayed across time through Scripture, teaching, and appropriate forms of ecclesial authority—whatever those may be! Apostolicity looks backwards, to the church's origins; forward, to the faithful transmission of apostolic teaching across generations; and outwards, to the church's diaspora scattering among the Gentiles. Finally, we must remind ourselves that the church's apostolicity is not a substitute for the presence of Christ within it, but precisely an expression of Christ's continued guidance and rule of his community through the Spirit. It is the living Lord Jesus Christ who gathers, upholds, and sends the apostles as his witnesses in the time between the Ascension and his second coming.[3]

Like the church itself, all of Scripture is apostolic; but not all parts of Scripture *about* apostolicity speak with equal clarity or force. Within the New Testament we think first of Paul, whose self-consciousness about his apostolic identity and mission was acute and, at times, defensive ("Am I not free? Am I not an apostle? Have I not seen Jesus our Lord?"—1 Cor 9:1) and secondly of the synoptic writers, especially Luke, whose idea of the Twelve exerted such a decisive influence on later ecclesiology. It is striking how New Testament authors as different as Luke and John the Seer should both emphasize the apostles' role as guarantors of the church's continuity with Israel, the first by stressing a single salvation history, the second by fusing imagery of the twelve tribes with that of the twelve apostles, the church, then, as a consummated Israel singing hymns to God and the Lamb (Rev 4:4, 7:1–8, 21:14).

Conspicuously absent in this brief survey is the Fourth Gospel. Unlike what we see in the synoptics, the Johannine disciples are never called apostles. John's references to the Twelve are few, concentrated in a single episode (John 6:67, 70, 71; cf. 20:24), and seemingly without programmatic intention. But semantics alone do not tell the whole story. Elsewhere in the New Testament apostolicity is closely connected with the ideas of witness—specifically, being a witness to the resurrection—and sending,

---

2. The best recent theological account of these matters is Jenson, *Canon and Creed*.

3. This scheme of gathering, upholding, and sending is central to Barth's ecclesiology. The theme has been further developed by Demson, *Hans Frei and Karl Barth*.

apostolos (emissary, delegate, representative) being linked to the verb *apos-tellein*. Both are *Ur*-Johannine notions. These notions are linked early on, for example in the character of John the Baptist, "a man sent [*apestalmenos*] by God" who "came as witness, to bear witness to the light, that all might believe through him" (John 1:6–7). The primordial act of sending in the Fourth Gospel is of course the mission of the Son, dispatched by the Father into the world in order to effect the world's salvation. We might hazard that the Evangelist's attitude toward "the" apostles as described in the gospels and Acts is similar to his attitude toward sacraments. Notoriously, John never describes the institution of the Eucharist; what he does instead is display the deeper logic of divine presence that makes the Eucharist and other sacraments possible. In a similar way, the apostles' sending across time is, for our author, a function of a more primordial Sending that originates beyond time and irrupts *in* time in the incarnation of the Word.

There is a telling episode in the Fourth Gospel where this deeper logic of sending may be observed. It is, in its own way, an apostolic and therefore ecclesial story . . . but I must not try to interpret the narrative before telling it. There is nothing for it but to plunge directly into the text:

> As he [Jesus] passed by, he saw a man blind from birth. And his disciples asked him, 'Rabbi, who sinned, this man or his parents, that he was born blind?' Jesus answered, 'It was not that this man sinned, or his parents, but that the works of God might be displayed in him. We must work the works of him who sent me while it is day; night is coming, when no one can work. As long as I am in the world, I am the light of the world.' Having said these things, he spat on the ground and made mud with the saliva. Then he anointed the man's eyes with the mud and said to him, 'Go, wash in the pool of Siloam' (which means Sent). So he went and washed and came back seeing.[4]

The immediate background to this story is Jesus' long, involved controversy with the Pharisees in the previous chapter. That debate reached its climax in Jesus' claim "I am the light of the world" (one of the seven Johannine "I am" sayings followed by a predicate). In the Prologue of the gospel the reader was told that "the light shines in the darkness, and the darkness has never overcome it." The Word is the light. Jesus is the light. It is the nature of light to illuminate darkness. In our present story Jesus offers the practical display of his identity as the Light, by bringing light into the darkness of a

4. John 9:1–7.

particular human life. He spits on the ground and makes mud—an action that seems almost vulgar, after all this talk of light!—and sends the man off to wash at Siloam, the pool whose name means "Sent."

The Fourth Gospel delights in place names: think of Cana, Bethesda, Tiberias, Bethany, Gabbatha, Golgotha. The topography of first-century Palestine is the site where the glory of the eternal Word displays itself in time. In our text Siloam is an actual pool or spring in Jerusalem, mentioned in an oracle in the book of Isaiah: "Because this people have refused the waters of Shiloah that flow gently, and rejoice over Rezin and the son of Remaliah," therefore the LORD will bring the waters of the River to inundate them—the king of Assyria (Isa 8:6–7). It might be possible to conduct a figural reading of John 8 in counterpoint with this Isaiah passage, perhaps focusing on the ambivalent water (=baptismal?) imagery, water being seen as an agent of both grace and destruction. Yet I think such a reading would be forced. The evangelist himself sets the direction of interpretation invoking a wordplay on the name Siloam, which he interprets as a form of the Hebrew root *shalaq* or send, rendering it in Greek as *apestalmenos*—literally "the One who has been Sent." This etymology is dubious; but then John is writing a gospel and not a Hebrew-Greek lexicon. As I have already noted, in the Prologue John the Baptist is described as an *apestalmenos*. Yet surely the Sent One of our text is not the Baptist but rather Christ himself. Jesus' identity as sent by the Father is a constant theme in the controversy with the Pharisees, which occupies the chapter immediately preceding our story. The language appears again in Jesus' and the disciples' initial encounter with the blind man: Jesus declares, "We must work the works of him who sent me while it is day; night is coming, when no one can work" (9:4). The sign Jesus is about to perform is one of these works, a display of the divine glory in the day leading up to the "night" of the passion, when the glory of the Son will be paradoxically displayed in his being lifted up on the cross.

Yet if Jesus is the Sent One, he also powerfully draws others into the history of his sending. As Peter Leithart comments:

> The fact that *apostello* is the etymological root of *apostolos* suggests that John is offering a double translation. Siloam equals sent, and sent links up with apostle. The blind man is being healed by the Sent One in the pool of sending, and thereby becomes one sent, a type of an apostle. He is plunged into the pool 'Sent' by the One Sent, immersed in the Sent One's sending.[5]

5. Leithart, *Deep Exegesis*, 102.

As Jesus' own identity coincides perfectly with his mission from the Father, in other words, so the former blind man is now nothing other than an *apestalmenos*. The question of identity looms large here. At the beginning of the story Jesus' disciples pose the question whether the man's blindness resulted from his own sin or the sin of his parents, a debate, however, that Jesus refuses to be drawn into (9:2–3). Moreover, in the narrative that follows the Pharisees characterize first Jesus and then the man born blind as sinners (9:24, 34)—an interesting negative tribute to the man's identification with Jesus! Not unlike the disciples, the Pharisees pose the question about identity with a view to the past; sin and blindness are conceived of as a kind of fate. But Jesus transforms the man's fate into destiny, or more specifically into his future as one who is sent—an apostle.

The man, indeed, not Jesus, is the central character in John 9, if by central character we mean the one who undergoes the most significant change or growth in the course of the story.[6] We can see this in the increasing complexity and boldness of his responses to the Pharisees. Asked about the one who had healed him he at first answers cautiously, using the cold language of facts: "the man called Jesus made mud and anointed my eyes" (9:11). On his second interrogation the Pharisees assert confidently that they "know" Jesus to be a sinner, to which the man replies: "Whether he is a sinner I do not know. One thing I do know, that though I was blind, now I see" (9:25). Note the asseveration *I do know*; he now backs up his claims with a first-person reference. At last the Pharisees lose all patience with him, crying out with exasperation, "You are his disciple, but we are disciples of Moses" (9:28). It is one of those delicious moments of Johannine irony, for the Pharisees are speaking the exact truth: they recognize that the man is well on the way to becoming a disciple of Jesus. At the very end of the story the man has begun to challenge the Pharisees on their own terms, declaring, "If this man were not from God, he could do nothing" (9:33). Jesus

---

6. Consider J.R.R. Tolkien's *The Lord of the Rings*, where by Tolkien's own admission the central character is not, as we might think at first, Frodo, but his servant Samwise Gamgee, who deepens in the virtues of courage and fidelity in the course of the tale, yet without losing his commonsensical outlook on life. Sam is clearly an English working class "type." If the battle for Middle Earth were the Great War of 1914 to 1918, Sam would have been Frodo's batsman. To be sure, this is a complex question where John's gospel is concerned. Jesus is surely the central figure in the Johannine narrative as a whole; but whether he is a "character" in the sense being discussed here is another matter. I simply note that by virtue of Jesus' singularity he does not rest easily with our ordinary understandings of genre or other categories of literary analysis.

is indeed from God; the reader has known this ever since the Prologue. It is only to be expected that in the coda to the story the now-sighted man bows down and worships Jesus.

What keeps all this from being a mere *Bildungsroman*—that eighteenth-century genre that narrates the sentimental, and so inferior, education of a young man—is the atmosphere of conflict in which the blind man is caught up by virtue of his connection with Jesus. If the truth in John is what makes you free, it is also what makes you suffer. This is recognized by Leithart, who notes that the Hebrew word *shalaq* can also carry the negative connotation of dismissal or expulsion, as in Adam and Eve's casting out from the garden (Gen 3:23; the Septuagint translates this passage using *exapostello*). Leithart goes on to say that Siloam is not merely the pool of the Sent One's sending but "a pool of expulsion, foreshadowing the blind man's expulsion from the synagogue (v. 34). The two sendings go together: the blind man can be sent out by the Sent One only if he is willing to be sent out of the synagogue by those who reject the One whom God sent."[7]

Readers familiar with the history of Johannine scholarship may catch an echo here of J. Louis Martyn's great *History and Theology in the Fourth Gospel*, which argued that John should be read as a two-level drama: a surface-level or ostensive drama concerning Jesus, and a secondary drama involving the separation between the nascent church and the synagogue.[8] The story of the man born blind was one of the central texts in Martyn's argument, given that certain features of the story—e.g., the odd word *aposynagogos*—fit better with late first-century realities rather than with Jesus' own historical setting. At the ecclesial level the text describes the story of an anonymous Christian healer who is hauled before the Jewish authorities, expelled from the synagogue, and eventually martyred. Martyn's thesis set the agenda in Johannine studies for an entire generation, seemingly giving a local habitation and a name to a gospel whose origins had long seemed obscure. More recently the thesis has fallen out of fashion. New Testament scholars today are less confident that we can reconstruct the historical setting of John with such precision, or that such is needed to make sense of the text. Moreover, critics have argued that there is a problem of genre, in so far as the evangelist clearly set out to faithfully reproduce the witness of the Beloved Disciple to Jesus—not to describe the travails of the

---

7. Leithart, *Deep Exegesis*, 102.

8. Martyn, *History and Theology in the Fourth Gospel*.

early church. "Two-level drama" was simply not a genre available to a first-century author.[9]

All this may well be true; but I do not think it gets to the heart of the matter. Critics of the Martyn hypothesis tend to cast it as an exercise in the hermeneutics of suspicion: "The Fourth Gospel says it is about Jesus, but when we look behind the text we can see that what is *really* going on is a power struggle between the church and the synagogue"—Christology as veiled ecclesiology. Yet I do not think we are obliged to read the hypothesis in this reductive way. Martyn, who was one of the twentieth century's most determined theological readers of the New Testament, invokes the two-level drama as a way of making sense of God's action as that which binds together Jesus' past and the church's present. It is the text of the Fourth Gospel itself that drives him to this conclusion: "Truly, truly, I say to you, whoever believes in me will also do the works that I do; and greater works than these will he do, because I am going to the Father" (14:12). Jesus' return to the Father, in other words, is the condition of possibility of the church and its missionaries performing these "greater works."

I am sympathetic to this program, but wonder whether Martyn was well served by speaking of two *levels* in John. Despite Martyn's theological intentions, such language suggests a static picture in which the meaning of the text is "fixed," referring to its historical circumstances of origin. The activity of the Spirit is constrained here, and the story of Jesus and the blind man becomes but a code for the church-synagogue struggle in the late first century. But what if we saw Jesus, the blind man, and the later church as bound together by a complex set of figural or typological relations? So Leithart: the man "becomes one sent, a type of an apostle." We are long past the day when figural reading is seen as inevitably "spiritualizing" in the bad sense. When it is performed well (and of course this is not always the case) a figural reading underscores the narrative and historical specificity of both poles in the figural relation. The blind man is not a mere symbol but a particular beggar whom Jesus "passed by" and engaged in conversation. It is in this specificity that he, immersed in and sent by the Sent One, becomes a type of the apostles.

I said earlier that John seems to have little sense of the Twelve as an institution in the church's life; yet toward the end of the gospel the spotlight

---

9. This is roughly the argument set forth by Richard Bauckham. See his *The Testimony of the Beloved Disciple*; more directly on Martyn, see the unsparing critique by Bauckham's former student Edward W. Klink III in *The Sheep of the Fold*.

falls more and more on Jesus' commissioning of the disciples for their life after his departure: "As the Father has sent me, even so I am sending you" (20:21). This theme culminates in the moving scene toward the end of the gospel, following Jesus' threefold question, "Simon, son of John, do you love me?" After Peter's pained insistence that he does, indeed, love the Lord, Jesus declares:

> 'Truly, truly, I say to you, when you were young, you used to dress yourself and walk wherever you wanted, but when you are old, you will stretch out your hands, and another will dress you and carry you where you do not want to go.' (This he said to show by what kind of death he was to glorify God.) And after saying this he said to him, 'Follow me' (21:19).

In light of passages like these, we would have to say that for the Fourth Gospel the church does not have a mission, it *is* its mission. And that mission is cruciform. In the title of this essay I have spoken of the "apostolic destiny of the church." The word "destiny" is meant to capture something of the givenness, the determinateness, even the elected and predestined character of the church's mission. For all that, destiny should not be taken to mean sheer impersonal fate. What binds the Father and the Son together is their love for one another; later Augustine of Hippo would identify that Love with the Holy Spirit. The Father sends the Son into the world out of sheer love—love both for the Son and for the world (3:16). The church participates in that love, being indeed the Beloved Community.[10] There is a practical counsel to be derived from all this: if members of the Christian community do not love the Father and Jesus, they should not bother to go out on mission. That is why Jesus' final conversation with Peter takes the form of this loving interrogation, so that Peter might understand why he is sent and Who is sending him.

Yet if apostolicity has to do with the church's existence in time, it must involve more than just mission in the sense of sheer garnering new members. The church in mission is expected to *say* something, in faithfulness to the same Jesus who healed the blind man and commissioned the twelve. Where in the Fourth Gospel in particular is the Irenaean concern for authentic tradition and succession in office that we usually associate with that

---

10. See Hinlicky, *Beloved Community*. The Fourth Gospel plays a key role in Hinlicky's account of continuity between the apostolic age and subsequent credal catholicism. His sage use of Sir Edwyn Hoskyns's commentary on John has shaped some of my comments below.

word? I think it is fair to say that the Fourth Gospel will not give us an ecclesiological blueprint: it would be anachronistic to ask questions of the book that it was not designed to give. "Apostolic succession" is Irenaeus's question; it is not yet John's. Nevertheless, there are plenty of signs in John of what might be called an emerging apostolic self-consciousness, an awareness that the church, if it is to go on *being* the church, must constantly test itself against the original deposit of faith. John may not be interested in modes or structures of apostolic continuity, but he is certainly interested in the apostolic basis of the Christian "thing." No one has seen this better than Sir Edwyn Hoskyns, whose great, unfinished commentary on the Fourth Gospel was published in 1940.[11] Hoskyns, an Englishman who had learned much from Barth, understood that the quest for the historical Jesus was a dead-end, not just theologically but historically. You can do it, of course, but you will not understand *these books* by doing it, given that they are about something else—they are about God. But Hoskyns also knew better than to flee the Jesus of history for the Christ of faith, an equally abstract and modern construct. The Fourth Gospel is about neither the Jesus of history nor the Christ of faith, but about the Word made flesh. The incarnation—assuming it occurred—eludes reduction to either the empiricist or the idealist option. If God entered our history, history itself looks different.

It is often supposed that the synoptic gospels operate on a more or less descriptive and historical plane, while John imposes theological or mystical meaning on them; hence, "the spiritual gospel." Hoskyns' commentary scrambles this simple-minded view. It is John, he argues, who presses the historicity of the Christian claim in an unrivaled way. Of course John has a high Christology, the highest of all, and that is important. But what makes the Fourth Gospel's high Christology potentially offensive is its identification of the eternal Word *with the human and Jewish Jesus*. Hoskyns saw earlier than almost anyone else that the provenance of John is that of Palestinian Judaism. It is a Jewish work "all the way down." Remember all those place names? John is a book not of sheer theological construction but a book of memory. The point, as Hoskyns saw so well, was not mainly the Fourth Gospel's reliability as a historical source, but its anti-gnostic and anti-docetic insistence on the human character of the Word. One of the things the gospel has in common with the Johannine letters is its vivid use of the first-person plural: "*We* have beheld his glory." "*We* know that his testimony is true," and so on. It would be very easy, Hoskyns says, for this

11. Hoskyns, *The Fourth Gospel*.

"we" to be a kind of self-assertion on the part of the evangelist or of his church. It is worth noting that he was writing for his fellow Anglicans, who on the one hand have a weakness for all things apostolic, but who on the other hand are constantly tempted to submerge Christ's identity into that of the community.[12]

Schooled by Barth, Hoskyns would not allow this sort of easy elision between divine and human reality. He argued that the Johannine "we" is precisely *not* an absorption of Christ into community, because the "we" that comes to expression here is that of the apostles. In the Johannine literature, the apostles' authority

> so far from being submerged by the vigorous faith of later Christians, becomes central, precisely in order that exuberant independence in the Church may be subjected to proper direction and control . . . The Church that authoritatively confronts the world must first have been confronted and created by the witness and apprehension of the apostles . . . .[13]

Who was the author of the Fourth Gospel? We simply do not know. Richard Bauckham thinks we should take the book's own claim seriously, and attribute authorship to the Beloved Disciple, a nameless disciple living in Jerusalem. Yet whoever the author may have been, the book proves its apostolic credentials by the role it has played in the subsequent life of the church. John has played a crucial role in the formulation of Christian trinitarian and Christological dogma. It is also, of course, a book that needs to be used very carefully. One need only think of its harsh language concerning "the Jews." But then there are few texts of Scripture that do not require handling with care.

As the church goes out on mission, it is constantly presented with the question as to who has authorized this mission, who "backs up" the church's claims. Apostolicity is the note of the church that directs us to the source from which such questions may be answered. We, like the man born blind, are placed under interrogation. Who healed you? The man Jesus put mud on my eyes . . . a prophet . . . a man from God. Before we know it, we find

---

12. In Hoskyns's day this would have taken the form of the remnants of English Hegelianism, a tradition all too prone to celebrate all things "incarnational." As Stanley Hauerwas somewhere writes, Anglicans should never be permitted to use the term "incarnation," because what they mean by it is "God became human and said 'this isn't so bad.'"

13. Hoskyns, *The Fourth Gospel*, 91.

that we are being questioned not by the Pharisees or their modern equiva-
lents but by the Lord himself: "Do you believe in the Son of Man?" And so
we offer our halting and always inadequate confessions of faith. We have
been baptized in the pool of Siloam, whose name means "Sent." We are
caught up in the Father's own sending of the Son into the world, a destiny
both constrained and joyful, looking ahead to that city whose foundations
bear the names of the twelve apostles of the Lamb.

One Holy, Catholic, and Missional Church

Hans Urs von Balthasar on the Church's Identity and Mission

—Eugene R. Schlesinger

Introduction[1]

The Nicene-Constantinopolitan Creed identifies the church as one, holy, catholic, and apostolic, and, of these, perhaps the church's apostolicity has produced the most controversy. Most discussions of apostolicity revolve around notions of apostolic succession. Those in churches such as my own which have retained the historic episcopate tend to stress the importance of bishops in maintaining the church's apostolicity.[2] Those who have dispensed with this venerable and time-tested form of church government tend to stress continuation in apostolic doctrine as the locus of succession.[3] I want to approach the question from a different angle, though,

---

1. A portion of my work in this essay was carried out during my tenure as a Rev. John P. Raynor, SJ, Fellow at Marquette University during the 2015 to 2016 academic year.

2. See, e.g., the discussion in ARCIC, *Church as Communion*, nos. 25–41; International Commission for Anglican-Orthodox Theological Dialogue, *Church of the Triune God*, 5.1–29. Even the discussion in the World Council of Church's document, *Baptism, Eucharist and Ministry*, while not insisting on a particular form of *episcopē*, nevertheless assumes that this is an integral component of the church's apostolicity, 3.9–14.

3. See, e.g., Calvin, *Institutes*, 4.2.1–4, 4.3.5–6. For a contemporary restatement see Horton, *The Christian Faith*, 880–92. Michael Ramsey presents an excellent synthesis of the viewpoints of apostolic succession as doctrinal and episcopal in *The Gospel and the*

one that sees the Apostles fundamentally as missionaries (indeed, it is built into their name: Sent Ones). Christ's commission to the Apostles is to send them out into the entire world to proclaim the gospel (Matt 28:16–20; Luke 24:44–49; John 20:19–33; Acts 1:8). The Acts of the Apostles details the church's initial missionary expansion. Therefore, apostolicity is perhaps best understood as carrying forward the apostolic mission.[4]

These considerations lie in the background of this chapter, which investigates an aspect of Hans Urs von Balthasar's ecclesiology: the church's identity in mission. Though he never wrote an ecclesiology, the church was essential to Hans Urs von Balthasar's theology. In particular, Balthasar's ecclesial leitmotif was mission. This missional preoccupation led to a "theoretical disinterest" in the typical ecclesiological and missiological questions, giving rise instead to a "theology *for* mission."[5] And yet, the particular shape of the church's mission remains undeveloped in Balthasar scholarship, which, in ecclesiological matters, tends to focus on Balthasar's famous Marian and Petrine dimensions of the church.[6] In this essay, I attempt an articulation of the church's identity and mission, indeed, the church's identity in mission. I shall develop my argument by way of another constitutive element of Balthasar's theology: the Eucharist, which Mark Miller and Roch Kereszty have suggested forms part of the deep structure of Balthasar's thought, despite its lack of systematic treatment.[7]

I argue that for Balthasar the church's mission is constitutive of her identity, that there is no abstracting the church away from her mission in and to the world. I further argue that the shape of this mission is at once disclosed and given in the Eucharistic action, which is another way of saying

---

Catholic Church, 55–85.

4. This perspective is not necessarily inimical to questions of episcopal or doctrinal succession, but rather supplements them. For instance, in its chapter on the Episcopacy, the Roman Catholic Dogmatic Constitution on the Church, *Lumen gentium*, explicitly roots the office of bishops in the apostolic mission (nos. 18–21). Meanwhile, questions of doctrinal continuity can be understood in terms of proclaiming the same gospel as the Apostles, which is a missionary enterprise. Keeping apostolic mission at the forefront prevents either of these understandings of apostolicity from becoming overly inward in their orientation.

5. Peelman, "Théologie pour la mission," 127 (my translation).

6. Koerpel, "Form and Drama of the Church," 82–88; Oakes, *Pattern of Redemption*, 252–54; McPartlan, "Who is the Church?," 271–88; Chapp, "Who is the Church?," 322–38; Casarella, "*Analogia Donationis*," 152; and Kereszty, "Eucharist and Mission," 7.

7. Miller, "Sacramental Theology of Balthasar," 55; Kereszty, "Eucharist and Mission," 4.

"at the cross." Moreover, the shape of this missional identity is thoroughly dispossessive, as the church is expropriated by the expropriated Christ. This enables me to put Balthasar's account of ecclesial identity in mission into conversation with the recent missional ecclesiology articulated by Nathan R. Kerr.[8] Kerr's apocalyptically tinged account of the church's mission allows (and demands) a further refinement of Balthasar's. At the same time, however, I demonstrate that Balthasar's ecclesiology is not subject to Kerr's critiques, and that Balthasar's account of the relation between liturgy and mission offers its own challenge to ecclesiologies like Kerr's.

In my investigation, I shall concern myself primarily with three volumes of Balthasar's trilogy: *The Glory of the Lord* 7, the New Testament Theology, in which the Christ form and the mission of Jesus are developed; *Theo-Drama* 3, which develops the account of mission and calling, as well as the relationship between human actors and Christ; and *Theo-Drama* 4, which articulates Balthasar's soteriology.[9] Focusing on these volumes, which are representative of Balthasar's thought as a whole, allows me to account for the most immediately relevant data. As mentioned above, the Marian and Petrine dimensions of the church are quite important for Balthasar, and are well attested in the scholarly literature. However, I shall not make much use of them. My hope is that by bracketing this conversation, I can foreground other dimensions of Balthasar's thought that have otherwise remained underdeveloped. I am not articulating a total ecclesiology, but rather giving an account of the dispossessive shape of the church's mission and arguing that the church is constituted in her identity by this dispossession.

Christ's Identity in Mission

According to Balthasar, Christ's existence is determined by his mission from the Father.[10] His identity as the one sent by the Father is so strong that "his mission [*Sendung*] coincides with his person."[11] An adequate account of this identity in mission is essential to a proper understanding of the church's mission. In this section I attempt to provide that account. In

8. Kerr, *Christ, History and Apocalyptic.*

9. Balthasar, *Glory of the Lord*, vol. 7; *Theo-Drama*, vol. 3; *Theo-Drama*, vol. 4.

10. Balthasar, *Glory of the Lord* 7:247; *Theo-Drama* 3:150–54, 167. See also *Mysterium Paschale*, 91.

11. Balthasar, *Theo-Drama* 3:150 (bracketed German original).

doing so, I take my cues from Balthasar's statement about Christ's mission: "we must see the doctrine of the Trinity as the ever-present, inner presupposition of the doctrine of the Cross. In the same way, and symmetrically to it, the doctrine of the covenant or of the church (including sacramental doctrine) must not be regarded as a mere result of the Cross-event but as a constituent element of it."[12]

Among other things, this shows that ecclesiology cannot be a mere afterthought to an understanding of Christ's mission. Indeed, it cannot even be considered a result of it. The church is somehow intrinsic to Christ's mission. Additionally, this means that when we turn to consider the church's mission, we will not be departing from a consideration of Christ's mission, but rather continuing it. Before making this turn, though, we must understand Christ's identity in mission against the backdrop of the triune life, and trace it through the cross and into the church.

Eternal Dispossession

The eternal relationship between the Father and the Son in the immanent Trinity is fundamentally dispossessive. The Son *receives* himself in his entirety from the Father in his eternal generation. His existence then is not his own, and he eternally returns the gift to the Father in thanksgiving and love.[13] The movement is one of reception-and-return-of-gift in the Holy Spirit. The movement, then, is an eternal Eucharist. However, the Son's reception and re-donation of being is not the only dispossessive movement. In generating the Son, the Father also eternally gives himself away entirely.[14] The Father's primary kenosis is the ground of all the other kenosis that will ever occur.[15] When the Son Eucharistically returns himself to the Father in the Holy Spirit, this self-dispossession images the Father's own dispossession.[16] None of the divine persons keeps the divine nature for himself. Rather, each one expropriates himself into and for the others.[17]

---

12. Balthasar, *Theo-Drama* 4:319.

13. Balthasar, *Theo-Drama* 4:325–26.

14. Balthasar, *Theo-Drama* 4:52.

15. Balthasar, *Theo-Drama* 3:323, 331.

16. Also noted by Casarella, "*Analogia Donationis*," 163.

17. Balthasar, *Theo-Drama* 4:324. Throughout, it must be stressed that the sort of intra-divine kenosis that Balthasar has in mind is not a negative reality, but is rather identical to the divine life. Within the Trinity, dispossession cannot be understood simply

It is within this eternal expropriation that Balthasar finds the condition of possibility for creation. Because the Father is able to have a divine other, it is possible for there to be a non-divine other. Creation takes place within the eternal generation of the Son. However, it does not unfold just in the eternal reception of being, but in the eternal Eucharistic re-donation. "The world can only be created within the Son's 'generation;' the world belongs to him and has him as its goal; only in the Son can the world be 'recapitulated.'"[18] Lawrence Chapp notes that it is for this reason that Christ's mission is able to be universal, because the world finds its place (as it were) in him.[19]

There is a dark side to all of this, though. In giving himself away, the Father produces a good "(divine) God-lessness (of love . . .)."[20] This God-lessness is in no way identical to the sinful godlessness that arises within the creation. However, the sinful godlessness finds its condition of possibility in this prior and eternally good God-lessness.[21] Even so, sin is not ontologized. Creation's No unfolds within the Son's eternal Yes. "The creature's No is merely a twisted knot within the Son's pouring-forth; it is left behind by the current of love."[22] Because the creation exists in the interval between the divine persons, its distortions also occur in this interval. This means, then, that if those distortions are to be overcome, the solution must occur in this same interval as well.[23]

Economic Dispossession: Obedience Unto Death

All this leads to the Son's Incarnation, his temporal mission, which is itself grounded in his eternal procession.[24] As the eternal Son is entirely dependent upon the Father for his being, the Incarnate Son is entirely dependent

---

as "loss." Rather, the triune dispossession is a positive reality according to which those who dispossess themselves also fulfill their being. This is well documented in Martin, "Balthasar's Gendered Theology," 1–29; Healy, *Eschatology of Balthasar*, 128–34.

18. Balthasar, *Theo-Drama* 4:326.

19. Chapp, "Who is the Church?," 328.

20. Balthasar, *Theo-Drama* 4:324.

21. Balthasar, *Theo-Drama* 4:324, 328–29.

22. Balthasar, *Theo-Drama* 4:329–30 [330].

23. Balthasar, *Theo-Drama* 4:333.

24. Balthasar, *Theo-Drama* 4:330–33; *Glory of the Lord* 7:214–15. See further Williams, "Balthasar and the Trinity," 37–50; Kilby, "Balthasar on the Trinity," 208–22; Hunt, *The Trinity and the Paschal Mystery*, 60–81; Healy, *Eschatology of Balthasar*, 118–37.

upon the Father for the shape of his mission. Particularly in *The Glory of the Lord 7*, Balthasar belabors the point that the revelatory function of the Incarnation consists in Jesus's transparency to the Father.[25] It is by his perfect, dispossessive obedience that the Son perfectly discloses the Father.[26] Here two themes converge. On the one hand the Son's non-determination of his own mission takes up the theme of his eternal reception of being from the Father. On the other hand, transparency to the Father in every aspect of his being reprises the motif of the coincidence of person and mission in Christ. The two of these together give a thoroughly dispossessive account of the Incarnation. Jesus *is* the one at the Father's disposal.[27] He *is* the one who exists in total dependence upon the Father.[28]

This dispossessive identity in mission is seen most clearly in the orientation of Jesus's life to the cross. His life was oriented towards death, and this death is a total self-abnegation.[29] Christ allows his "hour" to be determined by God in both its "time and content,"[30] while at the same time the cross was the "inner form" of his life.[31] So then, Jesus allows himself to be transparent to the Father to the extent that he is inwardly determined by his death on the cross, while also allowing the content of that death which forms its own inward determination to be determined by the Father. This dispossession and passivity is exemplified by the descent into Hell in Balthasar's theology of Holy Saturday.[32]

Cross as Eucharist

However, the foregoing only gives a partial account of the Son's identity in mission. As I noted above, the creation (and the Son's mission in that creation) takes place within the contours of the Son's eternal Eucharist. Sin enters as a "knot" disrupting the flow of reciprocal donation, and the Son enters the creation in order to untie the knot, as it were.[33] Without the

---

25. Balthasar, *Glory of the Lord* 7:125, 142–47, 290–92.

26 Balthasar, *Glory of the Lord* 7:283, 323.

27. Balthasar, *Glory of the Lord* 7:247; *Theo-Drama* 4:330.

28. Balthasar, *Glory of the Lord* 7:265.

29. Balthasar, *Glory of the Lord* 7:80–81; *Theo-Drama*, 4:323.

30. Balthasar, *Theo-Drama* 4:324.

31. Balthasar, *Theo-Drama* 4:495.

32. Balthasar, *Glory of the Lord* 7:288–90.

33. Balthasar, *Theo-Drama* 4:329–30.

return gift, the Incarnation's telos would be incomplete. This is why the church and sacraments must be not merely results of the cross and resurrection, but rather intrinsic elements of it.[34] The dispossessive logic of Christ's mission reaches its fullest expression in the collocation of cross and Eucharist. And this collocation in turn sets the stage for our consideration of ecclesial mission.

Balthasar describes the event of the cross in dramatic and Eucharistic terms: "God's anger strikes him instead of the countless sinners, shattering him as by lightning and distributing him among them; thus God the Father, in the Holy Spirit, creates the Son's Eucharist. Only the Eucharist really completes the Incarnation."[35] The reason the Incarnation is not complete apart from the Eucharist is twofold. On the one hand, it is in the return gift that the eternal dynamic of the immanent Trinity is completed, and this too must be transposed into the economy, untying the knot of humanity's No along the way. On the other hand, it is in the Eucharistic distribution of his flesh and blood that the dispossessive logic of Christ's incarnate mission reaches its fullest expression.

This second facet helps guard against a misunderstanding of the first. The Eucharistic component of Christ's mission, with its return of the gift could seem to indicate leaving behind the movement of dispossession. Instead, it deepens it. As Balthasar writes, Jesus gives himself over into "powerlessness in the Eucharist," handing himself over to the Holy Spirit and to the disciples.[36] In giving the Eucharist, Christ is "'liquefied' in his self-abandonment."[37] In the "Eucharist of the Cross . . . the kenosis has reached its fulfilment [sic]."[38] Here in the Eucharist, Jesus' placing himself "at the Father's disposal" and his gift of life to humanity coalesce.[39] As the Eucharistic distribution is the culmination of kenosis—by which Christ allows himself to be fully determined by his Father, fully constituted by his redemptive mission—it is entirely fitting to see Christ has himself summed up in the Eucharist. "Bread and wine . . . reveal precisely in what an essential

---

34. Balthasar, *Theo-Drama* 4:319.
35. Balthasar, *Theo-Drama* 4:348.
36. Balthasar, *Glory of the Lord* 7:149.
37. Balthasar, *Glory of the Lord* 7:151.
38. Balthasar, *Glory of the Lord* 7:226.
39. Balthasar, *Theo-Drama* 3:39, 243 [39].

manner Christ wills to be nourishment for us, how deeply he incorporates himself in us in order to take us up into himself," writes Balthasar.[40]

So then, it is in the Cross-Eucharist that Christ fulfills the mission that constitutes his person. The Eucharistic distribution of his body and blood at once completes the logic of dispossession, and demonstrates the inner heart of the cross: to give life to humanity. The cross is what the Eucharist is all about, and the Eucharist in turn is what the cross is all about. Moreover, this Eucharistic account of the crucifixion helps to tie Christ's economic kenosis to his Eucharistic expropriation in the eternal life of the immanent Trinity. What Christ does on earth is fully consonant with his eternal place in the divine life. And Christ's eternal place in the divine life is one of dispossessive expropriation, which mirrors his Father's own primary kenosis. Because the Eucharist is itself part of the inner logic of the Christ event— not merely a result, but rather a constituent element—it is necessary to also consider the mission of the church in connection with Christ's mission. To this task I now turn.

The Church's Identity in Mission

My stated aim is to give an account of the church as constituted by its mission. Such a goal immediately runs into an obstacle, however. Balthasar explicitly states that "it is a fundamental characteristic of all those who thus step onto the theological stage *en Christōi* that, in contrast to Christ, there is no identity between their (eternal) election and their (temporal) vocation and mission."[41] Instead, the creaturely actors in the Theo-Drama must be called to their mission in time and history, and their bestowal of mission occurs only in Christ.[42] However, Balthasar is clear elsewhere that the creature, and especially the church, must likewise find her identity in mission.[43] Indeed, "man [*sic*] can and must find his identity in his mission. This mission is constitutive of the person, within the mission of Christ."[44]

---

40. Balthasar, *Glory of the Lord* 7:540.

41. Balthasar, *Theo-Drama* 3:263.

42. Balthasar, *Theo-Drama* 3:263–65, 269–71.

43. Balthasar, *Glory of the Lord* 7:96–97, 414, 486; *Mysterium Paschale*, 262–63.

44. Balthasar, *Theo-Drama* 4:62. Also noted by Chapp, "Who is the Church?," 326–29; Miller, "Sacramental Theology of Balthasar," 55; Peelman, "Théologie pour la mission," 123.

In fact the church's missionary orientation is "in accord with her inner con-stitution—that is, not in a merely accidental way."[45]

Clearly then, there is a caesura in place when it comes to the church's mission. And yet, it is equally clear that Balthasar sees this caesura as over-come. In this section, I trace out how it is overcome, demonstrating that the Eucharist is the decisive link. Doing so will allow me to offer a final, synthetic account of the shape of Balthasar's missionary ecclesiology.

Free Response and a Share in Christ

The creature's free response to the Creator is a major emphasis of Balthasar's theology. It is this that above all drives his consideration of the Marian *fiat* and the Immaculate Conception, which, for the Roman Catholic Balthasar, renders it possible.[46] It is no accident that Mary's assent to the advent of grace in the blessed fruit of her womb is foundational to Balthasar's eccle-siological vision.[47] The importance of creaturely response owes primarily to the fact that humanity is created within the event of the Son's eternal generation, the movement of which is completed by the Eucharistic return-gift. Ontologically grounded in this dynamic, the creature, in its innermost being, ought to freely and joyfully respond to its creator. It is the failure of this response, the "knot" in the eternal Eucharist, that Christ comes to remedy.

In remedying this failure to return the gift, though, Christ cannot sim-ply *replace* the creature, for that would only compound the problem, leaving humanity out of the movement which constitutes its very being. "God does not step onto the stage to show contempt for his vanquished opponent. In an action that man [sic] could never have anticipated, he steps to his op-ponent's side and, from within, helps him to reach justice and freedom."[48] The response *must* be genuinely the creature's. In *Theo-Drama* 4, Balthasar notes five motifs, all of which must be given proper weight in an adequately dramatic soteriology. The third is the theme of redemption, of human-

---

45. Balthasar, *Theo-Drama* 3:435.

46. Balthasar, *Glory of the Lord* 7:60–64, 93–94.

47. Balthasar, *Glory of the Lord* 7:475–76; *Theo-Drama* 4:351–61, 394–400. See also Oakes, *Pattern of Redemption*, 252–54; Chapp, "Who is the Church?," 336; Casarella, "*Analogia Donationis*," 152; Kereszty, "Eucharist and Mission," 7; Koerpel, "Mary, Peter, Eucharist," 82–88.

48. Balthasar, *Theo-Drama* 4:201.

ity's liberation, which in its very nature demands that there be a genuinely human response. If one is set free, but that freedom is not operative, then in what sense has a liberation occurred?[49] So the creature must respond freely and in a genuinely creaturely way. How, though, is this achieved?

A partial answer has been sketched already: Christ enters into the creation in order to restore his own eternal Eucharistic dynamic (the dynamic in which creation lives and moves and has its being). So we are brought into Christ's own filial relationship.[50] Christ becomes what we are—sin, death, and alienation from God—so that we might now become what we are in him.[51] This recalls the principle above that the creature's identity in mission occurs "within the mission of Christ." [52] The original Trinitarian "distance" between the Father and the Son, prevents us from being obliterated or swallowed up into the giver when this gift is given.[53] So, the condition of possibility for genuine creaturely response is in the Son's generation. However, this alone does not suffice to account for that response. It is distinctly the role of the Holy Spirit to bring about this creaturely response, which occurs as we are given a share in Christ. The Spirit brings the work of the Son *extra nos* into us, making the possibility accomplished by Christ a reality for us.[54] He "makes the life of love well up, not in front of us nor above us, but in us, and thereby empowers us to 'glorify' through our life the glory that has been given to us *as our own*."[55]

Perhaps the clearest explanation of the principle comes in Balthasar's frequently used image of the vine and branches from John 15:

> The vine needs the grapes as its organs if it is to bear fruit; nonetheless it has produced them itself and saturated them with its own juices, thus enabling them to reach the desired condition . . . The branch's fruitfulness is indivisibly twofold: on the one hand, it is its *own* fruitfulness; but, on the other, it is a fruitfulness that has been given to it, entrusted to it.[56]

49. Balthasar, *Theo-Drama* 4:317–19.

50. Balthasar, *Glory of the Lord* 7:311–12, 405. This, by the way, is the fourth of Balthasar's soteriological criteria: inclusion in the divine life (*Theo-Drama* 4:317).

51. Balthasar, *Glory of the Lord* 7:395. This is the second of the soteriological criteria: the exchange of places (*Theo-Drama* 4:317).

52. Balthasar, *Theo-Drama* 4:62.

53. Balthasar, *Glory of the Lord* 7:396.

54. Balthasar, *Glory of the Lord* 7:390–91.

55. Balthasar, *Glory of the Lord* 7:389 (emphasis mine).

56. Balthasar, *Theo-Drama* 4:410 (emphasis original).

The relationship is intrinsic, then. The image allows Balthasar to envision us as forming a "single principle of fruit" together with Christ.[57] So then Christians' fruitful responses are at once and equally the work of Christ and of the individual. There is a certain asymmetry—the branch cannot produce grapes without the vine—but this asymmetry does not obliterate the equality just disclosed. The point of the image is to highlight both.

All of this only gives part of the picture, though. For it is not just fruitfulness that is produced, but rather a Christic fruitfulness. That believers are made actors in Christ means that it is the Christ form that is reproduced in them as the free response proceeding from their inmost depths. Humanity now "enjoys an inner participation in the attitude of divine selflessness," sharing in Christ's poverty.[58] Christ was perfectly transparent to the Father, and the church is conformed particularly to this.[59] "The form of the church is transparent to the very form of God's self-disclosure in the person of Jesus Christ."[60] Which means that the church has no form of her own.[61] However, as Chapp notes, it is because of the church's formlessness that "everything that Christ manifests to the world can also be manifested by the church."[62]

Eucharist as Cross

Thus far, I have dealt mainly with creaturely response in general, with references to the church qua church here and there. This is justified for two related reasons: first, both the church and the individual believer are formed inwardly by the Christ form; second, Mary's *fiat*, which itself shares in the Christ form, stands at the headwaters of both generic creaturely response and ecclesiology. It might also be noted that the faithful, as the *congregatio fidelium*, are an indispensable component of the church. Now, though, it is time to consider the church more explicitly.

Above I noted that the free creaturely response occurs as Christ's inward disposition (which is dispossession) becomes one's own. This is heightened when we recognize that even one's reception of God is dispossessive:

57. Balthasar, *Glory of the Lord* 7:420.

58. Balthasar, *Glory of the Lord* 7:429.

59. Balthasar, *Glory of the Lord* 7:96–97, 290–93.

60. Casarella, "*Analogia Donationis*," 150.

61. Chapp, "Who is the Church?," 323.

62. Chapp, "Who is the Church?," 323.

it is "Appropriation as Expropriation."[63] And the individual is expropriated into the church specifically by baptism and the Eucharist.[64] "The church's own form" is given sacramentally: "baptism *is* a conforming to the death and Resurrection of Christ . . . The Eucharist *is* the expropriation of the individual into the fellowship."[65] Reception is expropriation for two reasons: first, because faith is itself a passive reception of the act of God; second, because it is in the fellowship of the church that Christian identity is found. Therefore, in coming to faith we find an "expropriation of our privacy," we now belong to this community in a fundamental way.[66]

The passive, receptive character of faith is highlighted in the receptivity of the sacraments and the primacy of ecclesial faith, within which individual faith is always included.[67] The church itself, born through Christ's wounded side in the issue of water and blood, is instituted by the Cross-Eucharist, and "is only called into life when Jesus implants himself into her in the *triduum mortis et resurrectionis*."[68] So then, Jesus' self-gift in the Eucharist Cross corresponds to the *opus operatum*, while the church's response to this gift and ratifying reception of it corresponds to the *opus operantis*, though it must be noted that for Balthasar these two remain inseparable.[69]

When it comes to the *opus operantis* of the church's response, once more passivity is the distinguishing mark, and once more Mary is the exemplar. The church's Eucharistic sacrifice is not foreign to her, but rather intrinsic, because it consists primarily in the sort of passive acquiescence we have been noting.[70] Mary, at the foot of the cross, acquiesces to her Son's suffering, and it is by this acquiescence that she becomes fecund with the

---

63. Balthasar, *Glory of the Lord* 7:400. The phrase "Appropriation as Expropriation" is found on 399. Noted also in Peelman, "Théologie pour la mission," 137.

64. Balthasar, *Glory of the Lord* 7:312, 405.

65. Balthasar, *Glory of the Lord* 7:506 (emphasis original).

66. Balthasar, *Glory of the Lord* 7:400, 403 [403].

67. Balthasar, *Glory of the Lord* 7:306, 404–5.

68. Balthasar, *Theo-Drama* 3:426. See further *Glory of the Lord* 2:174. See also Peelman, "Théologie pour la mission," 140–41; Koerpel, "Mary, Peter, Eucharist," 71, 91; Casarella, "*Analogia Donationis*," 153.

69. Balthasar, *Theo-Drama* 3:429–30. On the inseparability of the two see *Glory of the Lord*, 2:175.

70. Noted by Howsare, "Eucharist as Sacrifice," 278–79; Bründl, "Braucht Gott Opfer?," 524–25.

seed of the Eucharist.[71] In her assent, the community's passive assent has already been perfectly realized.[72] And because Christ had previously handed himself over to Mary, being conceived in her womb, nursed at her breast, and raised under her care, he is able to hand himself over to the church for the Eucharistic action.[73] However, this action is only possible on the basis of the objective work already accomplished by Christ. Sacrifice is made possible by a previous communion. The *opus operantis* depends upon the *opus operatum*.[74]

This last point is reminiscent of the vine and branches imagery explored above. There is an asymmetry, but also an equality. Even the vine image involves a double expropriation: "first . . . when God lays claim to him as a field for his seed, and a second time, when the fruit that is borne is taken from him so that it might be brought into God's granary."[75] Christ alone is the redeemer. However, he includes his body in his work, "and this becomes more fruitful the more a member conforms itself to the selflessness that is Christ's disposition, and the less he exercises reserve in putting his existence at the service of universal redemption."[76] One's "bearing of fruit is not for oneself: it is for the kingdom of God."[77]

Missionary Identity

The kenotic mission of Christ produces the church's own free response, which conforms to that dispossession. This is realized in the Eucharist, which itself is interior to the Cross, and completes the latter's kenotic logic in the distribution of Christ's flesh and blood for the life of the world. In her reception of this life-giving work of Christ, the church is inwardly conformed to his form, which enables the bearing of fruit. And this fruit is itself expropriated, put at the service of Christ's redemptive work. Just as the Incarnation reaches its completion in the Eucharistic distribution, the church's response is not for herself, but for others. With this recognition,

71. Balthasar, *Theo-Drama* 4:360–61. See also Balthasar, "Eucharistic Sacrifice," 143–45.

72. Balthasar, *Theo-Drama* 4:395–98.

73. Balthasar, *Theo-Drama* 4:396–99.

74. Balthasar, *Theo-Drama* 4:394–95, 402–5.

75. Balthasar, *Glory of the Lord* 7:420.

76. Balthasar, *Glory of the Lord* 7:465.

77. Balthasar, *Theo-Drama* 4:388.

we are prepared to discuss the church's identity in mission and the shape of that mission.

Just as Jesus does not exist for himself, but for the world he was sent to redeem, so the church does not exist for herself but for that same world.[78] "The church has a form only so that she may transcend herself ever afresh and give the world transcendent form."[79] This transcendence is "in accord with her inner constitution—that is, not in a merely accidental way . . . her goal is the entire human world."[80] Balthasar contrasts this particularly with the centripetal mission of Israel and the synagogue. In contrast, the church's mission is self-transcending and centrifugal.[81] While Israel had a stable center of Land, Law, and Temple, the church lacks these things. Instead, the world is her altar, a point which Balthasar draws from Paul's liturgical description of his own ministry in Romans 15:15–16.[82] The liturgy is intrinsically connected with mission: "There is no hiatus between worship and service."[83] Indeed, all of life is meant to be liturgy.[84]

"The Woman [i.e., the church, see Rev 12:13–17] remains utopian and without form [Gestalt]: the 'place' God has provided for her cannot be found on earth, just as her true face cannot be seen."[85] Christ's entrance into the world has brought about an "immense movement . . . between the presence of the eschaton and its future, and this movement is the church, which essentially is an institution that never rests for a single moment but must always be breaking off and setting out."[86] The church has no place of its own. It lacks any stable center, save Christ himself, who carries it along as part of his movement into the world. As Matthew Miller observes, "the church exists in mediating Christ."[87] And this mediation occurs in via, in the church's missionary engagement with the world.

---

78. Note the way that all of this mirrors the Father's determination to "not be God for himself alone," but instead to generate the Son. Balthasar, Theo-Drama 4:324.

79. Balthasar, Glory of the Lord 2:486.

80. Balthasar, Theo-Drama 3:435. So also Mysterium Paschale, 263.

81. Balthasar, Theo-Drama 3:405–6, 435; Theo-Drama 4:464.

82. Balthasar, Glory of the Lord 7:488–89.

83. Balthasar, Theo-Drama 2:35.

84. Balthasar, Prayer, 119–23.

85. Balthasar, Theo-Drama 4:448 (bracketed German original; the other brackets are mine).

86. Balthasar, Glory of the Lord 2:485.

87. Miller, "Sacramental Theology of Balthasar," 55.

Church as Utopia[88]

With all these pieces in place, a distinctive picture of the church's mission emerges. "The goal of the church is to make herself superfluous," writes Balthasar.[89] Grace leads to mission, which involves sociality, sharing, and self-distribution.[90] The church's mission, then is kenotic, dispossessive, and Eucharistic. It must be because it is the extension of Christ's mission, which was all these things. While others have noted the intrinsic connection between Eucharist and mission, little attention has been given to this mission's radically kenotic shape. Instead, the focus has been upon sharing in Christ's work of returning the Eucharistically transformed cosmos to God.[91] This is not wrong, but it does miss a significant component of the church's identity in mission, which I have just delineated. In this section, then, I synthesize Balthasar's account of the church's dispossessive mission and put it into conversation with Nathan R. Kerr's apocalyptically missional account of the church's essence.

Kerr's Ecclesiology of Apocalyptic Rupture

Nathan Kerr's recent *Christ, History and Apocalyptic: The Politics of Christian Mission* stands as a challenge to all notions of stability in ecclesiology. Drawing from the apocalypticism of J. Louis Martyn, Kerr offers trenchant critiques of Ernst Troeltsch, the later Barth, and Stanley Hauerwas as all too easily captivated by ideology in their accounts of the church's mission.[92] Having offered these criticisms, Kerr turns to the constructive task, arguing that "our own participation in the politics of Jesus emerges as a *missionary* politics of liturgical *encounter* with the world."[93] This involves two primary moves: first is the turn from ideology to doxology, the latter of which refers to the prioritization of the reign of God, divine initiative, patterning of the

---

88. I intend "utopia" in the sense of *ou-topos* (without a place), rather than in the sense of *eu-topos* (a good place).

89. Balthasar, *Glory of the Lord* 7:506.

90. Balthasar, *Theo-Drama* 3:350.

91. Healy and Schindler, "Balthasar on Church as Eucharist," 51–63; Kereszty, "Eucharist and Mission," 3–15.

92. Kerr, *Christ, History and Apocalyptic*, 23–126.

93. Ibid., 161 (emphasis original).

self and church according to the cross, submission to the sole lordship of Jesus Christ, and dependence upon the Holy Spirit's work.[94] So far there are obvious continuities between Kerr's concerns and Balthasar's project.

The second move is "From 'church-as-*Polis*' to 'Mission Makes the church.'"[95] While at first blush, this might seem to work rather nicely with the Balthasarian notion of the church's identity in mission, Kerr's understanding diverges significantly from Balthasar's. What drives him in this shift are his "worries . . . with the political *ontologization* of the church, on the one hand, and a concomitant *instrumentalization* of worship, on the other hand."[96] Ontologizing the church, granting it a givenness, a "solid, stable 'centre,'" runs the twofold risk of "intensifying the Christian community's concern for its own interior *identity* overagainst [sic] the world," and of necessitating so much focus on the church's own internal dynamics that "its engagement with the world cannot help but be conceived in a subsidiary and conjunctive way."[97] It is precisely this that leads, in Kerr's opinion, to an instrumentalized notion of worship. Worship is now for counter-formation, serving the internal culture of the church. It leads to an understanding of "ecclesiological . . . 'gathering' that occurs *in advance of* encounter with 'the world.'"[98]

Instead of this, Kerr contends that the church's identity ought to arise precisely in its engagement with the world. Abstracting a prior moment for the church to be the church apart from missionary engagement will invariably lead to a domestication of Christ and the Spirit and a demotion of mission from the church's constitutive center.[99] To avoid this, Kerr insists that church must be modeled upon the diasporic dispossession of exilic Judaism (the original seedbed of apocalyptic thought).[100] The church occurs in the irruptive singularity of Christ's mission to the world, particularly as the people called church find themselves in engagement with the poor and marginalized.[101]

---

94. Ibid., 162–67.

95. Ibid., 169.

96. Ibid., 169 (emphasis original).

97. Ibid., 170–71.

98. Ibid., 171–73 [173].

99. Ibid., 175, 189.

100. Ibid., 181–88.

101. Ibid., 190–96.

Balthasar's Utopian Ecclesiology

As should be clear from my analysis of the constitutive character of the church's mission and especially the dispossessive nature of that mission, there is much in Kerr's project that Balthasar could have affirmed. The church does indeed lack her own form, her own place, her own telos. The church exists to transcend herself, even to lose herself in Eucharistic self-distribution to the world because the Christ form, which reaches its fullest expression in the Cross-Eucharist, forms her inmost reality. Indeed, even the church's unity is not her own, but is solely "in Christ . . . Only by carrying out this commission [to engage the world in Christ's mission] does she actually realize her unity."[102] So the church is not complete, is not herself, apart from missionary engagement. She exists *in her mission*, as the "movement . . . that never rests for a single moment, but must always be breaking off and setting out."[103] With Good Friday and Holy Saturday at her center, "the church can only be the 'tent' of a wandering people, a tent that is continually folded up anew, in order to be erected anew somewhere else."[104] The church is continually handing herself over, an act "that leaves the church no time to reflect upon herself."[105]

Where Balthasar differs strongly from Kerr is in his insistence that there be some respect in which the church is "over against the world." This is required, though, not as a prior moment for the church to be herself apart from missionary engagement, but rather in order for the church to be able to fulfill her missionary vocation. The church needs "to be able to address the world," and it is this mandate of addressing the world that requires the over-against-ness. Further, such positioning must be "without for a moment abandoning solidarity with that aim of her mission, viz. the world she is addressing."[106] Moreover, Balthasar sees the church's mission not simply in her external actions, but rather in a dialectic between her being built up and her missionary self-transcendence:

> To divorce the church's transcendence or her missionary thrust
> from her immanence or from the inner structure of the Body of
> Christ . . . is to fail to grasp that the church has no other mission

---

102. Balthasar, *Theo-Drama* 3:422.
103. Balthasar, *Glory of the Lord* 7:486.
104. Balthasar, *Glory of the Lord* 7:541.
105. Balthasar, *Glory of the Lord* 7:506.
106. Balthasar, *Glory of the Lord* 7:507.

but that which she has received from Christ, who is himself sent by the Father; she can only carry out her mission by receiving and assimilating the *pneuma* of Christ ever more profoundly. And it is through living out the mystery of her inner life that she assimilates the Spirit of Christ: through dying and rising with Christ; through a prayerful and contemplative listening to his word (like the listening Mary as compared with the busy Martha); through the believing, 'discerning' (I Cor 11:29) performance of the sacraments, most of all the Eucharist; and through the building up of the Body of Christ in selfless and mutual love, putting others' concerns and needs before one's own.[107]

In this situating the church over against the world and in granting a certain priority to the liturgical and sacramental has Balthasar either (1) taken with one hand what he has given with the other in terms of identity in mission, or (2) fallen prey to Kerr's critiques of ideology? I contend that the answer to both questions is *No*. With regard to Balthasar's consistency vis-à-vis the church's identity in mission, we must note two related items. First, as I pointed out, these moves are motivated not by a desire to abstract from the church's mission (a move that Balthasar explicitly disallows), but rather by a desire to serve the church's mission. Both the over-against-ness and the liturgical priority are there precisely for and as components of the church's mission. Second, identity in mission is not native to creatures.[108] Instead, it is bestowed in the Eucharistic action through Christ in the Spirit. In that light, then, Balthasar's moves in this regard are actually in service to the "singularity" of Christ.

How, then, do we conceptualize this relationship between internal and external movement, between liturgy and mission, in Balthasar's account of the church? I suggest that a hermeneutical circle may be the best metaphor for the dynamic. In order to engage a text, one must indeed engage with it. And yet, in one's engagement one must constantly be refining one's interpretation, particularly the prejudices with which one is always already laden in one's encounter with the text. The reflection by which one refines one's interpretation is not somehow prior to or separate from one's

107. Balthasar, *Theo-Drama* 3:435–36. Similarly in *Love Alone*, Balthasar writes against the view that Christians "only encounter Christ in their neighbor" that "they soon cease to be able to draw any distinction between worldly responsibility and the Christian mission. No one who does not know God in contemplation can recognize him in action" (89).

108. Balthasar, *Theo-Drama* 3:263–71.

act of interpretation, but rather belongs to that very act. In a similar way, the over-against-ness and the liturgical enactment belong to the event of missionary engagement. They should not be occurring in a state somehow prior to or separate from engagement with the world, but are rather part of that movement itself.

This, then, answers the second question raised above: whether Balthasar's moves in this regard fall prey to Kerr's critique of ideology. The understanding of liturgical priority from which Kerr demurs is one according to which this priority is somehow above, separate from, or prior to missionary engagement. That is not Balthasar's understanding, though. There is "no hiatus between worship and service,"[109] and the liturgy is not "an opportunity for 'refueling.'"[110] Priority does not equal *prior to*. Whether or not this understanding of the relation between the church's internal life and her mission *ad extra* has been consistently adhered to or put into practice is another matter, but clearly Balthasar is up to something different than what Kerr fears. And the way in which Balthasar does this turns the question back upon ecclesiologies like Kerr's: how, apart from something akin to Balthasar's hermeneutical circle of mission and liturgy, can they guarantee that their engagement with the world is Christian mission, in conformity to the form of the cross, and not itself captive to some worldly ideology? The answer is not immediately clear.

Conclusion

According to Hans Urs von Balthasar, the mission of the church is rooted in the mission of Christ, which is rooted in his eternal generation and finds its highest expression and inmost form in the event of the cross and the Eucharistic self-distribution. In Christ, identity and mission coinhere. He *is* the one who receives all that he is and has from the Father and who gives himself up in dispossession for the life of the world. As Christ's mission was constitutive of his identity, so is the church's, though in a derivative manner. Moreover, the church's mission is itself determined by the dispossessive logic of the Christ form and realized in the reception of that form in the Eucharist. This dispossession for the life of the world, then, *is* also what the church is.

---

109. Balthasar, *Theo-Drama* 2:35.
110. Balthasar, *Love Alone*, 89.

My treatment of the church's identity in mission has made more explicit what has often been muted in other treatments of ecclesial mission in Balthasar: namely its dispossessive and expropriated character. It is not just that the church exists in her mission, but that the form of her mission is the formless transparency to the divine love that characterized Christ's own mission. This, then, calls for greater humility on the part of the church in cultural engagement. She offers not herself, but Christ.

Engagement with the apocalypticism of Nathan Kerr has helped to refine our understanding of Balthasar's account of identity in mission. The liturgical priority Balthasar posits and insists upon must not be seen as in any way separate from or prior to the church's missionary encounter with the world. Rather, it functions like a hermeneutical circle, always itself part of the church's missionary dynamism. This is, I am convinced, Balthasar's intention, but this precise articulation of the relationship emerges through engagement of Kerr's concerns and critiques, and needs to be taken into greater account in our conceptions of liturgy and mission.

Finally, by interfacing Balthasar and Kerr, an important concern for "missional" ecclesiologies emerges. It is all well and good to posit the church's existence as arising precisely in her encounter with the world. However, apart from the hermeneutical circle proposed by Balthasar—apart from some over-against-ness of the church and some priority of internal life—it seems all too easy for such missionally-arising churches to themselves be swallowed up by whatever prevailing ideologies they encounter in the world. This need not mean that the missional theologians adopt Balthasar's formulations, but some account of this is needed, and I, for one, find Balthasar's persuasive. Moreover, the fact that Balthasar's understanding of the church avoids the pitfalls enumerated by Kerr, while also maintaining the elements missional theology has thought must be dispensed with, indicates that in the future missional ecclesiologies ought to take much greater account of Balthasar's contributions.

"Christ Clothed with His Gospel"

Apostolicity and the Deposit of Faith in the Thought of T. F. Torrance

–Joel Scandrett

I want to frame this chapter with some beginning and concluding observations about the significance of the apostolic character of the church for American Evangelical theology—or at least for one important movement within American Evangelical theology. For anyone who has been paying attention over the last few decades, these observations will come as no surprise. But people often are not paying attention, or at least not attending to the greater import of certain developments. Consequently, I think it will be helpful to begin with a brief survey of the recent historical-theological landscape, in order to locate the discussion of apostolicity within that landscape.

We can observe a distinct movement within Evangelical theology in the last several decades: a movement that has increasingly acknowledged the *ecclesial* character of the Christian faith, and increasingly emphasized the *unity and continuity* of the Christian ecclesial tradition. While this movement has been decades in the making, its more recent growth has been substantial, and is broadly demonstrated by a marked surge of interest in early Christian literature,[1] an increase in the use of liturgical forms in Evangelical worship,[2] a burgeoning interest among younger Evangelicals

---

1. Strikingly evinced by the success of InterVarsity Press's Ancient Christian Commentary on Scripture. Other projects of similar emphasis include the Evangelical Ressourcement series by Baker Academic and The Church's Bible by Eerdmans, as well as an increasing number of monographs in patristic theology.

2. Among those directly involved in the liturgical aspects of this movement, Robert Webber may be the most widely recognized. See, e.g., *Worship is a Verb* and *Worship*

in liturgical and sacramental traditions,[3] and recent key developments among Evangelicals working in the theological disciplines.

This movement first gained a modest foothold in mainstream American Evangelical theology in the 1970s and 1980s. The late Robert Webber and Methodist theologian Thomas Oden were key figures among others[4] who called Evangelicals to greater awareness of the unity, holiness, catholicity, and apostolicity of the church. Webber published and taught Evangelicals in this vein, especially at the popular level, until his death in 2007. Most popular perhaps is his 1985 *Evangelicals on the Canterbury Trail*,[5] and most notable perhaps is his more recent Ancient-Future series published by Baker.

Also in the 1970s, Thomas Oden turned his back on the Bultmannian-Tillichian synthesis of his earlier years and embraced the ancient theological consensus of creedal Christianity. Out of this conversion, Oden wrote his 1979 *Agenda for Theology*, later revised and retitled *After Modernity, What?*, which called theologians out of their modernist presumptions and back to the classic roots of Christian theological consensus. Oden subsequently published his three-volume systematic theology composed mostly of patristic sources and broadly organized around the Nicene Creed. On the heels of that work, he launched the twenty-nine-volume Ancient Christian Commentary on Scripture, and continues to work at present to reintroduce patristic thought to the churches of Africa through the Center for Early African Christianity, now housed at Yale University. Followed by younger Evangelical scholars such as Jeffrey Bingham, Donald Fairbairn, Christopher Hall, George Kalantzis, Daniel Williams, and behind them a veritable generation of younger Evangelical patristics scholars, Thomas Oden has been a pioneer of patristic retrieval among American Evangelicals.

In addition to these leading proponents, we see other correlative Evangelical developments in subsequent decades. These include the Evangelicals and Catholics Together initiative of Charles Colson and Richard John Neuhaus, which recently marked its twentieth year of ongoing ecumenical

---

Old and New.

3. See, e.g., Webber, *The Younger Evangelicals*; and Carroll, *The New Faithful.*

4. E.g., Howard, *Evangelical Is Not Enough.*

5. Now revised and updated: Webber and Ruth, *Evangelicals on the Canterbury Trail.*

dialogue, and has featured such Evangelical heavyweights as Gerald Bray, Timothy George, Mark Noll, Richard Mouw, Thomas Oden, and J. I. Packer.

On the Packer note, the important contributions of three Vancouverites are also worthy of mention. The work of the late Stanley Grenz was characterized by a deep ecclesial orientation that sought to recover the centrality of the community of God.[6] The ongoing work of Hans Boersma is focused on the *ressourcement* of a sacramental theology informed by a Platonist-Christian sacramental ontology under the impress of the *nouvelle théologie*, and calling Evangelicals to reclaim participation in a re-sacramentalized ecclesiology.[7] Somewhere between Stanley Grenz and Hans Boersma falls the recent work by Packer calling Evangelicals to recover the ancient church's practice and pattern of catechesis.[8]

Several more recent developments in Evangelical theology are worth highlighting. In biblical theology, the recent work of Evangelicals in the theological interpretation of Scripture looks to recover Christocentric, canonical, and figural hermeneutics that are in continuity with patristic and medieval approaches. In dogmatic theology, the recent resurgence in Reformed circles of the primacy of the doctrine of union with Christ certainly carries profound ecclesiological implications. And in philosophical theology, the recent work of James K. A. Smith[9] in recovering the inherently liturgical character of Christian life and formation is evocative of Webber's earlier popular work, while constructively speaking to the necessity of ecclesial life in relation to postmodernity. These recent developments, as well as their antecedents, might well be typified by the title of a recent book from Baker Academic written by Michael Allen and Scott Swain, *Reformed Catholicity: The Promise of Retrieval for Theology and Biblical Interpretation.*

We could adduce other examples, but these are sufficient to identify what has clearly become an ecclesially-oriented movement among a subset of American Evangelicals. The question is: what does it mean? How are we to understand it? And what does it portend for the future? As a historical theologian and participant in many of these developments, these are my recurring questions. While this movement is to my mind a work of the Holy Spirit, that answer alone lacks sufficient explanatory specificity.

---

6. See, e.g., Grenz, *Theology for the Community of God.*

7. See, e.g., Boersma, *Heavenly Participation.*

8. Packer and Parrett, *Grounded in the Gospel.*

9. See, e.g., Smith, *Desiring the Kingdom.*

We could look to antecedent influences in the twentieth century, especially the ecumenical movement of the early and mid-century, as well as the Second Vatican Council and its aftermath. These certainly are prominent features of the historical-theological terrain in view. We could identify the influence of ecclesially-minded non-Evangelical thinkers, such as Alasdair MacIntyre and Stanley Hauerwas. We could also understand this movement as one outcome, theologically speaking, of what Donald Dayton calls the "*embourgeoisement* of American evangelicalism," whereby Evangelicals have moved in increasing numbers into institutions of higher theological learning and come under the influence of Roman Catholic, Orthodox, and ecumenically-oriented Protestant theologies.[10]

All of these influences are likely required to answer the question, but none of them is sufficient to explain why Evangelicals appear to be compelled in increasing numbers in this ecclesiocentric direction, both at the popular and scholarly levels. What is the ingredient in these approaches that especially younger Evangelicals find missing in their own Evangelical heritage?

I have for some time now found the thought of Thomas Forsyth Torrance to be especially helpful in thinking through these matters. I have found Torrance's understanding of apostolicity to be of particular value in fundamental matters of ecclesiology, as well as in providing a helpful theological paradigm for understanding and framing this ecclesial Evangelical trend. I am inclined, à la Torrance, to believe that it is *the rediscovery by Evangelicals of the inherently apostolic character of the Christian faith* that lies, at least in part, behind these developments.

T. F. Torrance is widely considered the most important English-speaking theologian of the latter half of the twentieth century. Ecumenical theologian George Hunsinger considers Torrance the single most significant contributor to Nicene Christianity in that period, and considers Torrance's *The Trinitarian Faith: The Evangelical Theology of the Ancient Catholic Church* to be the most important work in theology of the last twenty-five years.[11] Torrance was a massively important figure for ecumenical theology in the twentieth century, and especially for his work with Georges Florovsky in spearheading dialogue between Reformed and Orthodox churches.

---

10. Dayton, "The *Embourgeoisement* of a Vision." See also the Marsden-Dayton debate in *Christian Scholars Review* 23.1 (1993), and Dayton and Johnson, eds., *The Variety of American Evangelicalism.*

11. Hunsinger, "5 Picks."

(For those interested in any ecumenical consideration of the *filioque*, Torrance's work on this issue is paramount.[12]) Torrance was also a leading figure in ecumenical efforts between his own Reformed tradition and Roman Catholics, Lutherans, and Anglicans.

Torrance was also a leading figure in the relationship between theology and science. Engaging the work of Albert Einstein, James Clerk Maxwell, Michael Polanyi, and others, Torrance sought to frame a constructive theology grounded in a unified understanding of reality that would overcome the modern divide between science and theology. Alister McGrath's work in this area is highly dependent upon Torrance, whom McGrath acknowledges as being of landmark significance for any subsequent efforts in this direction.[13]

While, on the surface, Torrance's efforts in theology and science may appear unrelated to his work in ecumenical theology, they are entirely of a piece at the foundational level. This is because Torrance is fundamentally committed to a *critical theological realism*, which undergirds everything he does as a theologian. In both arenas, as well as all his other theological endeavors, Torrance sought to identify the essential nature of the reality of God in light of the biblical witness of God's self-revelation in Christ, and to allow the objective features of that reality to form and inform his thought as a dogmatic and constructive theologian. In doing so, he sought persistently to move beneath, as it were, the competing doctrinal systems, especially of the Western theological tradition, in order to identify and delineate the basic ontological structures of the reality of God and of God's saving economy. He does this both in order to identify the proper ontological ground of all Christian theology, and to identify an actual, real basis from which to adjudicate and resolve matters of doctrinal dispute. Torrance's theological realism is therefore both a fundamental epistemological and theological conviction that informs the entirety of his work. So, says Torrance:

> In objective knowledge the realities we seek to know inevitably break through any frame of concepts and statements which we use to describe them even though they are developed under the constraints of those realities. Concepts and statements of this kind do not have their truth in themselves but in the realities to which they refer. Hence if we are to do justice to the integrity and nature of the objects of our knowledge we must discriminate them from our

12. See especially Torrance, *Christian Doctrine of God*, 168–202.
13. McGrath, *Science of God*, 26.

knowing of them, and let them confer relativity upon our concepts and statements about them.[14]

This critical theological realism is a relentless commitment of Torrance: that all doctrinal statements and concepts must, if they are to remain faithful to God's self-revelation, be submitted and remain open to the divine realities which they purport to represent. Otherwise, they become captive to delimited and self-referential systems of thought that may fundamentally distort our understanding of those realities. Torrance finds this sort of theological realism richly evident in the early Eastern Christian theological tradition. He finds especially in the theologies of Irenaeus, Athanasius, and Cyril of Alexandria an axis of theological realism that remains unparalleled in the subsequent thought of both Eastern and Western traditions—with the possible exception of Karl Barth. It is from this vantage point of a theological realism rooted in Scripture and informed by the Eastern theological tradition that Torrance develops his understanding of the apostolic character of the Christian church and of the Christian faith.

Torrance's understanding of the church is perhaps best summed up in the following statement:

> One of the immense gains of the second Vatican Council was the recovery of the Greek patristic insight that the Church is *grounded beyond itself in the divine-human nature of Christ* and through Christ *in the transcendent communion of the Holy Trinity*, from which it derives its essential intelligible structure to which all its visible institutional structures in this world are subordinate.[15]

Thus for Torrance, "the Church is grounded in the Being and Life of God, and rooted in the eternal purpose of the Father to send his Son, Jesus Christ, to be the Head and Savior of all things." This means, on the one hand, that "the Church does not derive from below but from above," yet on the other hand, that the church "does not exist apart from the people that make up its membership." Rather, says Torrance, "Jesus Christ through the Spirit dwells in the midst of the Church on earth, making it His own Body or His earthly and historical form of existence."[16]

Torrance thereby insists that the church is a creation of God in history, mysteriously yet truly rooted in the Being of God through the reality of

14. Torrance, "Deposit of Faith," 1.

15. Torrance, *Theology in Reconciliation*, 64 (emphasis added).

16. Torrance, *Theology in Reconstruction*, 192–93.

the Incarnation and Christ's ongoing indwelling of the church by the Holy Spirit. At the same time and indeed by virtue of this very reality, he also insists that the empirical, visible church *is* the Body of Christ on earth—"His earthly and historical form of existence." Thus, says Paul Molnar:

> Torrance's view of the church . . . is at once ecumenically and theologically grounded in such a way that he is able to stress how the church is the visible presence of Christ on earth and in history, while at the same time avoiding any idea which would reduce the church's reality to its institutional structures.[17]

Such a perspective undercuts on the one hand any notion of a merely invisible church as a disembodied, spiritual reality, while on the other hand undercutting a merely sociological or anthropological approach to the church—as if the church were simply another human institutional aggregate of like-minded individuals. Unfortunately, much of Evangelical practical ecclesiology employs both of these concepts separately yet in parallel—in effect, a sort of Docetic ecclesiology. However, neither view does justice to the reality of Christ's real, personal presence in the empirical church. Says Torrance:

> For Nicene ecclesiology the focus of attention was on the incorporation of believers into the Body of Christ on the ground of the reconciliation with God which he had accomplished in and through his bodily resurrection. That is to say, it was precisely the visible, empirical Church in space and time that was held to be the Body of Christ . . . [A]ny failure to grasp the implications of this Nicene theology for a realist and unitary doctrine of the Church, opened the door for the identification of the real Church with a spiritualised, timeless, and spaceless magnitude, and for the ongoing life and mission of the empirical Church to be subject to the laws that control human society in this world. In other words, it would . . . inevitably entangle the Church in a distinction between a juridical Society on the one hand, and a mystical body on the other hand, but that would involve the rejection of the doctrine that through the sanctifying and renewing presence of the Holy Spirit, *the empirical Church is the Body of Christ.* Thus Nicene theology became strengthened in its belief that 'the reality of the Church is the earthly-historical form of the existence of Jesus Christ, the one holy, catholic, and apostolic Church.'[18]

17. Molnar, *Thomas F. Torrance*, 265.

18. Torrance, *Trinitarian Faith*, 276 (emphasis original). Torrance here quotes Karl

In light of this understanding of the church, what for Torrance does it mean to affirm the apostolic character of the church and of the Christian faith? Most simply put, of course, the apostolic faith is the faith of the apostles. But in light of Torrance's realist understanding of the ontological foundation of the church in Jesus Christ, this statement requires explanation.

Key to Torrance's approach is the early Christian understanding of the church's "relation to 'the Faith once for all delivered to the saints' (Jude 3), that is, to the original *datum* of divine Revelation in Jesus Christ and his Gospel."[19] The early church understood itself as having been entrusted with a sacred deposit (*paratheke, parakatatheke, depositum*; 2 Tim 1:14, etc.) given by Christ himself to the apostles, which it was to guard and to pass on to subsequent generations of faithful people.

What is that deposit? In keeping with his fundamental commitment to the ontological ground of the church's life in the person of Jesus Christ through history, Torrance is quick to insist that the apostolic deposit of faith cannot be reduced to anything less than *the actual object of the apostles' faith—our Lord Jesus Christ*:

> 'The Deposit of Faith,' as it came to be called, is to be understood as the whole living Fact of Christ and his saving Acts in the indivisible unity of his Person, Word and Life, as through the Resurrection and Pentecost he fulfilled and unfolded the content of his self-revelation as Saviour and Lord within his Church.[20]

Thus Torrance identifies the deposit of faith as the whole united reality of Jesus Christ together with his saving works definitively revealed by God to the apostles. Note especially Torrance's insistence that *the saving works of Christ are inseparably united in his Person*. And note that it is Christ himself, not merely information about him, that is revealed to the apostles. Thus, the entire complex of the revelation of Christ to the apostles is the "original datum" of which Torrance speaks.

Of paramount importance here is the absolute rejection within the deposit of faith of any dichotomy between the person of the living Christ and his self-revelation by the Holy Spirit to the apostles. While these may be distinguished conceptually, they may not be separated in the reality of the deposit of faith. Accordingly, says Torrance:

Barth, *CD* IV/1, 643.

19. Torrance, "Deposit of Faith," 1.

20. Ibid., 2.

> We do not have to do here with Christ apart from his Word or the Word apart from Christ, nor with Christ apart from his Truth or the Truth apart from Christ, for he is the incarnate embodiment of the Word and Truth of God in his own personal Being, who continues in the power of his resurrection to make his mighty acts of redemption effective in the life and faith of all who are baptized in his Name and who draw near to the Father through his atoning sacrifice.[21]

Thus, Torrance sees in the Acts of the Apostles the living Word of Christ at work in the growth of the church (Acts 6:7, 12:24, 19:20; cf. Col 1:5-6), communicating himself through the Spirit in the witness and preaching of the apostles, and letting his self-revelation take definitive shape in the apostolic mind and embody itself in the apostolic mission. He writes,

> Christ thus *clothed with his Gospel* indwelt the Church united to himself as his Body, [such that] the Word and Truth of the Gospel embodied uniquely in Christ also became embodied in a subsidiary way in the apostolic foundation of the Church.[22]

This means that Jesus Christ the Word cannot be resolved into the apostolic word such that the deposit of faith is simply identified with the preaching and teaching of the apostles. For the deposit remains *identical* with the incarnate self-communication of God in Jesus Christ, which is constantly being renewed in the life of the church by the Holy Spirit. However, it does mean that from this time onward people have access to the deposit of faith only in the form that it has taken in the apostolic tradition—that is, through the apostolic preaching and understanding of the Gospel mediated to us in the Scriptures of the New Testament, and through incorporation into Christ in the midst of his church through baptism.

Consequently, we can see that the deposit of faith must be understood to have a primary and a secondary level. At the primary level, it is identical with the whole saving person and work of our Lord Jesus Christ. But at the secondary level, it is identical with the faithful reception and understanding of the Gospel of Jesus Christ that took form in the apostolic foundation of the church, and is subsequently given to us in the New Testament and through the life of the church.

Torrance is insistent that these two levels of the deposit of faith must not be separated from one another. And he identifies in the thought of

21. Ibid., 2.

22. Torrance, *Trinitarian Faith*, 258 (emphasis added).

Irenaeus of Lyons a paradigmatic pattern for understanding this. For Irenaeus, the deposit of faith, entrusted once and for all to the church through
its apostolic foundation, continues to inform, structure, and enliven the life
and faith, and mission of the Body of Christ in the world. Thus, Irenaeus
operated with a concept of *embodied truth* or *embodied doctrine* which derived from his understanding of the deposit of faith. Says Torrance:

> It is in this light that [for Irenaeus] the historical tradition (*para-
> dosis*) of the Faith, and the historical succession (*diadoche*) of
> presbyters and bishops from the original Apostles . . . is to be un-
> derstood. But no less important for Irenaeus was the stress upon
> the empirical tradition and living reception of the faith through
> the ordinance of Baptism in the context of the worship of God,
> meditation upon the Holy Scriptures and instruction in the Gos-
> pel when salvation was written in the hearts of the faithful by the
> Spirit.[23]

Thus, we see in Irenaeus a rich understanding of the embodied character of the deposit of faith in the life of the church, whereby every aspect of
the church's existence and ongoing historical and spiritual life is informed
and enlivened by the living presence of Christ "clothed with his Gospel,"
which lies at the heart of the ontological reality that is the Body of Christ,
the earthly-historical form of his existence. Note that far from a mere claim
to historic continuity, Irenaeus understands the deposit of faith as a *living
reality* that is ever being renewed by the Spirit of God. And in each ongoing
moment of the church's life, the people of God receive that deposit anew
through the study of Scripture, through baptism, through Christian worship, and through catechesis. Through these God-ordained means and by
the power of the Holy Spirit, our Lord Jesus—"clothed with his Gospel"—
ever continues to make himself known in the midst of his church and to
constitute the church as his Body throughout history.

However, Torrance acknowledges that it was always possible for these
primary and secondary levels of the deposit to be separated. This happens
when the central points of truth are distilled or crystallized out of the deposit of faith and detached from their embodiment in the life of the church,
in order to be organized into an independent system of truth. This Torrance
sees as a critical error, which fails to retain the locus of truth embodied in
the person of Christ and the life of the church and instead identifies it with

---

23. Torrance, "Deposit of Faith," 5.

a particular "logico-deductive" system of thought held up independently as a body of belief.

This, in Torrance's view, is the general failing of the Western theological tradition on the whole. And in contrast to Irenaeus, he identifies Tertullian of Carthage as the originator of an unfortunate precedent in this regard, a precedent that lies at the roots of the Latin theological tradition. According to Torrance, this precedent comes into view when comparing Irenaeus' view of the Canon of Truth to Tertullian's understanding of the Rule of Faith. Says Torrance:

> While for Irenaeus the canon of truth was in fact the *Truth* itself . . . for Tertullian the rule of faith was consistently regarded as a fixed formula of truth for belief, which he claimed had been instituted by Christ himself and had been handed down entire and unchanged from the Apostles . . . In accordance with his conception of the Gospel as 'a new law' (*nova lex*) inaugurated by Christ, Tertullian spoke of 'the faith deposited in the rule' as constituting a 'law' (*lex*) which must be observed as a condition of salvation.[24]

To be clear, Torrance affirms that Irenaeus' Canon of Truth and Tertullian's Rule of Faith operate analogously. They both comprise core beliefs about the saving economy of God in Christ that are distilled into essential proto-credal statements, statements which serve both to articulate and to defend the apostolic *kerygma* of the Gospel, as well as to identify those Scriptures that are truly apostolic. However, Torrance asserts that for Irenaeus such statements "could not be abstracted from the objective substance of the whole coherent structure of the Faith," but are "ordered and integrated from beyond themselves by their common ground in the Apostolic Deposit of Faith, and in the final analysis in the objective self-revelation of God in Jesus Christ."[25] By contrast, in Torrance's view, Tertullian's understanding of the deposit

> tended to be restricted to a compendium of doctrines formulated in definitive statements which were regarded as themselves identical with the truths they were meant to express . . . abstractively derived from the original Deposit of Faith and formalized into a *system of doctrine* which must be imposed prescriptively upon the life and faith of the Church. The effect of this was to make the rule of faith no more and no less than a deposit of doctrinal

24. Ibid., 15.
25. Ibid., 7.

propositions, and indeed to make the very concept of the rule of faith itself into a doctrine.[26]

Whatever we may make of Torrance's contrast between Irenaeus and Tertullian on this matter, they typify his understanding of a general difference between Eastern and Western approaches to the deposit of faith.[27] This is not to denigrate the richness and importance of Tertullian's own faith and contribution to the life of the church. Nor is it to lionize the Eastern tradition. However, while Torrance is critical of the later Eastern tradition in important respects, he believes that it has generally maintained the Irenaean approach. By contrast, Torrance sees in Tertullian's approach a precedent that lies at the roots of much of the Western theological tradition, a precedent in which a reductive dichotomy is too often established between Scripture and tradition, between the so-called substance of the faith and dogmatic formulations thereof, and between the church as a mystical body versus a juridical society. For Roman Catholics in particular, he notes a collapse of the distinction between ecclesial tradition and Apostolic Tradition (he is sharply critical of Cyprian of Carthage on this front), and the emergence of a distinction between "passive tradition" and "active tradition." However, in Vatican II Torrance sees a recovery of the Irenaean Christocentric approach to the Roman Catholic understanding of the church, Scripture, and worship.

As for the churches of the Reformation, especially the Reformed and Lutheran churches, Torrance sees in them the same dichotomous tendencies that characterize the rest of the Western tradition. Despite the vital breakthroughs of the Reformers, he asserts that "a failure to appreciate the living embodiment of faith and truth in the corporate life and structure of the church allowed a serious tension to become established between Scripture and Confession."[28] On the one hand, the deposit of faith came to be identified with Scripture itself in a way that conflates the "canon of Scripture" with the "canon of truth." This reduces the deposit of faith to the text itself, and thereby constitutes a rejection of the role that the canon of truth played in the establishment of the canon of Scripture in the first five centuries of the church.

---

26. Ibid., 15–16 (emphasis original).

27. Though it is worth noting that he stresses this distinction less sharply in later publications.

28. Torrance, "Deposit of Faith," 22.

On the other hand, the Reformation churches produced confessions of faith that, in Torrance's view, were essentially constitutional and juridical documents that related to the church in an especially Tertullian-like fashion. For Torrance, the great majority of these were simply organized accounts of chief articles of belief enunciated as doctrinal positions. As such, they were not actual declarations of faith in and before God. The great danger here, of course, was that the confessions came to be treated as systems of doctrinal propositions which are held to be identical with the divine truths they are intended to express, rather than pointing beyond themselves—as the Nicene Creed does—to the living reality of those truths. Despite this criticism, Torrance also expresses great hope for the Protestant churches, because he sees in the best of the ecumenical movement and Protestant theology indications of a recovery of an Irenaean-like understanding of the deposit of faith.

With this, we come full circle to where this chapter began, and to the current ecclesially-oriented trend among American Evangelicals. What are we to make of Torrance's treatment of the apostolic deposit of faith? How might it shed light upon this movement? Many implications might follow from Torrance's argument, but the following strike me as the most salient.

First, Torrance's argument appears to confirm the perception held by a growing number of Evangelicals that they have, on the whole, inherited an impoverished ecclesiology. By contrast, this understanding of the apostolic character of the church has comprehensive implications for what many Evangelicals perceive as a deeply fragmented understanding of Christian faith and life. A proper understanding of the deposit of faith ascertains that the very existence and authority of the church, the truth of Scripture, the proper orientation and character of Christian worship, the ontology and teleology of Christian catechesis, and the rationale and motive for Christian mission and proclamation *all coinhere* in the sacred deposit of "Christ clothed with his Gospel," which is the apostolic faith. Given this understanding, the many dichotomies that define so much of common Evangelical theology and practice—between Scripture and tradition, between preaching and liturgy, between doctrine and spiritual life, between worship and mission, between Christian life and secular profession—are profoundly challenged by an understanding of the apostolic character of the church rooted in the real, living presence of our Lord. Some version of this understanding appears to undergird many of the various theological trends described at the beginning of the chapter, as well as the movement in general.

Second, and related: in light of Torrance's critique, Evangelicals are challenged to think more deeply about what it means to be apostolic in our church practice. Is our worship led by and centered on the living Christ, who is ever with and in his Body? Is our understanding of Scripture unified in him, the incarnate Word? Does our preaching direct others ever toward the living Christ? Does our discipleship form believers intellectually, spiritually, and morally in a Christ-rooted and Christ-directed manner? Is our mission understood as a participation in his mission? The apostolic character of the church has profound implications for every aspect of our practical theology.

Finally, if Torrance is right, then we have good reason to see the contemporary ecclesiocentric trend among Evangelicals as evidence of a recognition and longing for apostolicity—for a more embodied understanding of what it truly means to have "a personal relationship with Jesus Christ." And this should give us reason to hope. For while we may consider its human causes, a consistently Irenaean ecclesiology will also lead us to consider that this movement is but the latest evidence of the renewal of the church by the One who is ever renewing his church—for he always dwells within it because it is his Body.

Bibliography

Agamben, Giorgio. *The Highest Poverty: Monastic Rules and Form-of-Life*. Translated by Adam Kotsko. Stanford, CA: Stanford University Press, 2013.

Ahlstrom, Sydney E. "The Scottish Philosophy and American Theology." *Church History* 24.3 (1955) 257–72.

Allison, Gregg. "Theological Defense of Multi-Site." *9Marks eJournal* (May/June 2009) 7–18.

Anglican-Roman Catholic International Commission. *Church as Communion: An Agreed Statement*. London: Church House, 1991.

Annan, Kent. "Chaos and Grace in the Slums of the Earth." *Christianity Today*. August 29, 2013, http://www.christianitytoday.com/ct/2013/september/chaos-and-grace-in-slums-of-earth.html.

Augustine of Hippo. "Treatise on the Correction of the Donatists." In *The Political Writings of St. Augustine*, edited by Henry Paolucci, 207–40. Washington, D.C.: Regnery, 1962.

Avis, P. D. L. "The True Church in Reformation Theology." *Scottish Journal of Theology* 30.4 (1977) 319–45.

Avis, Paul. *The Church in the Theology of the Reformers*. Eugene, OR: Wipf and Stock, 2002.

Ballor, Jordan J., and W. Bradford Littlejohn. "European Calvinism: Church Discipline." In Irene Dingel and Johannes Paulmann, eds., *European History Online* (EGO). Mainz: Institute of European History (IEG), 2013. http://www.ieg-ego.eu/en/threads/crossroads/religious-and-denominational-spaces/jordan-ballor-w-bradford-littlejohn-european-calvinism-church-discipline.

Balthasar, Hans Urs von. *Love Alone: The Way of Revelation*. London: Sheed & Ward, 1982.

———. *The Glory of the Lord, Volume 2. Studies in Theological Style: Clerical Styles*, edited by John Riches. Translated by Andrew Louth, Francis McDonagh, and Brian McNeil. Edinburgh: T & T Clark, 1984.

———. *The Glory of the Lord, Volume 7. The New Covenant*, edited by John Riches. Translated by Brian McNeil. San Francisco: Ignatius, 1989.

———. "The Holy Church and the Eucharistic Sacrifice." Translated by Leonard P. Hindsley. *Communio: International Catholic Review* 12 (1985) 139–45.

———. *Mysterium Paschale: The Mystery of Easter*. Translated by Aidan Nichols. San Francisco: Ignatius, 2005.

———. *Prayer*. Translated by Graham Harrison. San Francisco: Ignatius, 1986.

——. *Theo-Drama, Volume 2. Dramatis Personae: Man in God*. Translated by Graham Harrison. San Francisco: Ignatius, 1990.

——. *Theo-Drama, Volume 3. The Dramatis Personae: The Person in Christ*. Translated by Graham Harrison. San Francisco: Ignatius, 1992.

——. *Theo-Drama, Volume 4. The Action*. Translated by Graham Harrison. San Francisco: Ignatius, 1994.

Banks, Robert. *Paul's Idea of Community: The Early House Churches in Their Historical Setting*. Grand Rapids: Eerdmans, 1980.

Barth, Karl. *The Epistle to the Romans*. Translated by Edwyn C. Hoskyns. New York: Oxford University Press, 1968.

——. "The New World in the Bible." In *The Word of God and Theology*. Translated by Amy Marga, 15–29. New York: T&T Clark, 2011.

Bass, Diana Butler. *Christianity after Religion: The End of the Church and the Birth of a New Spiritual Awakening*. New York: HarperOne, 2012.

Bauckham, Richard. *The Testimony of the Beloved Disciple: Narrative, History, and Theology in the Gospel of John*. Grand Rapids: Baker Academic, 2007.

Bender, Kimlyn J. *Karl Barth's Christological Ecclesiology*. Burlington, VT: Ashgate, 2005.

Berger, Peter L. *A Rumor of Angels: Modern Society and the Rediscovery of the Supernatural*. New York: Anchor, 1970.

Berkhof, Louis. *Systematic Theology*, 4th ed. Grand Rapids: Eerdmans, 1949.

Berry, Wendell E. "It All Turns on Affection," National Endowment for the Humanities Jefferson Lecture, Washington, DC, April 24, 2012. http://www.neh.gov/about/awards/jefferson-lecture/wendell-e-berry-lecture.

Bessenecker, Scott. *Living Mission: The Vision and Voices of the New Friars*. Downers Grove, IL: InterVarsity, 2010.

——. *The New Friars: The Emerging Movement Serving the World's Poor*. Downers Grove, IL: InterVarsity, 2006.

Bethge, Eberhard. *Dietrich Bonhoeffer: A Biography*. Rev. ed. Translated by Eric Mosbacher, Peter Ross, Betty Ross, Frank Clarke and William Glen-Doepel. Minneapolis: Fortress, 1970.

Billings, J. Todd. *The Word of God for the People of God*. Grand Rapids: Eerdmans, 2010.

Boersma, Hans. *Heavenly Participation: The Weaving of a Sacramental Tapestry*. Grand Rapids: Eerdmans, 2011.

Bonhoeffer, Dietrich. *Act and Being*, edited by Wayne Whitson Floyd. Translated by Martin H. Rumcheidt. Minneapolis: Fortress, 1996.

——. *A Testament to Freedom: The Essential Writings of Dietrich Bonhoeffer*. Rev ed., edited by Geffrey B. Kelly and F. Burton Nelson. San Francisco: HarperSanFrancisco, 1995.

——. *Berlin, 1932–1933*, edited by Larry L. Rasmussen. Translated by Isabel Best, David Higgins, and Douglas W. Stott. Minneapolis: Fortress, 2009.

——. *Christ the Center*. Translated by John Bowden. New York: Harper & Row, 1960.

——. *Creation and Fall*, edited by John W. De Gruchy. Translated by Douglas Stephen Bax. Minneapolis: Fortress, 1997.

——. *Discipleship*, edited by Geffrey B. Kelly and John D. Godsey. Translated by Barbara Green and Reinhard Krauss. Minneapolis: Fortress, 2001.

——. *Ethics*, edited by Clifford J. Green. Translated by Reinhard Krauss, Charles C. West and Douglas W. Stott. Minneapolis: Fortress, 2005.

———. *Letters and Papers from Prison*, edited by John W. De Gruchy. Translated by Isabel Best, Lisa E. Dahill, Reinhard Krauss, Nancy Lukens, Barbara Rumschiedt, Martin Rumschiedt and Douglas W. Stott. Minneapolis: Fortress, 2009.

———. *Life Together*, edited by Geffrey B. Kelly. Translated by Daniel W. Bloesch and James H. Burtness. Minneapolis: Fortress, 1996.

———. *Sanctorum Communio*, edited by Clifford J. Green. Translated by Reinhard Krauss and Nancy Lukens. Minneapolis: Fortress, 1998.

Bourdieu, Pierre. *The Logic of Practice*. Translated by Richard Nice. Stanford, CA: Stanford University Press, 1990.

———. *Outline of a Theory of Practice*. Translated by Richard Nice. Cambridge: Cambridge University Press, 1997.

Breshears, Gerry. "The Body of Christ: Prophet, Priest, or King?" *Journal of the Evangelical Theological Society* 37.1 (1994) 3–26.

Brown, Peter. *Augustine of Hippo: A Biography*. London: Faber and Faber, 2000.

Bruce, Steve. *God is Dead: Secularization in the West*. Malden, MA: Blackwell, 2002.

Brueggemann, Walter. "The Preacher as Scribe." In *Inscribing the Text: Sermons and Prayers of Walter Brueggemann*, edited by Anna Carter Florence, 5–19. Minneapolis: Fortress, 2004.

Bründl, Jürgen. "Braucht Gott Opfer? Zur theologischen Frage nach dem Wesen der Eucharistie." *Theologie und Glaube* 94 (2004) 509–25.

Bryant, David J. *Faith and the Play of the Imagination: On the Role of Imagination in Religion*. Studies in American Biblical Hermeneutics 5. Macon, GA: Mercer University Press, 1989.

Buckley, James J., and David S. Yeago. *Knowing the Triune God: The Work of the Spirit in the Practices of the Church*. Grand Rapids: Eerdmans, 2001.

Busch, Eberhard. *The Great Passion: An Introduction to Karl Barth's Theology*. Translated by Geoffrey W. Bromiley. Grand Rapids: Eerdmans, 2004.

———. *Karl Barth and the Pietists: The Young Karl Barth's Critique of Pietism and Its Response*. Translated by Daniel W. Bloesch. Downers Grove, IL: InterVarsity, 2004.

Buschart, W. David and Kent Eilers, *Theology as Retrieval: Receiving the Past, Renewing the Church*. Downers Grove, IL: IVP Academic, 2015.

Butterfield, Herbert. *The Whig Interpretation of History*. New York: W. W. Norton, 1965.

Calvin, John. "Calvin's Reply to Sadoleto." In *A Reformation Debate: John Calvin and Jacopo Sadoleto*, edited by John C. Olin, 49–94. Grand Rapids: Baker, 1966.

———. *Commentaries on the Catholic Epistles*. In *Calvin's Commentaries*, vol. 22. Translated by John Owen. Grand Rapids: Eerdmans, 1948.

———. *Commentaries on the Epistles of Paul*. In *Calvin's Commentaries*, vol. 21. Translated by William Pringle. Grand Rapids: Baker, 2009.

———. *Institutes of the Christian Religion*. Edited by John T. McNeill. Louisville, KY: Westminster John Knox, 1960.

Campbell, Heidi. *Exploring Religious Community Online: We are One in the Network*. New York: Peter Lang, 2005.

Capps, Walter. *The Monastic Impulse*. Lexington, KY: Crossroad, 1983.

Carroll, Colleen. *The New Faithful: Why Young Adults Are Embracing Christian Orthodoxy*. Chicago: Loyola, 2004.

Casarella, Peter. "*Analogia Donationis*: Hans Urs von Balthasar on the Eucharist." *Philosophy & Theology* 11.1 (1998) 147–77.

Casey, Michael. *Strangers to the City: Reflections on the Beliefs and Values of the Rule of St. Benedict*. Brewster, MA: Paraclete, 2005.

Certeau, Michel de. *The Practice of Everyday Life*. Translated by S. Rendall. Berkley: University of California Press, 1984.

Challies, Tim. *The Next Story: Life and Faith after the Digital Explosion*. Grand Rapids: Zondervan, 2011.

Chapp, Larry S. "Who is the Church? The Personalistic Categories of Balthasar's Ecclesiology." *Communio: International Catholic Review* 23 (1996) 322–38.

Claiborne, Shane, Jonathan Wilson-Hargove, and Enuma Okoro. *Common Prayer: Liturgy for Ordinary Radicals*. Grand Rapids: Zondervan, 2010.

Coakley, Sarah. "Living into the Mystery of the Holy Trinity: Trinity, Prayer, and Sexuality." *Anglican Theological Review* 80 (1998) 223–32.

The Constitution of the Presbyterian Church (U.S.A.). Part II, Book of Order 2011–2013. Louisville, KY: Office of the General Assembly, 2011.

Davies, J. G. *Members One of Another: Aspects of Koinonia*. London: A.R. Mowbray, 1958.

Dayton, Donald. "The *Embourgeoisement* of a Vision: Lament of a Radical Evangelical." *Other Side* 23.8 (1987) 19.

Dayton, Donald, and Robert K. Johnson, eds. *The Variety of American Evangelicalism*. Knoxville: University of Tennessee Press, 1991.

De Gruchy, John W., ed. *The Cambridge Companion to Dietrich Bonhoeffer*. Cambridge: Cambridge University Press, 1999.

De Lange, Frederik. *Waiting for the Word: Dietrich Bonhoeffer on Speaking about God*. Grand Rapids: Eerdmans, 2000.

Demson, David. *Hans Frei and Karl Barth: Different Ways of Reading Scripture*. Eugene, OR: Wipf and Stock, 2012 [1997].

Dever, Mark, and Paul Alexander. *The Deliberate Church*. Wheaton, IL: Crossway, 2005.

Dreyfus, Hubert L. *On the Internet*. New York: Routledge, 2001.

Driscoll, Mark, and Gerry Breshears. *Vintage Church: Timeless Truths and Timely Methods*. Wheaton, IL: Crossway, 2008.

Dulles, Avery. *Models of the Church*. Exp. ed. New York: Image, 2002.

Dupré, Louis. *Passage to Modernity: An Essay in the Hermeneutics of Nature and Culture*. New Haven, CT: Yale University Press, 1993.

Dyer, John. *From the Garden to the City: The Redeeming and Corrupting Power of Technology*. Grand Rapids: Kregel, 2011.

Ebersole, Samuel E., and Robert Woods. "Virtual Community: Koinonia or Compromise? – Theological Implications of Community in Cyberspace." *Christian Scholars Journal* 31 (2001) 185–216.

Edwards, Jonathan. *The Works of Jonathan Edwards*, 26 vols. New Haven, CT: Yale University Press, 1957–2008.

Eilers, Kent. "New Monastic Social Imaginary: Theological Retrieval for Ecclesial Renewal." *American Theological Inquiry* 6/2 (2013) 45–57.

Ellingsen, Mark. "Common Sense Realism: The Cutting Edge of Evangelical Identity." *Dialog* 24.3 (1985) 197–205.

Erickson, Millard J. *Christian Theology*. 2nd ed. Grand Rapids: Baker Academic, 1998.

———. *Christian Theology*. 3rd ed. Grand Rapids: Baker Academic, 2013.

Estes, Douglas. *SimChurch: Being the Church in the Virtual World*. Grand Rapids: Zondervan, 2009.

Evans, G. R. *The Roots of the Reformation: Tradition, Emergence and Rupture*. 2nd ed. Downers Grove, IL: IVP Academic, 2012.

Ewald, Owen, and Ursula Krentz. "Beauty and Beholders: Are Past Intuitions Correct?" *Essays in Philosophy* 13.2 (2012) 436–52.

Flanagan, Bernadette. *Embracing Solitude: Women and New Monasticism*. Eugene, OR: Cascade, 2014.

Floyd, Wayne Whitson. "Dietrich Bonhoeffer." In *The Modern Theologians: An Introduction to Christian Theology since 1918*, edited by David Ford and Rachel Muers, 43–61. 3rd ed. Malden, MA: Blackwell, 2005.

Freeman, Andy, and Peter Greig. *Punk Monk: New Monasticism and the Ancient Art of Breathing*. Ventura, CA: Regal, 2007.

Frei, Hans W. *The Eclipse of Biblical Narrative: A Study in Eighteenth and Nineteenth Century Hermeneutics*. London: Yale University Press, 1974.

Fry, Timothy. *RB 1980: The Rule of St. Benedict in Latin and English with Notes*. Collegeville, MN: Liturgical, 1981.

Frye, Brian. "The Multi-Site Phenomenon, 1995–2010." PhD diss., The Southern Baptist Theological Seminary, 2011.

Gehring, Roger. *House Church and Mission: The Importance of Household Structures in Early Christianity*. Peabody, MA: Hendrickson, 2004.

Geisler, Norman. *Church, Last Things*. Vol. 4 of *Systematic Theology*. Minneapolis: Bethany House, 2005.

Gillespie, Michael Allen. *The Theological Origins of Modernity*. Chicago: University of Chicago Press, 2008.

Green, Clifford J. *Bonhoeffer: A Theology of Sociality*. 2nd ed. Grand Rapids: Eerdmans, 1999.

Greig, Peter and Dave Roberts. *Red Moon Rising: How 24-7 Prayer is Awakening a Generation*. Lake Mary, FL: Relevant Media, 2003.

Grenz, Stanley J. *Theology for the Community of God*. Nashville: Broadman & Holman, 1994.

Groothuis, Douglas. *The Soul in Cyber-Space*. Grand Rapids: Baker, 1997.

Grudem, Wayne. *Systematic Theology: An Introduction to Biblical Doctrine*. Grand Rapids: Zondervan, 1994.

Hadden, J. K., and D. E. Cowan. "The Promised Land or Electronic Chaos? Towards Understanding Religion on the Internet." In *Religion on the Internet: Research Prospectus and Promises*. Amsterdam: JAI, 2000.

Hammett, John S. *Biblical Foundations for Baptist Churches: A Contemporary Ecclesiology*. Grand Rapids: Kregel, 2005.

Hampson, Daphne. *After Christianity*. London: SCM, 1996.

———. "Luther on the Self: A Feminist Critique." *Word & World* 8 (1988) 334–42.

———. "On Autonomy and Heteronomy." In *Swallowing a Fishbone? Feminist Theologians Debate Christianity*, edited by Daphne Hampson, 1–16. London: SPCK, 1996.

Hardy, Daniel W. "Sociality, Rationality, and Culture: Faith Embedded in the Particularities of History." In *Papers of the Nineteenth-Century Theology Working Group*, edited by Claude Welch and Richard Crouter, 1–19. Colorado Springs: Colorado College, 1992.

Harrison, Peter. *The Bible, Protestantism, and the Rise of Natural Science*. Cambridge: Cambridge University Press, 1998.

Harrison, William H. "Powers of Nature and Influences of Grace in Hooker's *Lawes*." In *Richard Hooker and the English Reformation*, edited by W.J. Torrance Kirby, 15–24. Dordrecht, Netherlands: Kluwer, 2003.

Harrold, Philip. "The 'New Monasticism' as Ancient-Future Belonging." *Theology Today* 67 (2010) 182–93.

Hart, D. G. *Deconstructing Evangelicalism: Conservative Protestantism in the Age of Billy Graham*. Grand Rapids: Baker Academic, 2004.

Hauerwas, Stanley. Review of *The Eucharist and Ecumenism: Let us Keep the Feast*, by George Hunsinger. *Christian Century* (October 20, 2009) 36–38.

———. *Sanctify Them in the Truth: Holiness Exemplified*. Nashville: Abingdon, 1998.

———. *With the Grain of the Universe: The Church's Witness and Natural Theology*. Grand Rapids: Brazos, 2001.

Haynes, Stephen R. *The Bonhoeffer Phenomenon: Portraits of a Protestant Saint*. Minneapolis: Fortress, 2006.

Healy, Nicholas. *The Eschatology of Hans Urs von Balthasar: Being as Communion*. New York: Oxford University Press, 2005.

———. "Practices and the New Ecclesiology: Misplaced Concreteness?" *International Journal of Systematic Theology* 5.3 (November 2003) 285–308.

Healy, Nicholas, and David L. Schindler. "For the Life of the World: Hans Urs von Balthasar on the Church as Eucharist." In *The Cambridge Companion to Hans Urs von Balthasar*, edited by Edward T. Oakes and David Moss, 51–63. Cambridge: Cambridge University Press, 2004.

Hellerman, Joseph H. *When the Church Was a Family: Recapturing Jesus' Vision for Authentic Christian Community*. Nashville: B&H Academic, 2009.

Hill, W. Speed, and Georges Edelen, eds. *The Folger Library Edition of the Works of Richard Hooker, vol. 1: The Laws of Ecclesiastical Polity: Pref., Books I to IV*. Cambridge, MA: Belknap, 1977.

Hill, W. Speed, ed. *The Folger Library Edition of the Works of Richard Hooker, vol. 2: The Laws of Ecclesiastical Polity: Book V*. Cambridge, MA: Belknap, 1977.

Hinlicky, Paul. *Beloved Community: Critical Dogmatics after Christendom*. Grand Rapids: Eerdmans, 2015.

Hipps, Shane. *Flickering Pixels: How Technology Shapes Your Faith*. Grand Rapids: Zondervan, 2009.

———. *The Hidden Power of Electronic Culture: How Media Shapes Faith, the Gospel, and Church*. Grand Rapids: Zondervan, 2005.

Hirsch, Alan. *The Forgotten Ways: Reactivating the Missional Church*. Grand Rapids: Brazos, 2006.

Hodge, Charles. "Is the Church of Rome Part of the Visible Church?" *Princeton Review* (1846); http://www.hornes.org/theologia/charles-hodge/is-the-church-of-rome-a-part-of-the-visible-church.

———. "Validity of Romish Baptism." In *Discussions in Church Polity*, edited by William Durant, 191–215. New York: Westminster, 2001.

Holmes, Michael W., ed. *The Apostolic Fathers: Greek Texts and English Translations*. 3rd ed. Grand Rapids: Baker Academic, 2007.

Hoover, Stewart M., Lynn Schofield Clark, and Lee Rainie. "Faith Online: 64% of wired Americans have used the Internet for spiritual and religious purposes." http://www.pewinternet.org/files/old-media/Files/Reports/2004/PIP_Faith_Online_2004.pdf.pdf.

Horton, Michael. *The Christian Faith: A Systematic Theology for Pilgrims on the Way.* Grand Rapids: Zondervan, 2011.

Hoskyns, Edwyn Clement. *The Fourth Gospel,* edited by Francis Noel Davey. London: Faber and Faber, 1940; rev. ed. 1947.

Howard, Evan. "Introducing New Monasticism." http://spiritualityshoppe.org/wp-content/uploads/2013/01/intnm1.pdf.

Howard, Thomas. *Evangelical Is Not Enough: Worship of God in Liturgy and Sacrament.* San Francisco: Ignatius, 1984.

Howsare, Rodney A. "The Eucharist as Sacrifice: A Marian Dimension." *Josephinum Journal of Theology* 9.2 (2002) 267–81.

Hunsinger, George. *The Eucharist and Ecumenism: Let us Keep the Feast.* Cambridge: Cambridge University Press, 2008.

———. "5 Picks: Essential Theology Books of the Past 25 Years." *The Christian Century* 127, no. 21 (October 19, 2010) 38.

Hunt, Anne. *The Trinity and the Paschal Mystery: A Development in Recent Catholic Theology.* Collegeville, MN: Liturgical, 1997.

International Commission for Anglican-Orthodox Theological Dialogue. *The Church of the Triune God: The Cyprus Statement.* London: Anglican Communion Office, 2006.

Jacobs, Alan. "Do It Yourself Tradition." *First Things.* January 2009. http://www.firstthings.com/article/2009/01/002-do-it-yourself-tradition.

Jenkins, Simon. "Rituals and Pixels: Experiments in Online Church," *Online—Heidelberg Journal of Religions on the Internet* 3.1 (2008) 95–114. http://archiv.ub.uni-heidelberg.de/ojs/index.php/religions/article/view/390http://archiv.ub.uni-heidelberg.de/ojs/index.php/religions/article/view/390.

Jenson, Matt. *The Gravity of Sin: Augustine, Luther and Barth on* homo incurvatus in se. New York: T&T Clark, 2007.

Jenson, Robert W. *Canon and Creed.* Louisville, KY: Westminster John Knox, 2010.

Kant, Immanuel. *Philosophical Writings.* Translated by James Creed Meredith and Lewis W. Beck. The German Library 13, edited by Volkmar Sander. New York: Continuum, 1986.

Kelly, Douglas F. "Scottish Realism." In *Evangelical Dictionary of Theology*, edited by Walter A. Elwell, 2nd ed. Baker Reference Library. 1079. Grand Rapids: Baker Academic, 2001.

Kelly, J.N.D. *Early Christian Doctrines.* 5th ed. A & C Black, 1977. Reprint, New York: Continuum, 2011.

Kereszty, Roch. "The Eucharist and Mission in the Theology of Hans Urs von Balthasar." In *Love Alone is Credible: Hans Urs von Balthasar as Interpreter of the Catholic Tradition,* edited by David L. Schindler, 1:3–15. Grand Rapids: Eerdmans, 2008.

Kerr, Nathan R. *Christ, History and Apocalyptic: The Politics of Christian Mission.* Eugene, OR: Cascade, 2009.

Kilby, Karen. "Hans Urs von Balthasar on the Trinity." In *The Cambridge Companion to the Trinity,* edited by Peter C. Phan, 208–22. Cambridge: Cambridge University Press, 2011.

Kirkpatrick, Frank G. *The Ethics of Community.* Oxford: Blackwell, 2001.

Klink, III, Edward W. *The Sheep of the Fold: The Audience and Origin of the Gospel of John.* Cambridge: Cambridge University Press, 2007.

Koerpel, Robert C. "The Form and Drama of the Church: Hans Urs von Balthasar on Mary, Peter, and the Eucharist." *Logos* 11.1 (2008) 70–99.

Kuyper, Abraham. *De Gemeene Gratie*, 3 vols. Kampen, Netherlands: Kok, 1931–1932.

Larsen, Elena. "CyberFaith: How Americans Pursue Religion Online." http://www. pewinternet.org/2001/12/23/cyberfaith-how-americans-pursue-religion-online.

———. "Wired churches, Wired temples: Taking congregations and missions into cyberspace." http://www.pewinternet.org/files/old-media//Files/Reports/2000/PIP_ Religion_Report. pdf.pdf.

Leeman, Jonathan. *The Church and the Surprising Offense of God's Love: Reintroducing the Doctrines of Church Membership and Discipline*. Wheaton, IL: Crossway, 2010.

Leithart, Peter. *Deep Exegesis: The Mystery of Reading Scripture*. Waco, TX: Baylor University Press, 2009.

Lindbeck, George A. "The Church." In *The Church in a Postliberal Age*, edited by James J. Buckley, 145–67. Grand Rapids: Eerdmans, 2002.

Littlejohn, W. Bradford. *Richard Hooker: A Companion to His Life and Work*. Eugene, OR: Cascade, 2015.

———. "The Use and Abuse of John Jewel in Richard Hooker's Defense of the English Church." In *Defending the Faith: John Jewel and the Church of England*, edited by Angela Ranson. Kirksville, MO: Truman State University Press, forthcoming 2016.

Livingston, James C. *The Enlightenment and the Nineteenth Century*. Minneapolis: Fortress, 2006.

Locke, John. "A Letter Concerning Toleration." In *The Selected Political Writings of John Locke*, edited by Paul E. Sigmund, 125–67. New York: W. W. Norton, 2005.

Lumpkin, William L., ed. *Baptist Confessions of Faith*. Rev. ed. Valley Forge, PA: Judson, 1969.

Luther, Martin. *Luther's Works*. American Edition, 55 vols. Edited by J. Pelikan and H. Lehmann. St. Louis: Concordia and Fortress, 1955–1986.

———. *On Christian Liberty*. Translated by W. A. Lambert and Harold J. Grimm. Minneapolis: Fortress, 2003.

MacIntyre, Alasdair. *After Virtue: A Study in Moral Theology*. 3rd ed. Notre Dame, IN: University of Notre Dame Press, 2007.

Margolis, Mac. "Brazil's Celebrity Priest." *Newsweek* (2013); http://mag.newsweek. com/2013/07/17/father-marcelo-rossi-brazil-s-celebrity-priest.html.

Marsden, George. "Everyone One's Own Interpreter? The Bible, Science, and Authority in Mid-Nineteenth Century America." In *The Bible in America: Essays in Cultural History*, edited by Nathan O. Hatch and Mark A. Noll. 79–100. New York: Oxford University Press, 1982.

———. *Fundamentalism and American Culture: The Shaping of Twentieth-Century Evangelicalism 1870–1925*. New York: Oxford University Press, 1980.

Martin, Jennifer Newsome. "The 'Whence' and the 'Whither' of Balthasar's Gendered Theology: Rehabilitating Kenosis for Feminist Theology." *Modern Theology* 30 (2014) 1–29.

Martin, Ralph P. *The Family and the Fellowship: New Testament Images of the Church*. Grand Rapids: Eerdmans, 1979.

Marty, Martin E. *Dietrich Bonhoeffer's Letters and Papers from Prison: A Biography*. Princeton: Princeton University Press, 2011.

———. *The Place of Bonhoeffer: Problems and Possibilities in His Thought*. Eugene, OR: Wipf & Stock, 1962.

Martyn, J. Louis. *History and Theology in the Fourth Gospel*, 3rd ed. Louisville, KY: Westminster John Knox, 2003.

Maruyama, Tadataka. *The Ecclesiology of Theodore Beza: The Reform of the True Church.* Geneva, Switzerland: Librairie Droz, 1978.

McCall, Bradford. "A Contemporary Reappropriation of Baconian Common Sense Realism in Renewal Hermeneutics." *Pneuma* 32.2 (2010) 223–40.

McGrath, Alister. *The Science of God: An Introduction to Scientific Theology.* Grand Rapids: Eerdmans, 2004.

McLulan, Marshall. *Understanding Media: The Extensions of Man.* New York: McGraw Hill, 1964.

McLuhan, Marshall, and Quentin Fiore. *The Medium is the Message: An Inventory of Effects.* New York: Bantam, 1967.

McPartlan, Paul. "Who is the Church? Zizioulas and von Balthasar on the Church's Identity." *Ecclesiology* 4 (2008) 271–88.

Meeks, Wayne. "A Hermeneutics of Social Embodiment." In *Search of Early Christians: Selected Essays,* edited by Allen R Hilton and Gregory H. Snyder, 185–95. New Haven, CT: Yale University Press, 2002.

Meilaender, Gilbert. "The Catholic That I Am." *First Things* (February 2011) 28.

Melanchthon, Philipp. *The Augsburg Confession.* http://bookofconcord.org/augsburgconfession.phphttp://bookofconcord.org/augsburgconfession.php.

Metaxas, Eric. *Bonhoeffer: Pastor, Martyr, Prophet, Spy.* Nashville: Thomas Nelson, 2010.

Michalson, Carl. *Worldly Theology: The Hermeneutical Focus of an Historical Faith.* New York: Charles Scribner's Sons, 1967.

Milavec, Aaron, ed. *The Didache: Text, Translation, Analysis, and Commentary.* Collegeville, MN: Liturgical, 2003.

Miller, Mark. "The Sacramental Theology of Hans Urs von Balthasar." *Worship* 64 (1994) 48–66.

Milton, Anthony. "Puritanism and the Continental Reformed Churches." In *The Cambridge Companion to Puritanism,* edited by John Coffey and Paul C. H. Lim, 109–26. Cambridge: Cambridge University Press, 2008.

Milton, John. *Paradise Lost.* Oxford: Oxford University Press, 2008.

Moll, Rob. "The New Monasticism." *Christianity Today.* September 2, 2005, http://www.christianitytoday.com/ct/2005/september/16.38.html.

Molnar, Paul. *Thomas F. Torrance: Theologian of the Trinity.* Burlington, VT: Ashgate, 2009.

Mooney, Ginney. "Is 'the Culture' Really the Church's Problem?" *The Christian Post* (May 3, 2012). http://www.christianpost.com/news/is-the-culture-really-the-problem-74261/.

Nevin, John Williamson. *The Anxious Bench, Antichrist, and the Sermon Catholic Unity,* edited by Augustine Thompson. Reprint, Eugene, OR: Wipf and Stock, 1999.

———. "The Christian Ministry." In *The Mercersburg Theology,* edited by J. H. Nichols, 349–71. Eugene, OR, 2004.

———. "The Church." In *The Mercersburg Theology,* edited by J. H. Nichols, 56–76. Eugene, OR, 2004.

———. "Cyprian: Second Article." *Mercersburg Review* 4 (1852) 335–87.

———. "Hodge on the Ephesians." *Mercersburg Review* 9 (1857) 46–82.

———. "The Sect System, Article 1." *Mercersburg Review* 1 (1848) 482–508.

———. "The Sect System, Article 2." *Mercersburg Review* 1 (1848) 521–39.

———. "Thoughts on the Church." *Mercersburg Review* 10 (1858) 169–98.

Newbigin, Lesslie. *The Reunion of the Church: A Defense of the South India Scheme*, rev. ed. Eugene, OR: Wipf & Stock, n.d. [1960].

Nietzsche, Friedrich. *Human, All Too Human: A Book for Free Spirits*. Translated by R.J. Hollingdale. Cambridge: Cambridge University Press, 1986.

Oakes, Edward T. *Pattern of Redemption: The Theology of Hans Urs von Balthasar*. New York: Continuum, 1994.

Oden, Thomas C. *Life in the Spirit*. San Francisco: HarperSanFrancisco, 1992.

Okholm, Dennis. *Monk Habits for Everyday People: Benedictine Spirituality for Protestants*. Grand Rapids: Brazos, 2007.

Olson, Roger E. *The Story of Christian Theology: Twenty Centuries of Tradition and Reform*. Downers Grove, IL: InterVarsity, 1999.

Otto, Tim, Jonathan Wilson-Hartgrove and Jon Stock. *Inhabiting the Church: Biblical Wisdom for a New Monasticism*. Eugene, OR: Wipf and Stock, 2007.

Owens, L. Roger. *The Shape of Participation: A Theology of Church Practices*. Eugene, OR: Wipf and Stock, 2010.

Packer, J. I. and Gary Parrett. *Grounded in the Gospel: Building Believers the Old-Fashioned Way*. Grand Rapids: Baker, 2010.

Pangritz, Andreas. *Karl Barth in the Theology of Dietrich Bonhoeffer*. Translated by Barbara Rumscheidt and Martin Rumscheidt. Grand Rapids: Eerdmans, 1989.

Peelman, Achiel. "Une théologie pour la mission; Aperçu des préoccupations ecclésiologiques de Hans Urs von Balthasar." *Kerygma* 10 (1976) 123–49.

Peters, Greg. *Reforming the Monastery: Protestant Theologies of the Religious Life*. Eugene, OR: Cascade, 2014.

Phillips, Richard D., et al. *The Church: One, Holy, Catholic and Apostolic*. Phillipsburg, NJ: P & R, 2004.

Plant, Stephen. *Bonhoeffer*. London: Continuum, 2004.

Postman, Neil. *Amusing Ourselves to Death: Public Discourse in the Age of Show Business*. New York: Penguin, 1986.

———. *The Disappearance of Childhood*. New York: Vintage, 1994.

Putnam, Robert D. *Bowling Alone: The Collapse and Revival of American Community*. New York: Simon and Schuster, 2000.

Quine, W. V. O. *Methods of Logic*. New York: Holt, Rinehart and Winston, 1959.

Radner, Ephraim. *The End of the Church: A Pneumatology of Christian Division in the West*. Grand Rapids: Eerdmans, 1998.

Ramsey, Michael. *The Gospel and the Catholic Church*. Cambridge, MA: Cowley, 1990.

Reno, R. R. *In the Ruins of the Church: Sustaining Faith in an Age of Diminished Christianity*. Grand Rapids: Brazos, 2002.

———. "Out of the Ruins." *First Things* 150 (February 2005) 11–16.

Rice, Jesse. *The Church of Facebook: How the Hyperconnected Are Redefining Community*. Colorado Springs: David C. Cook, 2009.

Robinson-Neal, Andreé. "The Impact of Virtual Worship on the Real World Church Expereince," *Online—Heidelberg Journal of Religions on the Internet* 3.1 (2008) 228–242.

Romero, Simon. "A Laboratory for Revitalizing Catholicism." *New York Times* (2013); http://www.nytimes.com/2013/02/15/world/americas/in-brazil-growing-threats-to-catholicisms-sway.html?pagewanted=1&_r=0.

Rutba House, ed. *School(s) for Conversion: 12 Marks of a New Monasticism*. Eugene, OR: Cascade, 2005.

Ryken, Philip Graham. *The Communion of Saints: Living in Fellowship with the People of God*. Phillipsburg, NJ: P&R, 2001.

Sartre, Jean-Paul. *No Exit and Three Other Plays*. New York: Vintage, 1949.

Sartwell, Crispin. *Six Names of Beauty*. New York: Routledge, 2006

Scarry, Elaine. *On Beauty and Being Just*. Princeton: Princeton University Press, 1999.

Schaff, Philip. *The Principle of Protestantism*, edited by Bard Thompson and George H. Bricker. Translated by John W. Nevin. Eugene, OR: Wipf and Stock, 2004.

Schlingensiepen, Ferdinand. *Dietrich Bonhoeffer: 1906–1945: Martyr, Thinker, Man of Resistance*. Translated by Isabel Best. New York: T&T Clark International, 2010.

Schmemann, Alexander. *For the Life of the World: Sacraments and Orthodoxy*. Crestwood, NY: St. Vladimir's Seminary, 1988.

Second Vatican Council. Dogmatic Constitution on the Church. *Lumen gentium* (November 21, 1964). In *Decrees of the Ecumenical Councils*, edited by Norman Tanner. 2 vols. Washington, DC: Georgetown University Press, 1990. 2:849–900.

Seerveld, Calvin. *Rainbows for the Fallen World: Aesthetic Life and Artistic Task*. Toronto: Tuppence, 1980.

Simpson, Ray. *High Street Monasteries. Fresh Expressions of Committed Christianity*. Stowmarket, UK: Kevin Mayhew, 2009.

Smith, James K. A. *Desiring the Kingdom: Worship, Worldview, and Cultural Formation*. Grand Rapids: Baker Academic, 2009.

———. *Imagining the Kingdom: How Worship Works*. Grand Rapids: Baker Academic, 2013.

———. *Introducing Radical Orthodoxy: Mapping a Post-secular Theology*. Grand Rapids: Baker Academic, 2004.

Smith, James K. A., and David I. Smith. "Introduction: Practices, Faith, and Pedagogy." In *Teaching and Christian Practices: Reshaping Faith and Learning*, edited by James K. A. Smith and David I. Smith, 1–23. Grand Rapids: Eerdmans, 2011.

Smith, Ronald Gregor, and Karl Barth. eds. *World Come of Age: A Symposium on Dietrich Bonhoeffer*. London: Collins, 1967.

Solzhenitsyn, Alexandr. "Nobel Lecture in Literature 1970." www.nobelprize.org.

Sproul, R. C. *Are We Together? A Protestant Analyzes Roman Catholicism*. Orlando, FL: Reformation Trust, 2012.

Stuart, Hunter. "Alabama Government Agency Holds Prayer against Abortion, Gay Marriage"; http://www.huffingtonpost.com/2013/07/25/alabama-prayer-gay-marriage_n_3651756.html.

Surratt, Geoff, and Greg Ligon. *A Multi-Site Road Trip: Exploring the New Normal*. Grand Rapids: Zondervan, 2009.

Surratt, Geoff, Greg Ligon, and Warren Bird. *The Multi-Site Church Revolution: Being One Church in Many Locations*. Grand Rapids: Zondervan, 2006.

Sykes, Norman. *Old Priest and New Presbyter: Episcopacy and Presbyterianism Since the Reformation with Especial Relation to the Churches of England and Scotland*. Cambridge: Cambridge University Press, 1956.

Taliaferro, Charles. "Beauty and Aesthetics in Theology: The Art and Beauty of Wisdom." In *The Wisdom of Christian Faith*, edited by Paul K. Moser and Michael T. McFall, 197–217. Cambridge: Cambridge University Press, 2012.

Tanner, Norman P., ed. *Decrees of the Ecumenical Councils*. Vol. 1, *Nicaea I–Lateran V*. Washington, DC: Georgetown University Press, 1990.

Tapscott, Don. *Growing Up Digital: The Rise of the Net Generation*. New York: McGraw-Hill, 1998.

———. *Grown Up Digital: How the Net Generation is Changing Your World*. New York: McGraw-Hill, 2009.

Taylor, Charles. *A Secular Age*. Cambridge, MA: Belknap, 2007.

———. *Modern Social Imaginaries*. Durham, NC: Duke University Press, 2004.

Thayer, Joseph H. *Thayers Greek-English Lexicon of the New Testament*. Peabody, MA: Hendrickson, 2007.

Thérèse of Lisieux, *The Autobiography of Saint Thérèse of Lisieux: The Story of a Soul*. Translated by John Beevers. New York: Image, 1989.

Thomas Aquinas. *Summa contra Gentiles*. Translated by Charles O'Neil. http://dhspriory.org/thomas/ContraGentiles4.htm.

Tinder, D. G. "Denominationalism." In *Evangelical Dictionary of Theology*, edited by Walter A. Elwell, 335–37. 2nd ed. Grand Rapids: Baker Academic and Carlisle, UK: Paternoster, 2001.

Torrance, T. F. *The Christian Doctrine of God: One Being Three Persons*. Edinburgh: T&T Clark, 1996.

———. "The Deposit of Faith." *Scottish Journal of Theology* 36 (1983) 1–28.

———. *Theology in Reconciliation: Essays Towards Evangelical and Catholic Unity in East and West*. London: Geoffrey Chapman, 1975; reprinted Eugene, OR: Wipf & Stock, 1996.

———. *Theology in Reconstruction*. London: SCM, 1965; reprinted Eugene, OR: Wipf & Stock, 1996.

———. *The Trinitarian Faith: The Evangelical Theology of the Ancient Catholic Faith*. Edinburgh: T&T Clark, 1991.

Tveldten, Benet. *How to Be Monastic and Not Leave your Day Job: An Invitation to Oblate Life*. Brewster, MA: Paraclete, 2006.

Van Gelder, Craig. "How We Hear Mission in North America: Critical Reflections on the Presentations at the 2009 ASM Meeting." *Missiology: An International Review* (2010) 51–60.

Veith, Gene Edward Jr., and Christopher L. Stamper. *Christians In a .com World: Getting Connected Without Being Consumed*. Wheaton, IL: Crossway, 2000.

Wainwright, Geoffrey. *Doxology: The Praise of God in Worship, Doctrine, and Life*. Oxford: Oxford University Press, 1984.

Ward, Graham. "Becoming Holy: The Process of Sanctification." Presidential Address to the Society for the Study of Theology, York University, United Kingdom, March 26–28, 2012.

Webber, Robert E. *Worship is a Verb*. Peabody, MA: Hendrickson, 1992.

———. *Worship Old and New*. Grand Rapids: Zondervan, 1994.

———. *The Younger Evangelicals: Facing the Challenges of the New World*. Grand Rapids: Baker, 2002.

Webber, Robert E., and Lester Ruth. *Evangelicals on the Canterbury Trail: Why Evangelicals Are Attracted to the Liturgical Church*, Revised Edition. New York: Morehouse, 2013.

Webster, John. *Confessing God: Essays on Christian Dogmatics II*. Edinburgh: T&T Clark, 2005.

———. *Holiness*. London: SCM, 2003.

———. *Word and Church: Essays in Church Dogmatics*. New York: T&T Clark, 2006.

Wenger, Etienne. *Communities of Practice: Learning, Meaning, and Identity*. Oxford: Oxford University Press, 1998.

White, Thomas, and John M. Yeats. *Franchising McChurch; Feeding an Obsession with Easy Christianity*. Colorado Springs: David. C. Cook, 2009.

Williams, Colin W. *The Church*. Philadelphia: Westminster, 1968.

Williams, Rowan. "Balthasar and the Trinity." In *The Cambridge Companion to Hans Urs von Balthasar*, edited by Edward T. Oakes and David Moss, 37–50. Cambridge: Cambridge University Press, 2004.

———. *Why Study the Past? The Quest for the Historical Church*. Grand Rapids: Eerdmans, 2005.

Willis, David. *Notes on the Holiness of God*. Grand Rapids: Eerdmans, 2002.

Wilson, Jonathan R. "Introduction." In *School(s) for Conversion: 12 Marks of a New Monasticism*, edited by Rutba House, 1–9. Eugene, OR: Cascade, 2005.

———. *Living Faithfully in a Fragmented World: From "After Virtue" to a New Monasticism*. Eugene, OR: Cascade, 2010.

Wilson-Hartgrove, Jonathan. "Advent 2009: The End of the World as We Know It." *Tikkun*, November 2009, 37–41.

———. *The Awakening of Hope: Why We Practice a Common Faith*. Grand Rapids: Zondervan, 2012.

———. "Economics for Disciples." *The Christian Century*, August 11, 2009, 22–27.

———. *God's Economy: Redefining the Health and Wealth Gospel*. Grand Rapids: Zondervan, 2009.

———. "Money Enough/Rediscovering Our Values." *The Christian Century*, May 4, 2010, 42–43.

———. "New Monasticism and the Resurrection of American Christianity." *Tikkun*, September 2009, 52–55.

———. *New Monasticism: What It Has to Say to Today's Church*. Grand Rapids: Brazos, 2008.

———. "Together on the Ark: The Witness of Intentional Community." *The Christian Century*, August 11, 2009.

———. *The Wisdom of Stability*. Brewster, MA: Paraclete, 2010.

———, ed. *The Rule of St. Benedict: A Contemporary Paraphrase*. Brewster, MA: Paraclete, 2012.

Wilson-Hartgrove, Jonathan, and Shane Claiborne. *Becoming the Answer to Our Prayers: Prayer for Ordinary Radicals*. Downers Grove, IL: InterVarsity, 2008.

———. "A Liturgy for Our Whole Life." *Liturgy* 26.2 (April 2011) 46–52.

Winship, Michael. *Godly Republicanism: Puritans, Pilgrims, and a City on a Hill*. Cambridge, MA: Harvard University Press, 2012.

Wittgenstein, Ludwig. *Lectures and Conversations on Aesthetics, Psychology and Religious Belief*. Oxford: Blackwell, 1966.

Wolfe, Gregory. *Beauty Will Save the World: Recovering the Human in an Ideological Age*. Wilmington, DE: Intercollegiate Studies Institute, 2011.

Wolterstorff, Nicholas. *Art in Action: Towards a Christian Aesthetic*. Grand Rapids: Eerdmans, 1980.

Wood, Jr., John Halsey. "The New Testament Gospels and the *Gospel of Thomas*: A New Direction." *New Testament Studies* 51(2005) 579–95.

World Council of Churches. *Baptism, Eucharist and Ministry*. Geneva, Switzerland: World Council of Churches, 1982.

Wuthnow, Robert. *Sharing the Journey: Support Groups and America's New Quest for Community*. New York: Free, 1994.

Yong, Amos. "The Spirit Poured out on All Flesh." In *A Reader in Ecclesiology*, edited by Bryan P. Stone, 259–61. Burlington, VT: Ashgate, 2012.

Ziegler, Philip. "Dietrich Bonhoeffer—An Ethics of God's Apocalypse?" *Modern Theology* 23:4 (2007) 579–94.

Subject Index

Name Index

Scripture Index